Coming of Age Handbook
for Congregations

Coming of Age Handbook for Congregations

Sarah Gibb Millspaugh

Jessica York and Judith A. Frediani
Developmental Editors

Unitarian Universalist Association of Congregations
Boston

ISBN 1-55896-540-8
978-1-55896-540-9

Permission is granted to copy handouts and leader resources within the context of a Unitarian Universalist Coming of Age program.

10 9 8 7 6 5 4 3 2 1
10 09 08

We gratefully acknowledge permission to use the following material: "Slowly" by Marianna Ballou; chalice lighting by Lindsay Bates; "Opening Words/Call to Worship" by Paul H. Bicknell; "Ritual Addressed to a Teenager" from *The Art of Ritual* by Renee Beck and Sydney Barbara Metrick, copyright © 1990, 2003 by Renee Beck and Sydney Barbara Metrick, Celestial Arts, Berkeley, CA, www.tenspeed.com; "Gem Mining" from *Rollerskating as a Spiritual Discipline* by Christopher Buice, Skinner House Books, all rights reserved; "Grief and Mourning" and "Tools for Coping" from the Centre for Living with Dying, a program of Bill Wilson Center; "The Secret Desire of Fear" from *Grasslands* by Jim Cohn; credo by Catie Eichberg; credo by Austin Gay; "Grieving a Parent's Death," reprinted with permission from *Go Ask Alice!*, Columbia University's Health Q&A Internet Resource, at www.goaskalice. columbia.edu, copyright © 2007 by the Trustees of Columbia University; arrangement of chant based on psalm 121 by Shefa Gold, www.rabbishefagold.com; "Living by Choice" by Galen Guengerich; excerpt from *Peace Is Every Step* by Thich Nhat Hahn, copyright © 1991 by Thich Nhat Hahn, used by permission of Bantam Books, a division of Random House, Inc.; excerpt from *The Dancing Animal Woman* by Anne Hillman, Bramble Books; "Trash Talk," copied with permission from the website of the Institute for Peace and Justice (www. ipj-ppj.org); "A Wish for Our Children" by Bob Kaufmann; chalice lighting by Maureen M. Killoran; Coming of Age ceremony by David Maywhoor; "Tips for Working with BGLTQ Youth," by PFLAG, www.pflag.org; "Components of a Traditional Worship Service" by Barbara Pescan; "Confronting Evil: Has Terrorism Shaken Our Religious Principles" by Warren R. Ross, *UU World*, 16:1 (January/February 2002); "We Light This Chalice" by Natty Smith; "Dreamwork Tool Kit" by Jeremy Taylor, © 2006 by Jeremy Taylor, chalice lighting by Samuel L. Trumbore; chalice lighting by Susan Van Dreser; chalice lighting by Jean L. Wahlstrom; gathas from *Beginning Mindfulness* by Andrew Weiss, © 2004 by Andrew Weiss, published by New World Library, www.newworldlibrary.com; excerpt from *Simply Pray: A Modern Spiritual Practice to Deepen Your Life* by Erik Walker Wikstrom, Skinner House Books, all rights reserved; credo by Ian Wilson; "Blessing" by Dana E. Worsnop

CONTENTS

Introduction

Coming of Age Handbook for Congregations can be used to design a Coming of Age program that complements your religious education program. It is part of Tapestry of Faith, an integrated lifespan curriculum of the Unitarian Universalist Association of Congregations.

As youth prepare to leave childhood, they are maturing physically, cognitively, emotionally, and spiritually. This maturation opens the door for greater understanding of their faith, and Coming of Age programs address changes in youth's spiritual and faith development. This handbook will give you the tools to help youth grow more confident in their beliefs and deeper in their Unitarian Universalist faith.

Your program will offer new ways to experience Unitarian Universalism. It will ask youth to reflect upon what it means to be a Unitarian Universalist and provide a safe environment for questioning. Through activities, relationship building, and involvement in the broader community, it will accompany youth on their journeys of spiritual self-awareness.

The goal of Coming of Age is to help youth better appreciate Unitarian Universalism, their own beliefs and values, and how these intersect. It will enable them to grasp what it means to belong to a congregation so that they may become informed members. It will help participants recognize that as they grow and change, there is still a place for

them in their faith home: a new place, full of fresh opportunities and responsibilities.

Who Should Read This Book

Since you are reading this handbook, you are probably a religious educator (or religious education committee member) or Coming of Age program leader. While individual congregations will make different decisions concerning who will design the program, ultimately, both those responsible for lifespan religious education and the program leaders will need information contained in this handbook.

If you are the religious educator (or a religious education committee member), decide who will design the program. You may well be the best choice as you will have access to calendars, budgets, and other resources. You may also choose to bring others into the process, including a committee, minister, or lay leaders. Before beginning, it is crucial that you read the entire handbook to understand how the program elements fit together so that you can better decide which elements you wish to include. And whether or not others assist in designing the program, you will want them to read all the relevant sections of the handbook, including the first section, Program Participants.

If you are a Coming of Age program leader who has been asked to help design the program, it is very important that you read the entire handbook first as well. You will get a good idea of how the elements of the program fit together and be better able to decide which elements you wish to include. If the religious educator has already designed the program, read all of the first section, Program Participants, and those parts of the second section, The Program, that are included in your program. You will want to stay in close communication with the religious educator throughout the program. Consider a weekly or monthly report; add this report to your Coming of Age schedule.

How the Book Is Organized

The first section, Program Participants, contains information that will be useful when working with youth, leaders, mentors, and families. It includes developmental information on early adolescents; what to look for in adult leaders and mentors; how to recruit, train, and support leaders and mentors; and how to welcome families as full participants in the program.

The second section, The Program, is composed of nine chapters that detail the building blocks of the program. After reading this handbook, you will be ready to decide which to include in your program. Leader Resource 34, Sample Program Outlines (page 252), gives you a few suggestions on how to put them together. Your congregational calendar will probably not look exactly like the schedules in the outlines, and you will need to adjust for holidays and other weeks your program will not meet. You will want to decide which workshops are most important for your particular youth, and you may or may not include group trips or retreats. Because each congregation is unique, this handbook has been designed for the greatest amount of flexibility.

Designing and Preparing for Your Program

Over the years, congregations' Coming of Age programs have come to be appreciated for their transformative effects not only on young people but also on the mentors, leaders, and other adults involved. While the positive effects are lauded, these programs require more time and energy than most religious education programs. For that reason, they can be difficult to plan and recruit for, so it is helpful to begin at least six months in advance.

This handbook was designed with the expectation that users would choose from its various building blocks to create their own unique program. These suggested steps can help you with the significant task of designing a program compatible with your congregation's schedule, style, and needs:

Read the Handbook

The handbook includes building blocks to help you design your Coming of Age program, as well as specific content for that program. Reading the entire handbook first will help you understand how best to use these building blocks, how they interrelate, and how the content fits within the building blocks, so that you can choose what you wish to include.

Decide Which Ages Will Participate

Congregations can run Coming of Age programs for adolescents ages twelve to eighteen. The decision depends on a variety of factors, including the content of your congregation's religious education program in other grades, the number of children and youth in your congregation, and the perceived readiness of your congregation's youth.

The question we can ask ourselves as Unitarian Universalists is, "What is the best age for our young people to come of age religiously?" The response involves looking at your congregation's religious education program as a whole. What learning objectives do you have for youth who "graduate" from religious education at eighteen? For example, your congregation might have a strong investment in its children and youth being familiar with Unitarian and Universalist history, or in their embodying antioppressive values. Which of those goals are met by other religious education programs in the congregation, and which will need to be met by this program? Which can be met later? In several congregations, Coming of Age programs mark the end of formalized, classroom-style religious education for children and youth. What would your congregation like to make sure youth have experienced by the time they embark upon a Coming of Age program?

Many congregations mark completion of a Coming of Age program by offering membership in the congregation. If your program will include this feature, check age requirements for membership to ensure program graduates will qualify.

The activities and suggestions in this book are targeted to an eighth- and ninth-grade audience but can be tailored for any grade from sixth to twelfth. For example, a program offered to sixth-graders could focus on the emotional and spiritual sides of entering puberty and becoming a teenager. Offered to seniors in high school, the program could bridge participants into young adulthood and their new rights and responsibilities. Another example involves credos, which are statements of belief written by participants. Credo writing might be much more difficult for a youth in middle or junior high school than one in high school, so you might choose not to include it if participants will be younger than eighth grade. In each of these phases of life, young people hold different amounts of responsibility and approach religion in different ways.

Here are some possible adaptations for younger groups:

- no credos

- more focus on outdoor challenges, such as ropes courses

- more games, active community service, and service to the church

- more field trips

- fewer discussion-focused sessions

- more focus on rules/group covenant and consequences

- adaptation or elimination of reading assignments

These adaptations can be used for older groups:

- meetings scheduled to avoid conflict with youth group meetings

- more advanced reading assignments

- more time allotted for discussion

- deeper check-ins

- deeper credos

- involvement of youth in leadership of curriculum sessions and retreats

- more choice and depth in individual community service projects

Plan Your Program Length

While it's recommended that Coming of Age be a year-long program (fall through spring), some congregations choose to follow a semester schedule, generally January to May. Smaller congregations who offer the program in tandem with neighboring congregations may opt for a series of four or more weekend retreats or a weeklong camp.

The program's length is one of the biggest determinants of its content. If you choose a semester option, the program will be shorter on content, and mentor relationships will have less time to build. If you choose the year-long option, you may still be unable to lead all of the activities in this handbook, but you will have more time for youth to grow, form friendships, and develop their Unitarian Universalist identity.

Build a Preliminary Schedule

Once you have decided how long your program will run, consult congregational, religious education, and school calendars for holidays, vacations, activities, and congregational events that will conflict with Coming of Age activities. Note these on one calendar, and use this calendar to construct a preliminary schedule.

Set a schedule for regular meetings. Will the group meet during Sunday morning worship? Will it meet after church, or at another time? Will it meet nearly every week? Regular meetings will be the time for workshop activities, the foundation of your program. Weekly regular meetings give youth the greatest exposure to the material and the most time together for community building.

Next, decide the duration of these meetings. Most of the workshops in this handbook are designed for one hour. However, if you would like to regularly include circle worship, check-in, and journal writing, it is wise to plan for hour-and-a-half meetings.

Your program might also include elements that have special scheduling needs, such as retreats, trips, community service and social action projects, and a Coming of Age recognition service. It is especially important that you build time for these events into your schedule from the beginning, as they could possibly happen outside of the regular meeting time. Having read the entire handbook, you will be equipped to decide which building blocks, besides workshops, you will include in your program. Fit these building blocks into your schedule.

Once you have a basic idea of the overall time frame, list all the dates and times that you plan to hold meetings, retreats, and events. Check the dates against the calendars you consulted earlier to confirm the lack of conflicts.

Fill In Content

After the list of dates is set, determine the sequence of workshops, keeping in mind these helpful organizing principles:

- Create opportunities for youth to bond with each other—right away! Intentional bond-building activities, such as those in the Community Building unit, are an essential way to create a strong and coherent group and can have a positive effect on later activities.

- Include religious and spiritual content early on. Some youth might be turned off if they did not previously understand that the program involves more than getting to know other people; participants need to realize that Coming of Age is going to help them "go deep" and tend to their spiritual needs.

- Keep the group's energy in mind. What events and activities are likely to generate excitement and will to participate? Spread these events and activities out over the course of the year. If they are all in the fall, it could be difficult to sustain interest in the spring, or vice versa. It can also be helpful to think about the effect of holidays; for example, Christmas can generate a great deal of anxiety as well as a great deal of joy. A December session that teaches calming spiritual practices might be just what youth need in the holiday season.

- Find out what this group has already covered in religious education, and adapt the program accordingly. For example, if the group just finished taking *Traditions with a Wink*, they will likely know much more about Unitarian Universalist Principles and practices than a group that just finished *Our Whole Lives* or *Neighboring Faiths*. Such a group might be able to spend less time with some of the more basic program lessons about Unitarian Universalist values and beliefs. A group that has completed *In Our Hands* will already have a strong understanding of social justice, so you might abbreviate some of the social justice activities. Knowing where the youth have been will help you know where you want to take them.

- Remember that building blocks other than workshops can provide material for regular meetings. In particular, some of the work of preparing for and processing the community service and social action projects can happen during regular meeting time. Conversely, if your plans call for one or more retreats, workshops can be included in retreat activities.

Recruit Participants

Leaders play a tremendous role in the Coming of Age program, so you will want to give a great deal of thought to their recruitment. Plan to start at least six months before the start of the program. You may decide to recruit leaders at an earlier point so they can assist in scheduling and choosing content.

If your program will be assigning mentors, you will also need to start recruiting for these positions several months in advance. Though mentors may devote less time to the program than leaders, you will probably need to recruit more of them. See Leaders and Mentors (page 13) for more guidance on recruitment.

Youth will also need to be recruited. If your program is being offered for the first time, you will want to educate youth, families, and the entire congregation on Coming of Age. Including the entire congregation will make it easier to solicit support, find guest speakers, and hold fundraisers, and it might bring forth volunteers. Use all the outlets for communication within your congregation. See Recruitment (page 11) for additional suggestions.

Plan Your Budget

Because Coming of Age programs often involve field trips, overnights, meals, and gifts from the congregation, they frequently require additional funding. Therefore, religious education committees are wise to request funds in advance of the program.

The budgetary needs can be met with funds from the congregation's operating budget or participants' families, through fundraising, or through a combination of these sources.

Consider these potential expenses when drafting the budget:

- refreshments for meetings

- transportation, lodging, food, and supplies for retreats, overnights, and field trips

- photocopying of handouts

- art and craft supplies

- honoraria for guest speakers

- dinner/celebration at church for parents, youth, leaders, and mentors

- gifts for mentors and youth at the end of the program

- any books for participants, such as *The Unitarian Universalist Pocket Guide*

Consider offering a sliding scale for the funds from participants' families, or offering financial assistance for youth based on family need. A voluntary sliding scale is generally considered to be more sensitive, as it has less potential to inadvertently demean families that cannot afford the full cost of the program. An effective scale can be set by determining the actual per-participant share of the cost and making the maximum 25 percent higher and the minimum 50 percent lower.

Arrange Logistics

Refer to your schedule for other logistics that need handling before the program starts. These could include reserving space at your congregation for the regular meeting, reserving space at retreat centers, creating a comprehensive materials list, and other details. Get information on any special needs of your participants, and check all meeting spaces for accessibility.

Finalize Your Schedule

At least three months from the start of your program, try to finalize your schedule, including scheduling the mentor orientation and parent-youth orientation and making plans to include the parents' small group ministry sessions. If your program will start in September, you will want families to have schedule information before they leave for summer vacations, with the understanding that there might be changes. Of course, issues may arise that necessitate such changes, and the program designers will need to find the right balance in the schedule between flexibility and reliability.

Finally, understand that there is no one-size-fits-all approach. Each congregation is expected to use this handbook to create a program that makes sense for its size, its calendar, and its people. May you take these materials and build a meaningful, effective, personalized Unitarian Universalist Coming of Age program for the youth of your congregation.

Leader Resource List

Handout List

PROGRAM PARTICIPANTS

Plentiful resources and the best activities in the world would be of no worth at all without the right combination of people to use them, so it is fitting that the first element considered in your Coming of Age program be the participants: the youth, leaders, mentors, and families.

If you coordinate religious education or faith development in your congregation, you will want to read everything. You will also want to share the information on youth with other program leaders and mentors, and share the information on mentors and families with other program leaders.

Youth

So you have decided to work with youth who are coming of age. Congratulations! Many adults find this experience rewarding, but it has its challenges. Leading a Coming of Age program or mentoring a youth participant is hard work, and not only because of the logistics. It takes effort to reach out across the generations and build trust and understanding. Additionally, although all adults were teenagers once, many find it difficult to relate to teenagers in a natural and respectful way. The information included here will help in understanding early adolescents, by describing characteristics of the age group and various issues they might face and by outlining how adults can make youth feel more respected and affirmed.

Coming-of-age rites with long-standing traditions, such as bar and bat mitzvah, quinceañera, vision quest, and eunoto, recognize the passage of young people into greater maturity, responsibility, and spiritual commitment. In offering Coming of Age, our congregations seek to honor this passage as well. However, the definition of what youth are passing into is different in our congregations than it was when ancient rites originated. At the end of the program, our youth are not yet adults and are not passing into the rights and responsibilities of adulthood. Rather, when the program is offered in eighth or ninth grade, youth are transitioning from what psychologists call early adolescence to middle adolescence. They are leaving childhood and becoming youth.

Developmental Basics

From the physical changes brought on by puberty to the emotional changes brought on by increasing maturity, the challenges a typical young person faces during adolescence are numerous and profound. Adolescence can be understood as encompassing three phases: early, middle, and late. In *Nurturing Children and Youth: A Developmental Guidebook*, author Tracey Hurd notes these characteristics of the early adolescent (youth in sixth through ninth grades):

- seeks support for self-esteem and body image as he/she transitions into an adult body

- engages in abstract and hypothetical thinking

- concentrates on self and others' perceptions of the self

- engages actively with peers and social relationships

- tries to reconcile the inner self with the outer self

- explores gender, racial, and ethnic identities through affiliations

- expresses criticisms of self and others

- seeks belonging and membership and is concerned with social approval

- takes on others' perspectives and understands that sharing perspectives does not necessarily mean agreement

- demonstrates altruism, compassion, and an interest in ethics and justice

- expresses interest in religion that embodies values

- enjoys the presence or absence of religious creed

- sustains faith development by engaging with a community that allows questioning

- seeks love, understanding, loyalty, and support

Hurd also offers ways to support the early adolescent:

- Promote healthy body image and self-esteem.

- Affirm and support the adolescent's many physical, emotional, and cognitive changes.

- Model respect.

- Be flexible and responsive.

- Provide opportunities for complex thinking and the pondering of big questions.

- Respect and take seriously the adolescent's self-consciousness.

- Recognize that challenging authority provides an outlet for new cognitive skills.

- Maintain clear expectations enabling adolescents to make independent decisions.

- Keep some routines or rituals that provide continuity from childhood to adulthood.

- Be a sounding board for youth's exploration of ideas.

- Encourage involvement in multiple settings.

- Actively support the adolescent's exploration of identity.

- Provide repeated, sustained opportunities for engagement with ethnically and racially diverse peers.

- Encourage participation in a faith or religious community.

- Provide outlets for questioning faith, religion, and creed.

- Facilitate youth's work in the community.

- Celebrate both change and continuity.

- Have a sense of humor.

It is valuable for any adult working with early adolescents to remember these characteristics:

- Youth at this age are naturally fidgety. Their inability to sit still for long periods of time has nothing to do with you! It is helpful to plan one or more movement-based activities for each meeting.

- They are very self-conscious. What others think of them (or more precisely, what they *imagine* that others think of them) weighs heavily on their minds. They often carry around what child psychologist David Elkind refers to as an "imaginary audience." It is natural for them to feel that they are always being watched, that they are always on stage.

- They focus on their own present lives. Their self-conscious egocentrism, combined with difficulty thinking about the future, makes most early adolescents less interested in religious education subjects that do not apply to their life today.

- Bonds with adults make a difference. Despite what youth might say, they want adults to be involved in their lives, and to set boundaries and act in responsible ways.

Developing Self-worth

The Unitarian Universalist Association's first Principle recognizes the "inherent worth" of every person. Further, the Tapestry of Faith lifespan curriculum aims to help participants "know that they are lovable beings of infinite worth." For adolescents, self-worth varies with the social context, so any attempt to foster their self-worth must include an awareness of context.

It is also valuable to give attention to validation, or affirmation of the self. Validation is crucial to successful programs with youth; it makes young people feel better about themselves, and thus more at home, in Unitarian Universalism. Peers, adult leaders, and mentors can all serve this purpose. However, the validation that youth receive in Coming of Age will not necessarily make them feel better about themselves in all contexts. Adults often expect this will happen, but developmentally, early adolescents are still sorting their self-worth into contextual boxes. Coming of Age can positively affect self-worth in these primary contexts:

- in the Unitarian Universalist religious community

- among peers in the program

- between youth and mentors

Self-worth may grow with non-UU friends, parents, siblings, and romantic interests, though the increase may not occur until after the program is complete and participants mature.

While it would be difficult to imbue graduates of Coming of Age with a high level of self-worth that shows up in all contexts of their lives, the validation they receive in the program can affect them long after the program has finished.

Religious, Spiritual and Faith Development

Understanding some general background about youth and faith can be of great help to adults working with youth. James Fowler, a leading theorist of lifespan religious development, writes about how the experience of adolescence affects one's religious beliefs and longings. As young people are approaching puberty, he claims, they tend to have a very concrete and literal approach to religion. For example, they might believe that God is a concrete being, or that God does not exist at all. It is not uncommon for Unitarian Universalist children at this stage to reject the notion of divinity, because to them the concrete idea of an all-powerful, all-seeing, and all-good supernatural being does not make sense. In preadolescence, most are not yet able to claim an alternative view of the divine—one that is more flexible or more adaptable to their observations.

During middle school, some youth begin shifting to a different stage in their approach to religion. In this stage, Fowler theorizes, "the adolescent's religious hunger is for a God who knows, accepts and confirms the self deeply, and who serves as a guarantor of the self." Whether a Unitarian Universalist youth at this stage believes in God or not, the hunger to be deeply known, understood, and accepted is strongly displayed. It is spiritual, because although people play a role in providing this acceptance, the hunger goes beyond what mere people can provide. It has a cosmic element to it.

Fowler writes, "There are peers and adults . . . whose 'mirroring' of the young person has the power to contribute positively or negatively to the set of images of self and of accompanying meanings that must be drawn together in a forming identity and faith." That is, the way that other youth and adults treat the individuals in Coming of Age is part of those individuals' faith experiences. A personal and affirming relationship with the sacred is frequently manifested in the creation of intentionally accepting community for teenagers, such as Unitarian Universalist youth groups. When done well, Coming of Age enacts emotional intimacy, acceptance, and affirmation of the participants' deep selves. It also presents new ways of understanding the sacred within the Unitarian Universalist tradition, ways that can help break apart the concrete images held in earlier grades. These combined elements serve to deepen participants' spirituality and religious identities.

A purely developmental model, however, provides an inadequate understanding of young people's approach to religion. To fully grasp the religious development of youth in Coming of Age, it is valuable to take into account each individual's "socialization" within Unitarian Universalist religious community. How well do they know the congregation, its values, and its customs? How deeply do they identify as Unitarian Universalist? How much have they or their families ventured out into the larger UU world (attending General Assembly, family camps, conferences, etc.)? Although youth in the program are all of similar age, there will be differences in the expressed depth of their faith and commitment to the Unitarian Universalist faith. Further, some youth may have more extensive experience of Unitarian Universalism than the adults working with them in the program. It is therefore valuable to observe and listen to youth to determine "where they're at" religiously.

Adolescence is an important time for introducing youth to the ways of Unitarian Universalism. Many parents and youth believe that during this stage, Unitarian Universalism stops being solely the parents' religion or the family's religion. Through religious education and programs like Coming of Age, adolescents have the opportunity to make Unitarian Universalism *their own religion*. Through community building, as well as lessons on beliefs, rituals, and stewardship, the Coming of Age program helps youth find their place within Unitarian Universalism.

What to Expect of Adolescents

UU adults and youth "do" religion differently from each other. Adults generally personalize their religion and their values according to a sense of inner authenticity developed in their adulthood. This inner authenticity enables a self-authoring approach to religion—one in which they themselves are religious authorities and choose approaches that are right for them.

With the hope that young people will self-author, too, Unitarian Universalist adults offer youth space to form their own thoughts and to embark on a "free and responsible search for truth and meaning." However, because youth are at a different developmental place, they often do not interpret this freedom the way an adult would. When youth and children ask "What do Unitarian Universalists believe about _____," UU adults tend to respond with a question: "What do you believe?" This response is very well intentioned, and the motivation behind it is consistent with Unitarian Universalism. However, both developmental theory and experience suggest that adolescents often view it as a nonresponse. When

they ask questions, they concretely want to know what *this* faith they belong to—Unitarian Universalism—stands for. When well-intentioned adults do not respond with straight answers, youth can get the impression that we believe in nothing.

It is unrealistic to expect early adolescents to self-author their religion; most are not yet capable of doing so. Unitarian Universalist religious educator Kate Tweedie Erslev suggests, based on interviews with lifelong Unitarian Universalists, that religious education programs in the early teen years ought to include "Unitarian Universalist identity-specific subject matter." Early adolescents need to be exposed to their own faith tradition.

Integrating All Participants

Within any group of young people, you can find learning differences, gender differences, a variety of sexual orientations, ethnic and cultural differences, and a variety of family cultures and structures. A single approach cannot be effective for all the youth in your program; working with them requires adaptability and attention to individual needs. This section highlights some of the differences to be aware of.

Youth Who Seem "Behind" or "Ahead"

Because people develop at different rates, the mental and emotional skills of youth in your group are likely to vary. Along this spectrum, some youth are considered developmentally delayed; their communication abilities, learning progress, and/or motor skills are not as advanced as a "typical" young person their same age. Other youth are considered developmentally advanced, meaning that their cognitive and emotional abilities are considered advanced compared to their peers.

All young people have areas where they exhibit higher and lower competence. By the time youth with developmental delays enter Coming of Age, they have most likely already experienced being labeled for their deficits. It is therefore a real gift when leaders and mentors are able to create a Coming of Age experience that accepts developmentally delayed youth and focuses on their assets. Adapting a program to the individual learning needs of developmentally delayed youth can be a challenge, however. Parents are often quite knowledgeable about their children's abilities and can be allies in designing a successful program, although it is generally not advisable to have them actually present during the program. Their presence can make their children feel like babies and make other youth infantilize them. Leaders can recruit helpers—perhaps a youth's mentor—to companion developmentally delayed youth throughout the program, assisting them with participation and understanding.

On another side of the spectrum are youth who are considered developmentally advanced or gifted. Like those who are developmentally delayed, gifted children are out of sync with the majority of their peers in terms of cognitive development. Just as developmentally delayed youth cannot be assumed to be behind in all areas, developmentally advanced youth cannot be assumed to be ahead in all aspects of their development. An article in the *Roeper Review* reports that "gifted children tend to exhibit wide discrepancies in the development of intellectual, social, emotional, and physical areas. They may be many years above chronological age in intellectual reasoning, but closer to age peers in social and emotional functioning."

The experience of being gifted comes with several challenges for early adolescents. Kid Source Online identifies some of these challenges:

Young gifted people between the ages of eleven and fifteen frequently report a range of problems as a result of their abundant gifts: perfectionism, competitiveness, unrealistic appraisal of their gifts, rejection from peers, confusion due to mixed messages about their talents, and parental and social pressures to achieve, as well as problems with unchallenging school programs or increased expectations. Some encounter difficulties in finding and choosing friends, a course of study, and, eventually, a career.

Often ahead of their peers in the ability to express empathy and compassion, gifted chil-

dren can question the social practices they see at school, which is sometimes a socially isolating experience. As teenagers, they may feel ambivalent about being different from other kids and may choose to suppress their differences to gain acceptance.

Gifted children might feel like it is up to them to save the world. The Kid Source article continues: "A second basic pressure often experienced by gifted students is that, since they have been given gifts in abundance, they feel they must give of themselves in abundance. Often it is subtly implied that their abilities belong to parents, teachers, and society." As leaders and mentors work to develop social conscience in youth, it can be valuable to check in with participants about how they are internalizing the messages of the program. A gifted youth could take the social responsibility message to the extreme, feeling intense pressure and obligation to change society.

Additionally, if gifted youth seem unchallenged or bored by the program or a particular part of it, having a talk with them is a good idea. Often they can identify what they need to make the program more effective for them. Caring adults can help gifted youth own their gifts and develop coping strategies that will serve them beyond their life in the congregation. Coming of Age can be a place where they are valued for full personalities and a range of interests.

Learning Differences

Leaders and mentors are encouraged to take time to understand the learning differences of the youth involved in Coming of Age, so that they can more effectively be reached and included. For further information on learning differences, including those not discussed below, please see the website of the National Center for Learning Disabilities, *www.ld.org*.

Dyslexia. A language-processing condition that makes it difficult to read, write, and spell, dyslexia is not an indication of lower intelligence, but youth with dyslexia may need extra assistance with the segments of the program that require reading and writing. Classroom activities may require some adaptation, as well. For example, if each person in the class will be asked to read a paragraph aloud, a person with dyslexia may need time to review the text beforehand.

Young people with dyslexia can suffer from low self-esteem, especially if they have not received effective support at home or at school. Additionally, those who are enrolled in special education classes at their school may feel socially isolated. If leaders and mentors take care to consider the needs of youth with dyslexia, Coming of Age is a context in which they can feel affirmed and appreciated.

Attention deficit/hyperactivity disorder. AD/HD is a behavioral condition rather than a learning disability, but it is included here because it affects learning. Youth with AD/HD exhibit impulsivity, inattention, and (sometimes) hyperactivity to a higher degree than is typical of their peers. Many young people with AD/HD take medication that reduces the condition's symptoms.

Adult leaders can find the behavior of youth with AD/HD particularly challenging, because it can come off as disrespectful and destructive to the group's progress. Disciplinary action may be tempting but does not usually work; these youth may have trouble controlling their behavior. Often, they cannot help getting distracted, blurting out ideas, or pounding out a beat on the table. In *The Myth of the A.D.D. Child: 50 Ways to Improve Your Child's Behavior and Attention Span Without Drugs, Labels, or Coercion*, educator and psychologist Thomas Armstrong suggests that "what these kids really need are adults who will help internally empower them" and use the strategy he calls "the 'respect, listen, collaborate, and problem-solve' approach." This latter strategy is also more in line with Unitarian Universalist principles than a disciplinary approach.

It is up to leaders to model UU values not only in what they say, but also in what they do, but it takes skill to walk this talk. The youth may have built walls of defensiveness, depression, and negative self-esteem. You must be willing to truly engage with the youth who has AD/HD, as

well as with the whole group. It is an opportunity for building trust, inclusion, and affirmation. Further, inclusion can be built into the curriculum by ensuring that activities are varied in style and relevant to participants' lives. When programs are active and relevant, youth with AD/HD have an easier time focusing and being constructively involved.

Autism. Doctors and psychologists are just coming to understand the spectrum of conditions that are collectively called autism. Those diagnosed with autism exhibit a variety of behaviors, including inability to comprehend nonverbal social cues, difficulty understanding others' needs (and thus difficulty with empathy), and a restricted range of interests. They may demonstrate a high degree of intelligence in certain areas, but they are unable to understand the intricate subtleties of human interaction.

A Coming of Age program, therefore, has the potential to be an anxiety-provoking experience for youth with autism. They have learned patterns of behavior to protect themselves from hurt, and they may exhibit them. Pediatric neurologist Martin Kutscher identifies several secondary problems that result from the attempt to learn and socialize. These problems make youth with autism appear:

- Anxious, since they don't know where the next blunder will come from.

- Insistent on sameness and showing ritualistic behavior. Change means that previously hard-learned strategies will not help in this situation. These kids are barely hanging on. One new wrinkle can throw them over the edge. For example, Jill may know how to unpack her lunch from her backpack each day, but what happens if the lunch is missing? Now what does she do?

- Inattentive, since it's hard to pay attention to something you don't understand.

- Rude-appearing, since they don't understand rules of conversation such as waiting your turn.

- Interested in objects rather than people. After all, objects are more predictable.

- Hanging back from peers, for all of the above reasons, and from simply not knowing how to make conversation and relate.

- Out of it and odd looking

It is important for adults working with youth who have autism to understand that these behaviors are not fundamental aspects of their personalities, but reactions to living in a world that excludes them. If there are youth with autism in your group, they can be put at ease by a covenant that says "no teasing," mentors who can explain things to them in a more concrete and literal way, clearly announced expectations (including schedule), and youth who make an effort to include them.

Developmental and learning differences need not preclude youth from having a successful and meaningful experience in the program. Leaders, mentors, and religious educators can work together to attend to the diversity of developmental levels and learning differences in the classroom. The following model, which is built into many of the suggested activities in this manual, helps foster inclusion by ensuring variety in the style of activities.

Multiple Intelligences

Educational theorist Howard Gardner presents a model that can help in designing Coming of Age programs that are meaningful to a variety of young people. In Gardner's view, intelligence is about more than one's IQ or school grades. Rather, it can be described as a capacity for creating and problem solving in eight different areas. The first seven definitions are adapted from Thomas Armstrong's *Multiple Intelligences in the Classroom.*

- linguistic intelligence: effective use of language—oral or written

- logical-mathematical intelligence: effective use of numbers and capacity to reason well

- spatial intelligence: accurate visual and spatial perception and ability to problem-solve within those perceptions

- bodily-kinesthetic intelligence: effective use of the whole body to express oneself (acting, dancing, athletics) and ability to use one's hands to create or transform

- musical intelligence: capacity to perceive, discriminate, transform, and express musical forms

- interpersonal intelligence: ability to perceive emotions, intentions, and motivations of other people; the capacity for understanding verbal and nonverbal interpersonal cues

- intrapersonal intelligence: the capacity for self-understanding, self-discipline, and self-esteem, and the ability to act adaptively in response

- naturalistic intelligence: the capacity to identify plants, animals, and other components of a natural environment

Of these, linguistic, interpersonal, and intrapersonal intelligence are the three most heavily drawn upon in Unitarian Universalist religious education. Many have observed that at the eighth-grade level, these three forms of intelligence are often more evident in girls than boys. This can account for some gender differences in receptivity to religious education programs.

The activities in this manual seek to reach youth through activities designed to highlight a variety of intelligences. Logical-mathematical intelligence can be called upon to form a basis for moral and theological reasoning. Musical, spatial, and bodily-kinesthetic intelligences can be incorporated into games that are both fun and educational, as well as into retreat programming. Gardner's newest intelligence, naturalistic, can also be employed in Coming of Age programs: intelligence about flora and fauna can be very important in outdoor adventure–style retreats, and can serve as a source for inspiration in solo vigils in nature.

A program that acknowledges multiple intelligences benefits youth with learning differences. For example, dyslexia is a significant problem only when the activity focuses on reading and writing. Attention deficit/hyperactivity disorder becomes more of a problem when activities involve sitting still and listening to a lecture. Planning varied activities ensures that Coming of Age will be meaningful to a variety of young people.

Identity and Difference

In adolescence, young people begin to ask the question "Who am I?" in a whole new way. Rather than simply accepting the definitions of themselves imposed by family, friends, and culture, they begin to explore those definitions, engaging in a process of creating an identity. Surely, characteristics such as gender, ethnicity, and race have been fairly consistent throughout young people's lives so far. But as the hormones of adolescence affect the body and the brain, young people begin to explore these identities in a new way—a way that can involve experimentation, risk, and even drastic changes as they decide if and how they conform to the identities they've been assigned and the identities they've chosen.

Gender

The onset of puberty makes physical differences between the sexes more obvious. While adolescents have many characteristics in common across gender, they often act in ways that emphasize the differences. They frequently reevaluate their identities to become more feminine or masculine.

Gender is one of the most pronounced categories that early adolescents explore in forming their identity. In *Real Boys*, psychologist William Pollack describes how adolescent boys take on the "Boy Code," an informal set of rules that precludes anything "girly," like showing emotions, dependence, or vulnerability. They learn to bottle their true feelings and act like "everything is fine." Yet at the same time, Pollack finds that many boys are yearning for a safe space to talk about how they really feel. In *Reviving Ophelia*, psychologist Mary Pipher identifies early adolescence as a time when girls internalize the look-obsessed, media-saturated culture in a new way, seeking to be more feminine and at the same time suppressing those sides of themselves that don't conform with a feminine stereotype. In this process, girls can lose their confidence and their "voice."

For teenagers who are transgender, adolescence compounds the difficulties they face in reconciling their felt gender identity with the gender identity that society has assigned to them. For example, a young person who knows he is a boy despite his female body can find it traumatic to develop female secondary sex characteristics during puberty. In addition, the expectation that he conform to feminine gender stereotypes encourages him to further deny a very fundamental part of his identity. All teenagers face an increased risk for depression and self-destructive behavior as they enter adolescence; for transgender teenagers, this risk is acute.

Coming of Age leaders can help challenge gender stereotypes by confidently sharing those sides of themselves that are both "masculine" and "feminine." Perhaps you are a man who plays football and loves to knit; perhaps you are a woman who lectures on nuclear physics and gets her nails done every week; perhaps you are a transgender person whose simple presence challenges gender standards.

Everyone makes assumptions about people based on gender—that is what we are taught to do from day one. However, leaders who strive to make fewer gender assumptions make more space for youth to express their true selves. One way is by avoiding sexist division of tasks. For example, say, "I need some strong people to help me move this table" rather than requesting "strong guys."

Keep in mind that gender-segregated ritual and discussion groups pose a particular challenge to youth with a transgender identity.

Sexual Orientation

Early adolescents who are gay, lesbian, bisexual, or questioning also face an increased risk for depression and self-destructive behavior. Some seek to hide their sexual orientation by becoming involved in heterosexual dating relationships; some act asexual; some focus intensely on academics, sports, or other areas so they will be too busy to date. Some are fortunate enough to have supportive friends and family to whom they can come out, but few are in schools where they feel safe doing so. However, research shows that when youth are able to be out to themselves, they experience increased feelings of self-worth. Leader Resource 1, Tips for Working with GLBTQ Youth (page 24), offers several suggestions for making your meeting space safer for young people who are struggling with sexualities that go against the majority. Further, teaching *Our Whole Lives: Sexuality Education for Grades 7 to 9* in your congregation helps reduce the potential for homophobia and heterosexism among the youth in your group.

Program leaders have a real opportunity to create space for youth to take off their masks and truly be themselves. All youth—gay, straight, transgender, male, female—face pressures to suppress their true selves. Coming of Age can help them live in a more authentic way that honors all of their emotions and affections.

Race, Ethnicity and Culture

For youth who are in a minority in their neighborhoods, schools, or churches, race is a constant reminder of difference. Just as with all differences in early adolescence, some youth embrace this difference and others seek to minimize it. Psychologist Beverly Daniel Tatum notes that in racially integrated settings, children often have friends across color lines. However, in sixth and seventh grades, young people start to racially self-group. Black, Latino, Asian, American Indian, and other youth of color begin to look seriously to their peers of color to learn how to "be" members of their ethnic group. White children have less of a need to do this, as dominant American culture teaches them how to "be" white. As with gender, youth can begin to suppress those aspects of their personality that do not fit with their perceived notion of their race, and they can begin to embrace new styles and attitudes that they associate with their race.

It is important to let youth of this age define their own racial/ethnic/cultural identity. This can be challenging, especially if youth have different identity expressions than adults think they should. For example, an adult could get frustrated with a young woman who seems to be in denial about her Asian heritage, or annoyed with a young man who stops doing his homework in order to be "more Latino." Whatever expression (or lack of expression) youth have concerning their racial/cultural identity exists along a developmental continuum. Movement on the continuum needs to come from within; it cannot be imposed by another person. That said, mentors and role models can make a difference. Youth of color can especially benefit from mentorship and role modeling from adults of color who help them learn what it means to be of color and be themselves.

Multiracial/multiethnic youth face additional challenges in answering the question "Who am I?" Each parent may have roots in a different racial group (e.g., Latino and white) or a significantly different ethnic group within the same race (e.g., Bangladeshi and Indonesian or African American and Haitian). Additionally, some "monoracial" children adopted by parents of a different race consider themselves multiracial, as they identify with the racial/cultural backgrounds of their birth parents and adoptive parents. In a society that has not yet come to fully understand and accept multiple racial identities, multiracial youth often choose just one racial label to "wear" publicly. Perhaps it is the one that fits most closely with their skin tone, or the one with which they feel the greatest affinity. However, even if one label is worn in public, multiracial youth often cherish their multiple backgrounds in private.

Leaders must be careful not to make too much or too little out of participants' racial/cultural/ethnic identities. White Euro-American leaders, despite good intentions, can alienate youth of color by treating them as representatives of their race. Asking an African American girl to provide the black perspective on an issue singles her out, isolates her, and presumptuously asks her to speak for everyone who shares her identity. It is not welcoming behavior. But asking all participants, for example, to reflect on their heritage and how it informs their opinions and beliefs gives that same girl an opportunity to develop her ideas and share them with the group if she so chooses. If leaders make the space for it, Coming of Age can be a place where multiracial/multiethnic youth can uphold and celebrate all aspects of their identities.

Family Diversity

Youth in adolescence can struggle to figure out their roles in their families and their identities vis-à-vis their families' identities. Adopted youth often face a number of psychological issues and tasks that their nonadopted peers do not have to deal with in the same way. When youth who are adopted consider the universal teen question "Who am I?" they have an entire other dimension of identity to explore. Many are uncertain about what being adopted means to them. Some may begin to identify less with their adoptive families. Some may identify strongly with their adoptive families and not think about adoption much. Youth who were adopted cross-culturally or trans-racially can begin a search to figure out who they are in terms of their birth parents' race and culture as well as that of their adoptive parents. Sometimes program leaders mistakenly assume that a multiracial youth is adopted just because he/she is a different color from the parent who is known to the leaders. But for a leader seeking to be welcoming, it is a good practice to make no assumptions about family structure and history.

Youth of gay, lesbian, bisexual, or transgender parents can face unique issues, which include homophobia directed at their families, concerns about coming out as members of gay families, and concerns about being perceived as gay or lesbian. Research shows that children of gay parents are not significantly different from children of straight parents with regard to gender roles, self-esteem, psychological well-being, and likelihood of same-sex attraction. That said, it does not mean that having same-sex parents is a nonissue. It is a gift for youth with BGLT parents to be part of congregations where they are warmly accepted.

Sensitivity to family structure also helps leaders make the Coming of Age program a safer space for youth. Many of our congregations include youth of same-sex couples, youth of single parents, youth of divorced parents, youth in foster homes, and youth living with adults who are not their parents. Inclusive language, such as saying "families," "caregivers," and "parent or parents," rather than "mom and dad," can help. Youth might also be dealing with the stress of their parents' divorces while in Coming of Age. The program can provide a sense of stability and inclusion that they might not feel at home.

Safety and Abuse

All adults working with youth in Coming of Age are encouraged to consult the articles "Creating Policies with Youth Groups" and "Upholding Trust in the Religious Education Community" in *The Safe Congregation Handbook: Nurturing Healthy Boundaries in Our Faith Communities*. Congregations are strongly encouraged to implement safety policies that address abuse prevention, procedures in the event of abuse disclosure, and mandated reporting of abuse.

Recruitment

The program takes place during years when many young people become increasingly involved in extracurricular activities—for example, theatre, music, and sports—that also require considerable dedication. Because their commitment to these other activities may have already been made, their participation in this program cannot be taken for granted. Some are committed Unitarian Universalists who know they will always go to church, while others will need a compelling reason to commit their time and energy to Coming of Age. This actually involves more than just the youth: The family must also be on board. Aside from the need for families to bring youth to meetings, the complexity of the program needs support in the congregation and at home. Youth and their families must be recruited in much the same way as leaders and mentors.

The challenge in recruiting youth lies in maintaining a balance. It is important to emphasize that participation is a serious and meaningful commitment. However, if you emphasize this point too heavily, youth may begin to think that they are not up to the task. The program needs to be presented as both challenging *and* affirming, both serious *and* fun. The opportunities for learning and the opportunities for peer bonding can be emphasized together. Ideas for recruitment include the following:

- asking next year's Coming of Age leaders and "COA alumni" members of the youth group to make a brief presentation to the group containing next year's potential members (for example, the eighth-grade class)

- sending a flyer with a program description to the homes of all eligible youth in the congregation

- following up the flyer with phone calls to youth and their families to further discuss the program and respond to any questions

- encouraging youth from the congregation to invite their peers to join

Be sure to invite any youth who are attending your congregation without their families. You might have to make additional efforts to communicate with the families of these youth.

Some congregations ask youth to complete and sign an application that commits them to the program. Such forms can generate excitement and commitment. See Leader Resource 6, Sample Application for Participants (page 42).

Ministry to Youth

Working with youth is both a challenge and a joy. They will bring all their diverse identities, needs, and strengths to Coming of Age, which is designed to engage them on many levels and in many ways to better appreciate all their gifts. As you become more familiar with them, use the flexibility built into the program to design workshops that reflect their unique needs.

By working with early adolescents as they go through a coming-of-age process, you are engaging in an important ministry of your congregation. The program makes a true difference in the lives of young people: their self-esteem, ability to relate to others, faith development, ethical and spiritual development, and connection to Unitarian Universalism. When adults reach out to young people to build bridges of understanding and inspiration across the generations, lives are transformed.

Leaders and Mentors

Coming of Age programs require talented and hardworking adults. The information included here will help the religious educator decide how to best recruit, use, and support these adults.

The Role of Leaders

Leaders not only teach the material in the lesson plans, they also guide the program: working with mentors, planning for trips, problem solving. The role requires more intense commitment than typical religious education teaching, and more active leadership than typical youth group advising. But most of all, this role involves being a positive role model who can guide youth in becoming more mature and responsible Unitarian Universalists. Leaders will develop bonds of mentorship with the youth, even as they play a different role than the program's mentors do. It is a challenging, yet rewarding experience. To borrow a phrase from the Peace Corps, it is one of the "toughest jobs you'll ever love."

Recruitment must begin well ahead of the program launch. Religious educators will need to recruit more than one leader; two to four adults who can share the load and offer different perspectives would be an ideal configuration for most congregations. Recruit from a pool of adults with diverse identities, including gender, ages, affectional orientation, ethnicity, abilities, religious outlooks, and life experiences. Consider these characteristics in looking for leaders:

- organization and general competence
- confidence and capability with speaking in front of a group
- good rapport with youth
- strong understanding of Unitarian Universalism and solid identity as Unitarian Universalists
- solid ties to the congregation as members in good standing
- good personal support system
- ability to work collaboratively
- willingness to ask for help when it is needed
- proactive communication skills
- nonjudgmental listening skills

Parents often have conscious and unconscious investments in their children's identities that could block youth's efforts at developing a more mature personal identity, so it is best if leaders are not the parents of youth enrolled in the program. Part of the program's value lies in the kind of maturity youth can develop when they are mentored and guided by responsible adults other than their parents.

Consider asking a member of the congregation's professional staff—particularly a minister, intern minister, or religious educator—to join the team of leaders. If your congregation is lay-led, recruit among lay leaders you identify as possible role models for youth. Playing a key role in helping youth develop their UU identity is an experience that many congregational leaders would find spiritually rewarding.

As is the case for all adults who work with children and youth, potential leaders should undergo screening that involves a criminal background check. Such a check would find any convictions or civil penalties regarding felonies and sexual or physical abuse. Leaders must also sign a code of ethics. (See Leader Resource 2, Sample Code of Ethics, page 26.)

In recruiting leaders, be up front about what the role requires. Offering a job description to potential leaders is one effective way of achieving this goal. (See Leader Resource 3, Sample Job Description for Leaders, page 27.) Tailor this sample to the requirements of your particular program, but resist the temptation to downplay the level of commitment out of concern that leaders might be put off. Leaders will be happier throughout their tenure if they know at the beginning that the role requires commitment to weekends, overnights, and field trips, as well as regular weekly program leadership. Be honest about the amount of time you anticipate they will spend each week in preparation. Point them to people who can help them fulfill their role: parent volunteers, mentors, the director of religious education, and the religious education committee.

The Value of Mentors

Coming of Age mentors are adults from the congregation who commit to building a relationship with participating youth. David Oldfield, director of the Center for Creative Imagination at the Foundation for Contemporary Mental Health, says, "Not a friend. Not a teacher. Not a parent. Not an advisor. Not a coach. A mentor is one whose sole concern is the development of character in a young person. Acting on behalf of the community, the mentor's responsibility is to guide the young person on an inner journey of self-discovery, wherein one's unique gifts and insights can be claimed, and brought forth into the world. The mentor thus creates a bond of mutual benefit between a young person and the community; and by means of this bond, both the individual and the community are renewed." Since one goal of the Coming of Age program is to integrate youth into the community that is the congregation, mentors can play an especially unique role.

Mentorship of youth by adults in the community is a very traditional element of coming of age around the world. In Unitarian Universalist programs, mentors are able to offer individual attention to youth, helping them understand their gifts and reach a new level of maturity in faith and life. The focused relationships that mentors and youth build together have a different sort of impact from the relationships youth develop with program leaders or other youth participants. A mentor is an adult, other than a parent, who takes interest in a youth's growth and success. Many youth today do not know adults very well who are not members of their family. Further, mentors enhance a Coming of Age program by building a bridge between the world of the adult congregation and the world of children's religious education. Youth are able to become acquainted not only with their own mentors, but also the other adult mentors who volunteer with the program. As they build relationships with more adult members of the congregation, they begin to identify more with the congregation as a whole.

Mentorship can affect youth's lives beyond the congregation and beyond their teenage years. The Search Institute, an organization dedicated to positive youth development, has conducted research on the developmental assets that help people thrive. Their research indicates that young people who feel supported by three or more adults (besides parents) are more likely to grow up healthy, caring, and responsible.

Mentoring is also a rich experience. Adults who mentor youth often find that it enhances their own religious and moral understandings. They find enjoyment in getting to know a young person in their congregation: learning about a youth's personality, struggles, and concerns. For congregations that elect to have a Rites of Passage weekend, it can be deeply gratifying to create meaningful rites for youth. Adults benefit from serving on councils of elders and honoring young people's transitions.

But mentorship doesn't simply happen. The Search Institute has identified these key ingredients for success: appropriate screening, matching, and training; adequate support and communication structures; opportunities for social activities; and a good match between mentor expectations and program goals. A successful program depends on solid structure, thoughtful planning, clear definition of the role, and (last, but not least) selecting the right people for the job.

Characteristics of a Good Mentor

Mentors must be mature, emotionally secure adults with a good understanding of Unitarian Universalism. They must be able to uphold appropriate sexual and emotional boundaries. They must be able to share their own stories and ideas in a way that youth can understand and that helps them develop their own stories and ideas.

A good mentor remembers that we have one mouth and two ears so that we can listen twice as much as we talk. A good mentor is not in it for herself; she is able to center the relationship on the youth's needs. A good mentor respects youth and has a rapport with them. A good mentor is open to change in his mentee's behavior, attitudes, and ideas, but doesn't expect to be the architect of the mentee's transformation. A good mentor affirms youth as they are, and does not withhold affirmation until her mentee conforms to her standards. A good mentor has resolved his own issues and is not trying to relive or heal his own adolescence through his mentee.

In addition to these personality characteristics, some congregations require that mentors be age twenty-five or over and that they be members of the congregation for at least one year.

Finally, it is wise to choose mentors who are not currently parents of teenagers, especially those enrolled in the program. Parents of teenagers are often locked in power struggles that can play out in a mentor-mentee relationship. And parents of youth in Coming of Age have their own program to go through; it would be too confusing for one of them to also be a mentor.

How to Build Mentors Into Your Program

The configuration of your mentoring program affects both the role of mentors and the time commitment they make. A variety of models have been successful in Coming of Age programs developed by individual congregations. The Prairie Star District's Coming of Age program compiled descriptions of several ways to structure a mentor-mentee relationship. We present these as options so that religious educators can choose the model that will work best for your congregation.

One-to-one Mentorship in the Context of a Facilitated Program. Each youth is matched with an adult from the congregation, often of the same gender. The facilitated program provides structured opportunities throughout the year for youth and mentors to work together and get to know one another. Mentors participate in certain sessions of the curriculum with youth. They also have a role in retreats, overnights, and the final worship service and celebration at the end of the program. The structure of the program might allow for one-to-one social interaction between mentor and mentee outside of the workshops.

One-to-multiple Mentorship in the Context of a Facilitated Program. Each mentor is matched with two or more youth, often of the same gender as the mentor. Some congregations use this model because they have difficulty finding enough adult volunteers to create one-to-one relationships. Others choose this arrangement because it is perceived to reduce the probability of inappropriate behavior on the part of the mentor. A potential disadvantage of this model is that youth might feel more self-conscious about sharing their insecurities if other youth are present. On the other hand, the presence of a second or third youth might make some youth feel more comfortable sharing. In other ways, the model works in the same way as one-to-one: It offers structured opportunities for youth and mentors to work together.

Group-to-group Mentorship. In this model, a few adults serve as mentors to a few youth, meeting as a group. It bears some similarity to the small group ministry model that many Unitarian Universalist congregations have used for adults. An advantage of this program is that mentors and youth can meet off-site and still honor congregational safety policies that require two or more adults present at all times. The potential disadvantage is similar to that of the preceding model: Youth may be more self-conscious and less inclined to share things that they are insecure about if other youth are present.

Local Mentors for Cluster Program. In about a half dozen regions of the country, Unitarian Universalist congregations join together to offer Coming of Age as a series of joint retreats and events. These retreats and events are held off-site, at camps or conference centers away from local congregations. Mentors are drawn from the same congregation as their mentees. These mentors provide a local link for the youth and facilitate their mentees' integration within their congregation. The specific way the mentors relate to youth can be one-to-one, one-to-multiple, or group-to-group.

Individualized Program Conducted by Mentor-Youth Dyads. Several congregations, especially those with smaller religious education programs, have run Coming of Age programs that do not include a regular classroom element. Instead, youth are paired with mentors who conduct an individualized program based around certain expectations, checklists, and parameters. The interactions are structured around a list of required and/or suggested activities, such as "Discuss *The Unitarian Universalist Pocket Guide*" or "Volunteer at a homeless shelter together." The mentor role is different in this model because there are no leaders who conduct various lessons; the mentor takes more responsibility for creating and transmitting the content of the program, and the mentored activities are the lessons.

The Mentor's Role

The following questions can help your program's leadership come up with a shared understanding of the mentor's role, which you can use as the basis for a job description to be distributed during recruitment and training.

- What are the goals of the mentor-mentee relationship?

- What is the expected duration of the relationship?

- How is the mentor to assist the mentee's religious and spiritual development?

- How is the mentor to assist the mentee's emotional and social development?

- How often will mentors meet with mentees?

- In which of the following contexts will mentors spend time with mentees?

  a. during program workshops

  b. during program overnights and/or retreats

  c. at other congregational functions (e.g., serving together at coffee hour)

  d. in public places on their own time

  e. at the mentor's home

  f. at the mentee's home

Here are some sample articulations of mentor roles from congregations of different sizes and program styles. The first is adapted from materials provided by First Parish in Lexington, Massachusetts, a midsized congregation that used one-to-one mentors in the context of a facilitated program.

Mentors will concentrate their work with their mentees to help meet the following goals:

- Youth will be able to make rational decisions about whether they are ready to sign the congregation's membership book.

- Youth will explore their personal religious and spiritual beliefs, share them with each other, and learn to affirm those with differing beliefs.

- Youth will live their beliefs within the church and in the larger world. For this goal, you'll want to listen to the evolving religious and spiritual beliefs of your mentee and share your own religious and spiritual beliefs as appropriate. In this context, your primary responsibilities will be to listen without judging and to make affirming comments whenever possible to your mentee.

- Youth will understand what goes into creating and leading a UU worship service, and will experience and understand some of the variety possible in UU worship services. Your responsibility here is for the first half of this goal, helping your mentee to be able to contribute to an excellent and well-run Coming of Age service.

- Youth will build connections with other program participants and with members of the congregation, including people of all ages—children, other youth, adults, and older adults. Your primary responsibility here is simply to make contact with your mentee on a regular basis, and by so doing, to build a personal connection.

Another understanding of the mentor's role comes from First Parish in Stoughton, Massachusetts, a smaller congregation that used mentor-youth dyads in an individualized program. Mentees used checklists of possible activities to share with their mentor, similar to the list in Leader Resource 26, Sample Supplemental Activity Checklist (see page 218).

We are glad you have chosen the opportunity to form a warm and supportive relationship with one of our young people enrolled in the Coming of Age program. The role of the mentor is an important one and will need sincere dedication. Without you, the program would not be possible. As a mentor, you will be expected to do the following:

- Meet once a month for one hour with your candidate.

- Help your young person make choices to fulfill the requirements of the program in a timely fashion.

- Help them resolve logistical problems,

such as transportation, time conflicts, etc.

- Provide an outlet for the mentee to express feelings of accomplishment as well as feelings of frustration or confusion, and to help overcome negative feelings.

- Show enthusiasm for the program, the church, and the value of what they are doing.

- Be an adult in whom they can confide freely, trusting they will not be subjected to parental judgment.

- Check off the completed requirements with your initials and the date on the program checklist. Indicate any comments if you like.

- Help them with the short written or artistic expression of their religious belief to be used at a year-end recognition service.

- Act as their sponsor at that service.

A mentor is a person deeply committed to Unitarian Universalism and active in the church. Providing guidance to the youth assigned is your chief assignment. The role includes troubleshooting and directing the youth's growth. It also involves casual chats and informal get-togethers. You will also be involved in some group projects.

Mentor Recruitment

Early and effective recruitment ensures that a Coming of Age program will have an adequate number of mentors. Congregations benefit by getting started with this process as early as six months before the mentors' commitment begins.

These tips can help make recruitment effective:

- Make the mentor role visible to the congregation through announcements, newsletter articles, and participation in worship.

- Be straightforward about the commitment of time and energy that mentorship entails.

- Take advantage of high-profile events, such as Coming of Age worship services and teacher recognition ceremonies, to invite adults to apply to be mentors.

- Develop a list of adults in the congregation that you think would be good mentors. Approach them, tell them about the role and why you think they would be great in it, and ask them to apply. A direct and personal "ask" is typically much more effective than a general plea for volunteers.

- If your program starts in the fall, start recruiting mentors in the spring, or in the summer at the latest. That way, in the fall you will have applications from a number of mentors before you begin the training and selection process.

- Consider developing a job description for mentors similar to the one for leaders. See Leader Resource 3, Sample Job Description for Leaders (page 27) for ideas on what to include.

After recruitment, many congregations have found it valuable to ask potential mentors to fill out an information form that addresses their motivations, interests, and experience working with youth. The form can be used as a matching device to help connect suitable pairs. It can also be used as a screening device; it is fine to turn down an applicant whose answers are not appropriate. See Leader Resource 4, Mentor Information Form (page 39) for a sample.

Matching Youth and Mentors

Congregations have taken various approaches to assigning mentors to youth. Some allow youth to choose their mentors; others empower the program's leadership team and the religious educator to make matches without input from youth. Your congregation can select the system that best serves the spirit of your program.

Youth Select Mentors. Arrange a simple event to bring youth and mentors together. It could be over ice cream on a Sunday afternoon or a shared snack at the end of your first workshop. Once youth and potential mentors have had the chance to meet, youth can indicate preferences for mentors with whom they would like to work. Because two or more youth might want the same mentor, it's important to let them know that they may not get matched with their top preference. It is also important to let adults know that they might not be matched with a youth at all.

The advantage of such a system is that youth will feel a special investment in mentors of their choosing, so they are likely to take the relationship more seriously. In some congregations this investment is encouraged by having youth call the mentor they have been matched with to ask, "Will you be my mentor?" The disadvantage is that there could be adults in the mentor pool who are not chosen by any youth but may be needed, because of numbers, to be mentors, thus creating an awkward situation. That is why it is best in this system to have a pool of potential mentors that is much larger than the number that will be required.

Mentors Selected for Youth. Another way to approach the matching issue is to have the program leadership team decide which mentors and youth would go together well. Questionnaires such as Leader Resource 4, Sample Mentor Information Form (see page 39), can assist with this process. Caring adults who know the youth and the mentors can sometimes make better matches than youth can themselves. The disadvantage of this system is that youth may not feel as much investment in a relationship that is assigned to them as they will in one which they choose. Advantages include fewer "rejections" of potential mentors and perhaps more insightful matches.

Mentors, assigned or chosen, are often the same gender as their mentees. However, it is helpful to be flexible about the gender of mentors if all parties agree that the youth would be better served. For example, a young man who strongly identifies as an artist and musician might benefit from being matched with an adult woman in the congregation who is also an artist and musician; a young woman who is getting in touch with her Asian identity could learn a lot from a mentor who is also Asian, even if that mentor is male. In the case of a transgender youth, be cautious of making assumptions about the preferred gender of their mentor.

Safety

Because leaders and mentors are adults, they possess far more societal power than youth in the program, and they must take care to use this power wisely, respectfully, and responsibly. Good boundaries are necessary for effective youth-adult relationships. These boundaries include sexual boundaries, which are often discussed in congregational safety policies. Leaders and mentors are not to engage in any kind of sexual or sexualized behavior with youth. This includes sexual harassment, even if it does not involve touch. Other boundaries concern the emotional, spiritual, and physical safety of youth.

Structuring safety guidelines from the very beginning will give leaders, mentors, religious educators, families, and youth a greater feeling of assurance as to what is and is not appropriate. Many congregations have their own safety guidelines. Even if such guidelines are not required by the congregation, however, consider asking leaders and mentors to abide by and sign a code of ethics and submit to a background screening. Additionally, your program will need to set guidelines concerning the safe meeting between mentors and mentees. Each of these areas is covered below.

Code of Ethics

All of us, youth and adults, function best when expectations are clear. That is the role of the code of ethics that mentors and leaders sign: It lays out expectations for ethical behavior in the unequal relationship between youth and adults. Presenting a mentor or leader with a code of ethics to sign also provides a unique opportunity to discuss and agree upon what constitutes a healthy

relationship with youth. While a signature on a code of ethics cannot prevent all ethical violations, it does affirm a standard for this relationship that the signer has agreed to abide by. An adult who violates the standard can more easily be held accountable. See Leader Resource 2, Sample Code of Ethics (page 26), for an example.

Screening

A criminal background check on each leader and mentor is strongly advised, and it is helpful to have completed the background checks on potential mentors *before* the youth-mentor matching process begins. Sex offenders do not necessarily have criminal records, so a background check is an important safety measure, but not a guarantee that an individual is "safe." A congregation can be held liable if they accept a volunteer with a sex-offender record to work with youth. Please see *The Safe Congregation Handbook* for more information.

A criminal background check may reveal sensitive information that does not pertain to an adult's suitability for the position, such as a currently sober alcoholic's arrest for drunken driving ten years ago or an activist's trespassing conviction from a political protest. Whoever is reading the background check reports (most likely the religious educator) must be trusted to discern which kinds of criminal backgrounds should prevent an adult from being eligible to work with youth.

Additional Guidelines for Mentors

Individual Unitarian Universalist congregations set their own guidelines concerning safety in religious education programs. The congregation in San Jose, California, has a number of measures in place to help create safety in the mentor-mentee relationship. First, they want mentors to be mature and to be familiar with their congregation, so they set an age requirement of twenty-five and a congregational membership requirement of one year. Second, they request the names of four references in addition to the mentor's written application. The application and references help the program coordinators get to know the character of the applicants better. Third, they ask mentor applicants to agree to a criminal background check that would reveal any convictions for molestation, assault, rape, abuse, or other actions that would call the suitability of an applicant into question, and to agree to and sign a code of ethics that spells out the appropriate boundaries.

Youth may be discussing vulnerabilities, insecurities, and personal information with their mentors. Mentors are to understand that personal information is to be kept confidential. However, confidentiality is not equivalent to secrecy. If a mentee reveals something illegal or life-threatening—such as abuse, suicidal thoughts, or a serious drug problem—mentors need to discuss these matters with the congregation's minister or religious educator. Together, then, the mentor and the congregation's staff can determine if, when, and how to involve families or authorities. In most states, ministers and religious educators are mandated to report physical abuse to governmental authorities. Consult your congregation's safety policy, be in touch with your district office, or contact your state's office of child protection to learn more about what reporting procedures are mandated by law in your locality.

An appropriate mentor also upholds emotional boundaries. Mentors are not to treat their mentees as friends and confidants. Friendship is generally focused equally on both friends' interests and needs. The mentoring relationship is intended to focus on the mentee, and all conversations and interactions must be geared toward the mentee's needs and development. Any of the mentor's needs that get met in this interchange are secondary.

Concretely, this means that mentors share only personal information that is mostly resolved, meaning that the mentor has dealt with the issues at hand and received support from others on those issues. The risk here is of the mentor's leaning on the youth for affirmation or support. For example, if a mentor shared the details of her current break-up or vented about how horrible her teenage son was, her mentee might feel unduly pressured to care for the mentor's emotions. The dynamic of the relationship would shift in those moments, moving from being about the youth to being about the mentor.

Another valuable screen for personal sharing involves discerning what is helpful to youth. It can be of great comfort when mentors affirm youth's experiences by sharing their own stories. For example, if a mentee is upset because she doesn't fit in at school, a mentor sharing that she wasn't popular in school either can be very affirming. Sometimes figuring out what is helpful involves looking for the question behind the question. If a mentee asks, "Did most kids have sex in your junior high?" he probably does not really want to know about Burbank Junior High in the 1970s. He probably *does* want to talk about peer pressure and the sexual norms at his own school, and could be looking for some support in navigating through his own challenges. A possible answer to the question is: "There were some sexually active kids, but most were not. Kids at school talked about sex a lot, but it didn't mean they were doing it. What's it like at your school?" Every response a mentor makes to personal questions should lead back in the direction of the mentee's own growth and development.

Some programs are structured so that all meetings between youth and mentors happen within congregational programming. If your program encourages youth and mentors to spend one-on-one time beyond the congregation, additional boundaries come into play. As a way of decreasing the possibility of abuse, some congregations specify that one-on-one time should be spent in a public space, such as a restaurant or sporting event. Others allow home visits if at least one other adult is present. We recommend that explicit, informed parental consent be obtained for each meeting of mentors and mentees outside of the congregation.

In addition, if meeting outside of the congregation, it is important to be respectful of youth's boundaries in terms of physical risk. Taking a youth rock climbing, river rafting, or mountain climbing might be very exciting, but it is also risky. Any activities that involve physical risk must have the explicit, informed permission of parents and the youth. If the activity is far from home, mentors must bring a permission slip that includes medical information and authorizes the mentor to sign for emergency medical care for the mentee. Further, all cars that mentees ride in should have seat belts and be driven only by licensed drivers.

Mentors are discouraged from buying special gifts for mentees or treating them to expensive items. A relationship should be based on personal sharing and trust rather than expectations of goodies.

A final boundary concerns the relationship between the mentor and the family of the mentee. Some mentorship programs have found it valuable to discourage interaction between the mentor and the mentee's parents. Mentees need to know that mentors are there for them. In some situations, a mentor's friendship with the mentee's parents can confuse the dynamic of the mentoring relationship, making the mentor appear as an agent of the parents. In other situations, a mentor could be tempted to interfere with a family that is experiencing difficulties. Saving families is not part of the mentor's job description for good reasons: It's too much to take on, and it rarely works. A mentor serves a family well simply by being a mentor to their child. If mentors are friends with the mentee's parents, they are encouraged to state at the outset to parents and youth that they will uphold confidentiality and that during the duration of Coming of Age their primary allegiance will be to their mentee.

Just as lines on a highway help a truck driver drive, boundaries help leaders and mentors fulfill their roles more safely and effectively. And just as driving between the lines becomes instinctive for the driver, staying within appropriate boundaries becomes instinctive, too. It sets the stage for a good and healthy journey for all involved.

Training and Support

It is important to give leaders and mentors a better understanding of their roles and the specific commitments they are being asked to make and provide an outlet for their questions. Program leaders will benefit by participating in your religious education teachers' training; a different training will need to be designed for mentors. See the mentor orientation (page 31) for a sample.

A single training session is not enough to ensure that leaders and mentors feel adequately prepared to fulfill the obligations of their roles. We all do better in our roles when we are given support, and there are many ways that congregations can provide support. An informal mentor gathering every few months would offer mentors and leaders the chance to share frustrations, successes, and tips. Giving leaders and mentors permission to go to the parish minister or religious educator—staff who are held to confidentiality—is especially valuable if they find themselves dealing with complex issues. The advent of e-mail enables leaders to communicate easily with most mentors about upcoming events and expectations. Mentors, likewise, should be given permission to e-mail the leaders with any concerns or questions throughout the program. Some congregations require mentors to regularly report on their activities with their mentees. Responses to these reports can help support mentors throughout the joys and challenges of the mentoring relationship.

Leaders and mentors can also benefit from specific religious education programs geared toward their personal spiritual growth. Participating in adult religious education programs or small group ministry can complement Coming of Age in developing leaders' and mentors' faith.

With the proper attention to recruiting, training, and support of leaders and mentors, the program can be a rewarding experience not only for youth, but for adults as well. Building relationships with youth, families, and other adults is one reward; the opportunity to grow in one's own faith is another. Most important, leaders and mentors will experience the joy of knowing they have walked beside a young person on a spiritual journey along the road from childhood toward a path of deepening maturity and a more centered Unitarian Universalist faith.

Parents and Families

The National Study of Youth and Religion (*www.youthandreligion.org*) found that three in four youth say their beliefs are similar to their parents'. Parents play the most significant role in the spiritual and faith development of their children. If youth are to grow effectively into newfound maturity, they need the support of those who parent them, whether those be biological parents, adoptive parents, stepparents, grandparents, or guardians. Throughout this handbook, *parents* refers to the caregivers who do the work of parenting, whether they have the title *parent* or not.

Parents of youth need to be open to a new kind of relationship with their children: one that recognizes their adolescent children's growing capacities for responsibility and autonomy, yet still offers them the nurturing and protection they need as young people. In addition to supporting their children's growth, parents also play a crucial role in supporting the Coming of Age program. Their permission is required for youth to enroll, and they will likely be called on to drive youth to events, assist with fund-raisers, and pay a fee for their children to participate.

Yet these are not the only reasons to solicit support from parents. Their involvement offers youth an excellent example of how a community thrives when everyone assumes responsibility for its welfare. Throughout the program, youth will hear leaders voice this point; as they see parents, mentors, ministers, religious educators, and others from the congregation assist the program, they will see it in action.

Parents can use the Coming of Age program to infuse greater spirituality into their family life. Activities such as reading *The Unitarian Univer-* salist Pocket Guide together, spending time with mentors, attending worship together, and sharing of credos can help guide parents and youth to a new level of discussion about matters of faith. This is the ideal time for parents to share with their children what Unitarian Universalism means to them and the importance of belonging to a faith community. After all, the program will be complete in several months, but the family will be with participants always.

Supporting Parents

This handbook offers two resources to help cultivate parents' support for their children's growth and for the program itself: outlines for an orientation for parents and youth (see page 36) and for a five-session small group program for parents (see page 44). The parents' small group enables parents to connect, identify shared concerns, and help one another prepare for transition in their relationship with their children. It can be a very meaningful experience.

Parents might also appreciate periodic updates on topics covered in the workshops so that they can continue the conversations at home and help youth carry what they have learned into the wider world. You may also choose to involve parents in some of the larger activities. Workshop 31, Closing Celebration (see page 196), provides an occasion for parental participation, and parents can help with community service and social action projects. If you choose to hold a recognition service at the end of your program, consider asking parents to participate. (See Services of Recognition, page 242.)

Family Diversity

Sensitivity to diversity in family structure is especially important when you are in relationship with early adolescents. At a time when peer and other societal pressures are constantly driving youth to conform, belonging to a family whose structure is not average can be stressful. Unitarian Universalism is a welcome home for all families. As such, you should not be surprised by a myriad of family structures in your program: stepfamilies, one-parent families, two-household families, families with two moms or two dads, families headed by grandparents, foster families, and many others. A broad use of the words *parent* or *caregiver* instead of "mom and dad" is recommended. Do not be shy about asking which adult should be your primary communications link and what that person's relationship to the youth is. You will also need this information when signatures are required on Coming of Age forms.

Families play an important role in the religious education of youth, and welcoming them into the program affirms the reality that young adolescents still very much need and desire the love, support, and faith foundation that is found in a family setting. A Coming of Age program that intentionally deepens the connections between youth and their families better prepares youth to go out more fully and engage the world as people of faith.

Tips for Working with GLBTQ Youth

1. **Don't be surprised when a youth "comes out" to you.** They have tested you with a series of "trial balloons" over a period of time. Based on your previous responses, they've decided you can be trusted and helpful.

2. **Respect confidentiality.** If a gay, lesbian, bisexual, transgender, or questioning (GLBTQ) youth shares with you information about his/her sexual orientation or gender identity, you have a trust that must be respected. A breach of this confidence has led some to suicide.

3. **Be informed and examine your own biases.** Most of us are the products of a homophobic and transphobic society influenced by misinformation and fear. You can't be free of it just by deciding to. Read reliable sources and talk to qualified persons.

4. **Know when and where to seek help.** Know the reputable referral agencies and counselors in your area. Gay help lines can provide professional persons and organizations that are qualified to help. Tell them who you are and what kind of assistance you need.

5. **Maintain a balanced perspective.** Sexual thoughts and feelings are only a small (but important) part of a person's personality.

6. **Understand the meaning of sexual orientation and gender identity.** Each person's sexual orientation and gender identity are what is right for that person. It is not a matter of sexual "preference." In most cases, people do not choose to be gay or lesbian; they simply are. Understand that one's sense of gender identity is a separate issue with unique complexities and challenges.

7. **Deal with feelings first.** Most GLBTQ youth feel alone, afraid, and guilty. You can assist by listening, thus allowing them to release feelings and thoughts that are often in conflict.

8. **Be supportive.** Explain that many people have struggled with these issue in the past. Admit that dealing with one's sexuality or a gender identity that is different from one's birth sex is difficult. There are no easy and fast answers, whether heterosexual, bisexual, gay, lesbian, or transgender. Keep the door open for more conversations and assistance. Be aware that so-called "reparative therapy" has been discredited by all major mental health professional associations and can be harmful. While some groups promote it, it is not a credible way of offering support.

9. **Anticipate some confusion.** Most youth are sure of their sexual orientation by the time they finish the eighth grade, and the same appears to be true with gender identity. But some young people will be confused and unsure. They have to work through their own feelings and insights; you can't talk them into, or out of, being gay, lesbian, bisexual, or transgender.

10. **Help, but do not force.** If you are heterosexual or comfortable with your birth sex, you probably don't understand what it means to be different in these ways. Clues for how you can help will come from the young person. Don't force him or her into your frame of reference to make it easier for you to understand.

11. **Don't try to guess who's GLBTQ.** It is not helpful for you or for the youth you serve. We live in a world of stereotypes that do people an injustice; do not be tempted to perpetuate old myths.

12. **Challenge homophobic remarks and jokes.** Speak up when someone makes disparaging remarks about GLBTQ people, or thoughtlessly uses antigay language, just as you would any other slurs. Don't perpetuate injustice through silence.

—Parents, Families and Friends of Lesbians and Gays (PFLAG), *www.pflag.org*

Sample Code of Ethics

Adult leaders and mentors are in a position of stewardship and play a key role in fostering the spiritual development of both individuals and the community. It is, therefore, especially important that they be well qualified to provide the nurture, care, and support that will enable youth to develop a positive sense of self and a spirit of independence and responsibility. The relationship between young people and these adults must be one of mutual respect if the positive potential is to be realized.

There are no more important areas of growth than those of self-worth and the development of a healthy identity as a sexual being. Mentors and leaders who abuse their roles in these areas hurt not only the individuals involved, but also the whole community.

Experience dictates that all those involved suffer when adults become inappropriately involved or engage in negative or destructive behaviors with youth they are mentoring or leading. Inappropriate behavior includes the follwing:

- sexual, seductive, and erotic behavior

- physically or verbally abusive behavior

- inappropriate use of legal or any use of illegal substances while working with youth in a leadership position

- abuse of power or position within the youth community

Mentors and leaders need to be aware of the strong influence they have in the community. It is expected that their influence will be exerted in a positive manner.

By signing below, I agree to this Code of Ethics. I understand that if I am found to be in violation of this code, appropriate action will be taken. I also consent to the congregation's conducting a check to determine whether I have a criminal background that would interfere with my ability to be an appropriate mentor or leader to young people.

_____   _____
Name   Signature

_____   _____
Date of Birth   Social Security Number

_____
Today's Date

—"A Code of Ethics for Continental Young Religious Unitarian Universalists," Youth Office, Unitarian Universalist Association of Congregations, adapted by River Road Unitarian Church, Bethesda, Maryland

Sample Job Description for Leaders

The ideal candidate for this job will exhibit the following attributes:

- comfort in working with people with diverse theologies, identities, family structures, and multiple intelligences
- self-identification as a Unitarian Universalist
- ability to set appropriate boundaries in relationships with youth and their families
- knowledge about the workings of the congregation or willingness to attain such knowledge
- confidence and capability speaking in front of a group
- ability to work collaboratively

The leader's job duties will include the following:

- facilitating orientation sessions for youth and parents
- facilitating a training session for mentors
- facilitating workshops for youth on a regular basis (Specify how often.)
- preparing for such workshops by reading lesson plans in advance, meeting with co-leaders, and obtaining required resources
- coordinating the program's schedule
- working in conjunction with religious educator and/or religious education committee
- leading retreats and trips, including coordinating logistics (lodging, food, transportation), communicating with parents and families, and facilitating activities
- working closely with youth and mentors to ensure that youth accomplish the goals of the program
- communicating with community service sites and retreat centers to reserve space
- coordinating volunteers for events such as community service projects and fundraisers
- problem solving and handling difficult situations as they arise
- maintaining regular communication by e-mail, phone, or mail with enrolled youth, their parents, mentors, and the congregation's staff
- nurturing and guiding youth participants as they become more responsible and mature Unitarian Universalists
- having an incredibly rewarding experience and making a real difference in the lives of Unitarian Universalist young people and their families!

Successful applicants will be required to submit to a background check and sign a code of ethics for working with youth.

THE PROGRAM

Now that you have familiarized yourself with the people who will shape your Coming of Age program, let us take a closer look at the components, or building blocks, you can use to design your program. Leader Resource 34, Sample Program Outlines (page 252), offers ideas for individualizing these nine building blocks to meet the needs of your congregation:

- orientations
- small group ministry sessions for parents
- participant workshops
- community service projects
- social action projects
- supplemental activities
- group trips
- retreats and rites of passage
- services of recognition

Orientations

Your program will benefit from two orientation sessions: one for potential mentors and one for youth and their parents. An orientation session for all interested families enables you to present the program once instead of talking to each family, and it ensures that everyone gets the same information. These sessions also provide the involved parties an opportunity to get to know each other. Scheduling these orientations well in advance of the anticipated start of your program is highly recommended. See Orientations (page 31) for sample material.

Small Group Ministry Sessions for Parents

Because the program seeks to be inclusive of all its participants, parents are invited to participate in a small group ministry series. As children grow and transition into different roles in society, the job of parenting them does not lessen, but it does change. These sessions provide time for parents to support each other as they begin this adventure together. See Small Group Ministry for Parents (page 44) for a series of five sessions.

Workshops

The core building blocks of the program are thirty-one workshops that engage youth and leaders in topics ranging from spirituality to social action to congregational leadership. They are uniformly structured but vary somewhat in length and number of activities. Though most stand alone, there are key activities in some workshops—credo writing, journaling, check-in, worship, and mentor and *UU Pocket Guide* discussions—that need to be presented early in the program. Adding these activities to your workshops will strengthen your program. You will learn more about them in Workshops (see page 57).

Community Service Projects

To encourage participants to become involved in the wider community, opportunities for community service are written into the program. Parents are encouraged to plan a community service project during their small group sessions. Community Service Projects (page 200) guides youth, leaders, and mentors in designing a project that is meaningful for them and in reflecting on the event afterward.

Social Action Projects

To help youth distinguish between community service and justice work, Social Action Projects (see page 207) talks about more than taking social action. It also provides the framework for participants to examine justice issues that are a concern to them, deduce possible tactics to address these concerns, and put one into action.

Supplemental Activities

Many congregations have found it rewarding to ask Coming of Age youth to participate in activities outside of the regular meeting time. If your group meets during the same time as Sunday worship, you might especially want to consider this building block, as it encourages participants to engage with the congregation.

The approach to supplemental activities can be informal or formal. For example, it could simply involve letting youth know about congregational activities or inviting them to join in, or it could include a checklist of activities and a requirement that youth participate in a certain number or type of activity. Supplemental Activities (see page 217) contains a more detailed explanation of ways to use this building block.

Group Trips

One memorable feature of many Coming of Age programs is an extended road trip. The most common destination is Boston, for a Unitarian Universalist heritage tour. However, some groups have planned trips to the southern United States to immerse themselves in UU civil rights history, while others have learned about local UU history by visiting their neighbor congregations. Youth might decide to spend several days involved in a social action project or working with an organization like the Unitarian Universalist Service Committee or Habitat for Humanity. Coming of Age trips are another opportunity for participants to experience what it means to be Unitarian Universalist in the world. They also expand a participant's circle of friends. For more information on planning, see Group Trips (page 221).

Retreats and Rites of Passage

Retreats provide participants with the opportunity to spend longer periods of dedicated time together. A retreat can be for a weekend or just overnight. It can be held at a retreat center or campground, or at the congregational meetinghouse.

Many congregations have included a rite of passage as one of the culminating activities of their program. These rites place participants in an environment that is not part of their daily lives and invite them to spend time in solitary reflection. They use rituals to acknowledge the transition from childhood to adolescence, and these rituals frequently involve other members of the community, recognizing the transition on a communal and not just a personal level.

Retreats and Rites of Passage (see page 226) includes several resources you may use to shape a rites of passage retreat for your program.

Services of Recognition

A congregational worship service is one way to recognize the culmination of a Coming of Age program. Inviting the congregation to celebrate with Coming of Age participants reinforces the youth's sense of belonging and the congregation's sense of ownership of the program. The service is often a regular weekday worship service. Alternatively, it could be a special service offered in the evening and including a potluck dinner.

Orientations

Two sample orientations are included in this handbook. The first is for mentors and the second is for parents/caregivers and youth. Your Coming of Age leaders will probably participate in the teacher training for your religious education program and be in excellent contact with your congregation's religious educator throughout the Coming of Age program. If not, you might create an orientation session for your program leaders.

Orientation for mentors provides these benefits:

- a clear presentation of role expectations, including boundaries

- the chance for mentors to "try on" their role through interactive role-playing

- an opportunity to create community among mentors

- an opportunity for leaders to observe and screen potential mentors

In addition to orientation, we strongly recommend that mentors be screened and trained before actually working with youth. The specific elements in your orientation will depend on the role mentors will play in your program. For example, if the mentor has a role in directing the mentee's individualized program, that aspect will need to be discussed during orientation. Elements that pertain to role expectations, job description, boundaries, and safety are also essential. Exercises that acquaint mentors with the challenges of early adolescence, reconnect them with their own adolescence, and give them practice relating to youth are valuable. Leaders and Mentors (see page 13) includes suggestions on different models for the use of mentors, mentor job descriptions, and other useful information. The outline included here was adapted from a mentor training session at First Parish in Cambridge, Massachusetts.

The precise content of an orientation for parents and youth depends on which aspects of this manual you choose to include. Leader Resource 5, Sample Charts for Parent-Youth Orientation (page 40), is basic and will require the addition of material from the program's coordinators. Length of the program is variable. If all components of the outline are included, the program will be two to two-and-a-half hours long. Be sure to allow time for questions throughout the orientation.

Session for Mentors

Time   2 hours, 30 minutes

Participant Goals

- get to know each other and form a team

- become familiar with the goals and requirements of the program

- prepare for their upcoming relationships with eighth and ninth graders

Materials

- chalice, candle, and matches

- chalice reading

- newsprint and easel

- markers

- introduction sheet (see Preparation)
- "Parking Lot" sign (see Preparation)
- a few dozen sticky notes
- masking tape
- "Strongly Agree" and "Strongly Disagree" signs (see Preparation)
- cards for role-playing (see Preparation)
- an object, such as a fist-sized ball or beanbag, to pass for the sharing circle
- pens or pencils
- name tags
- small bell or chime
- mentor information forms (see Preparation)
- mentor information packets (see Preparation)

Preparation

- Create information forms for prospective mentors. See Leader Resource 4, Sample Mentor Information Form (page 39).

- Assemble information packets for mentors. These can include:
  - ~ program schedule
  - ~ mentor job description
  - ~ code of ethics
  - ~ material on youth from this handbook (see page 2)
  - ~ any other relevant information

- Select an appropriate reading for lighting the chalice.

- On a newsprint sheet, write "Introductions: Name, religious background, length of affiliation with congregation, something you love, something you dislike."

- On a second newsprint sheet, write "Parking Lot." Affix several sticky notes to the sheet, and post it on the wall.

- For the continuum game, use masking tape to create a straight line across the floor. Place a piece of tape crosswise at its center to mark the middle of the continuum. On the wall above one end of the tape, post the sign that reads "Strongly Agree." On the wall above the opposite end of the tape, post the sign that reads "Strongly Disagree."

- For the role-playing exercise, prepare one index card per participant, each with a different question or statement on it. You may use the following examples or create your own:
  - ~ I hate my parents! They are such jerks.
  - ~ I tried pot this weekend.
  - ~ Sometimes I just don't see the point in living.
  - ~ My father and sister had a huge fight, and he hit her.
  - ~ Everybody at the high school drinks.
  - ~ I think my mom is a major alcoholic.
  - ~ Were you sorry after you lost your virginity?
  - ~ Danny's dad is a fag.
  - ~ Did you ever tell your kid that he's a total idiot?
  - ~ Everyone in this town is so racist.
  - ~ I don't believe in God.
  - ~ God is kind of a stupid idea.
  - ~ Unitarian Universalists don't believe in anything.
  - ~ I think I'm a Trinitarian.

Welcome   5 minutes

Leaders introduce themselves. Light the chalice and offer a chalice lighting reading.

Group Introductions   15 to 20 minutes

Explain that this activity introduces sharing circles, one of the rituals of your Coming of Age program. Ask participants to form a circle with their chairs. Explain that in a sharing circle, an object is passed around from neighbor to neighbor, and the person who has the object is the only one who can speak.

Post the "Introductions" sheet and explain that participants will each have one minute to share their name, their religious background, how long they have been affiliated with the congregation, something they love, and something they dislike. You may want to identify a timekeeper who gently informs people when their minute is up.

Say some affirming words about the mentors as a group and express appreciation for their willingness to share of themselves and make a difference in young people's lives.

Parking Lot   5 minutes

Show the "Parking Lot" sheet. Explain that questions that can't be addressed immediately, because they are off-topic or call for a complex explanation, can be written down on sticky notes and "parked" until the next time the mentors gather. Ask if everyone understands and answer any questions.

Review of Information Packet   20 minutes

Distribute information packets and review the contents with mentors. Highlight the most essential information, and discuss any key points. If a long reading, such as the Youth portion of this handbook, is included, request that mentors read it after the session. Remind mentors that the Parking Lot is available for questions that cannot be addressed in this segment.

Guided Visualization   10 minutes

This activity asks participants to remember their lives at age fourteen. If you are offering the program to a different age, substitute that age. Read the following slowly, clearly, and calmly:

> To help us all get in touch with our own early adolescence, I'm going to lead you on a guided meditation. The memories, images, and emotions you experience are for your own learning. We will not be discussing what you see and feel. We simply believe that remembering what it is like to be a youth can help you be a good mentor. If unpleasant memories arise, feel free

to let your mind go elsewhere or stop the meditation.

> I invite you to stay seated and find a comfortable position for your body. Feel your spine relax, feel the muscles in your face begin to loosen and let go of tension. Take a deep breath into your belly, and let it go with a sigh. Take another deep breath, and exhale with a sigh . . .

> Now, let us go back in time, to the time when you were fourteen. Imagine yourself waking up one morning, fourteen again. You are in your bedroom. Look around. What do you see? Posters on your walls? What music is on your shelves?

> You get up and look at yourself in the mirror. What do you look like? Is your hair long or short? Straight or wavy or curly? Are you heavy? Skinny? Medium weight? Are there things about your appearance that you like? Things you dislike?

> As you take a shower, you are thinking about the day ahead. What will school will be like for you? Are there people you look forward to seeing? People you want to avoid? Do you feel a thrill of excitement? Or do you feel dread?

> As you get dressed, you begin to think about what will happen after school. Where will you go? To sports practice? To a relative's house? To some other activity? How do you feel? Is it something you look forward to? Something you resist?

> Now you're dressed. You go downstairs and encounter members of your family: maybe parents, maybe siblings, maybe other family members. How do you feel about them? What do you say to them? What do they say to you? How does it feel?

> Spend a few moments here, recalling as much as you can about what it felt like to be fourteen.

> When you are ready, come back to the present . . .

> Open your eyes. You are no longer fourteen.

Continuum Game   20 minutes

Ask participants to take a moment to stretch, then show them the masking-tape continuum. Explain that you will read statements and ask them to position themselves along the continuum based on how strongly they agree or disagree. After each statement is read, they will have the opportunity to briefly discuss their responses with others standing near them on the continuum. Then you will ask for volunteers from different places on the continuum to explain their positions.

Use the statements:

- When I was fourteen, I was comfortable in my body.

- When I was fourteen, I could go to my parents if I had a problem.

- When I was fourteen, I loved school.

- When I was fourteen, I had an adult in my life I could talk to openly and honestly.

- When I was fourteen, I had at least one best friend I could confide in.

- When I was fourteen, I felt affirmed, valued, and loved.

Reassemble the group in their chairs and ask, "What was it like to revisit this year of your life?" After a few people have responded, ask, "How will these memories affect the way you mentor?"

When you feel it is appropriate to move forward in the discussion, say something like the following: "Mentoring will indeed put us in touch with the issues we have about our own teenage years, or even the issues left over from our parenting teenagers. However, as mentors it is important to always focus on the mentee—on the young person. To do that, we put our own issues and experiences in our metaphorical back pockets. This means that we still have our experiences and issues with us, but they do not dominate our mentoring relationships. Instead, the mentoring relationship centers on the *youth's* needs. If you need support for dealing with your own issues, we encourage you to turn to adult friends or to our congregation's minister for support."

Boundaries Discussion   20 minutes

Explain that the setting of appropriate boundaries will play an instrumental role in defining the mentor-youth relationship, and invite participants to discuss these boundaries. If this concept is unfamiliar to some participants, share the following in your own words:

> In "Boundaries and Dysfunctional Family Systems" on *www.mentalhelp.net*, Dr. Mark Dombeck explains that psychological boundaries are constructed of ideas, perceptions, beliefs and understandings that enable people to define not only their social group memberships, but also their own self-concepts and identities. . . . Each person can be said to have a psychological identity boundary around themselves by which they distinguish themselves from other people. Like other boundaries, this identity boundary both separates people and also defines how they are linked together. This is to say that the act of drawing the boundary itself provides the basis for saying that one person is separate from another psychologically, but does so only by drawing a distinction between those two people, which implies a relationship, nevertheless. Self cannot exist without also "not-self" existing. Identity necessarily includes social relationships which are built into the self to varying degrees.

Ask participants to brainstorm a list of important boundaries for the mentor-youth relationship. If any of these important items are not mentioned, add them to the list:

- physical boundaries, including boundaries around sexualized behavior

- confidentiality

- emotional boundaries, including boundaries around looking to mentees for emotional support, sharing your own experience, and getting drawn into familial conflict

Familiarize mentors with the congregation's safety policy and code of ethics, and discuss any guidelines your congregation has developed for the mentor-youth relationship, such as limits on one-to-one time. Explain how mandated reporting of abuse works in your congregation.

Ask, "With these boundaries in mind, how is being a good mentor different from being a good friend?" Remind mentors that adult-youth relationships inherently carry a power imbalance. Because mentors are adults, their words and actions can have a profound influence upon youth. Rather than serving as friends, they are role models for youth growing into their Unitarian Universalist faith.

Highlight the following points, as articulated in a UU Coming of Age model from Minneapolis-St. Paul, Minnesota:

- Adolescence is a self-centered time. Youth are trying to figure things out, and their primary question is: Who am I? Mentoring is for youth first, and only secondarily for adults. Constantly be aware that this program is about them and for them.

- Think of yourself as a resource library, where youth will browse around, and take out what they are looking for right now. They won't need everything that is available. Do not dump the whole library on them.

- Try to keep your balance between being vulnerable and sharing, and your need for self-protection—you don't have to share everything with your youth.

- Screen what you do and say with your youth through the question: "Is this going to be helpful to this youth?"

- Remember that there is a difference between adults and teens. You have had many more experiences.

- This is a two-way street. You can be resources to each other.

Role Playing   25 minutes

Ask participants to form themselves into groups of three. One person will be A, one B, and the other C. Explain as follows:

> As and Bs will role-play being mentor and mentee. You will each be handed an index card with a challenging question or statement. Bs will begin as mentees and will read their cards to their partners; As will respond as if they were mentors. Pay attention not only to the literal question being asked, but also to the question that may be behind it. For example, a youth who asks "Did you feel depressed in high school?" might really want to know if it's okay for him to feel depressed. Cs will observe the process and make comments. You'll have two minutes for each question. When the bell rings, it is time to switch roles.

Pass out the cards, and ask if anyone has any questions.

After the last round, ask for one group to volunteer to demonstrate how they responded. Ask the larger group if they have any ideas for different ways of responding. Ask if anyone has any encouraging prompts that may be helpful, such as "Hmmm, what do you think?"

Point out any questions that asked mentors to share personal information, such as "Were you sorry after you lost your virginity?" Explain that mentors need to be comfortable telling youth that some questions are personal and that they are not comfortable answering them.

Remind mentors that they should not hesitate to say "I don't know, but I'll help you find out" if they cannot answer a question; they can call on the program leaders, other mentors, and the congregation's religious educator for help in responding.

If it has not already come up, explain your congregation's guidelines for mandated reporting of abuse.

Summary   5 minutes

Summarize by saying,

> This role play addressed challenging moments in the mentor/youth relationship, but be assured that not all moments are so challenging! I hope our time together has touched on all of these areas:
>
> - what is appropriate to share about oneself
> - what is appropriate modeling
> - phrases mentors can use to respond to difficult situations
> - what is supportive to youth but also respectful of their families
> - what "red flag" behaviors should be reported
> - our support structures in the parish
> - how you can support youth rather than giving answers or trying to "fix" them

Ask if there are any other questions or concerns, either about boundaries or any other aspect of the mentor duties.

Closing Circle   10 minutes

Invite participants to return to the circle. Remind everyone of the time and place of the next meeting, and thank them for coming. Ask participants to briefly share something they hope for or look forward to as mentors in the Coming of Age program. Pass the object used during the opening circle.

Mentor Information Forms   5 to 10 minutes

Ask mentors to stay for five minutes or so to complete a questionnaire that will assist in matching mentors to youth. Distribute forms and pens or pencils.

Session for Parents and Youth

Time   90 to 120 minutes

Participant Goals

- understand how the program will benefit participants
- meet other families and the leaders involved with the program
- register for the program

Materials

- name tags
- markers
- chalice, candle, and matches
- *Singing the Living Tradition* hymnal
- newsprint and easel
- Leader Resource 5, Sample Charts for Parent-Youth Orientation (page 40)
- informational handout for parents or overhead projector and water-soluble fine-tip markers (optional, see Preparation)
- registration and parent permission forms (see Preparation)
- program schedules (see Preparation)
- list of any materials parents are expected to provide and/or explanation of any fees associated with the program (see Preparation)
- ball of yarn (optional)
- art supplies and poster board for Coming of Age sign (optional)

Preparation

- Notify potential program participants. You might send invitations to all the families with youth in the appropriate age range. You might choose instead to advertise in the congregational newsletter, send e-mails, make announcements from the pulpit, and post on bulletin boards.

- Prepare a program schedule for Coming of Age. Even if it is tentative, a schedule gives parents and youth a sense of the commitment involved in participation.

- If the program includes a fee, be prepared to tell parents the amount of the fee and what it covers. If parents are expected to supply items for the program (such as *The Unitarian Universalist Pocket Guide*), prepare and photocopy a list of these items for parents to take home.

- Prepare registration and parent permission forms that are in line with those used for your congregation's religious education and youth programs. See Leader Resource 6, Sample Application for Participants (page 42). Consider covering these additional areas:

  ~ explicit permission for off-site field trips

  ~ a code of ethics for youth; for a sample, see the YRUU (Young Religious Unitarian Universalists) Code of Ethics at *www.uua. org/leaders/leaderslibrary*

  ~ parental permission for youth to spend one-on-one time with their mentors (if your policy allows for that)

  ~ dietary restrictions

  ~ health concerns and allergies

- Invite two or three high school youth who have successfully completed the program to come to the orientation and speak about their experience. Keep diversity—particularly gender diversity—in mind; potential male participants might be less likely to sign up if both speakers are female, and vice versa.

- Using Leader Resource 5, Sample Charts for Parent-Youth Orientation (page 40), as a reference, post on newsprint the information you want families to take with them, or design a handout and photocopy enough for every family to have one. Conversely, you may decide to use transparencies and an overhead projector for this presentation.

- Make a list of everything you need to cover logistically during the meeting.

- Decide if you will include the optional activity, Two Groups (page 38). If so, reserve additional meeting space. If not, make sure you inform parents of the small group ministry sessions at another time in your orientation.

Opening   15 minutes

Greet youth and their parents as they arrive and invite everyone to make a name tag.

Once everyone has arrived, lead the group in an icebreaker, possibly a game that parents, leaders, and youth can play to get to know one another's names. See the workshop Covenant and Community Building (page 61) for ideas, or look at "Deep Fun," an online games resource from the UUA Youth Office at *www.uua.org/documents/ youthoffice/deepfun.pdf* .

After the game, gather everyone for a chalice lighting. Use Reading 502 or other relevant words from *Singing the Living Tradition*.

What Is Coming of Age?   30 minutes

Introduce yourselves as leaders of the Coming of Age program. You might share with the group why you decided to work with the program. Inform the group that Coming of Age is a program that acknowledges that early adolescents are in a period of great change and maturation. As youth engage with their world in a new way, they have an opportunity to explore their beliefs, spirituality, and their Unitarian Universalist faith in a new way. Coming of Age will help them define what that new way will be.

Using the newsprint, transparencies, or handout you created from Leader Resource 5, Sample Charts for Parent-Youth Orientation, review the goals, components, and subject areas of your program. Periodically invite questions. Spend time on both the elements of the program that will provide unique learning opportunities (such as learning to lead worship) and those that will provide unique opportunities for fun (such as retreats and trips). Speak to both youth and their parents: you will need the support of both groups for a successful program.

Coming of Age Graduates   15 minutes

If graduates from a previous Coming of Age program are present, invite them to speak for a few minutes each on what they liked best about the program. Leave time for questions. Let the youth know that the graduates will be available for more questions when the youth and parents split into separate groups, if you are including this optional activity.

Logistics   20 minutes

Using your registration form and the list you prepared earlier, review important logistics with the families. You do not need to sign up drivers for a trip that is months away, but you will want to let parents know what is expected from them in the area of transportation. Other topics you might cover include the following:

- program schedule

- program requirements

- registration or other fees

- whether families are expected to provide any materials (such as *The Unitarian Universalist Pocket Guide* or food at retreats)

- expectations for youth participation in weekly meetings, retreats, and field trips, including any attendance requirements and behavioral standards

- whether youth and mentors will meet together outside of class

- whether youth can become members of the congregation after completing the program

Optional Activity

Two Groups   20 to 30 minutes

Separate parents and youth into two groups. One program leader should stay with each group, and graduates should be with the youth. One group will need to go to an alternate meeting space. It is best if the youth are in the space they will use for their regular workshops.

For parents, describe the concurrent five-session small group ministry program. Gather the names of interested parents and best times for meetings. Ask them to consider the question of facilitation: Would they like to rotate facilitation or should one person always facilitate? Invite them to decide the logistics of meeting and facilitating at this point, if they would like to.

If time permits, you might lead a sample activity from a youth workshop, such as Yarn Toss from Workshop 8, Unity and Diversity (see page 94). Answer any remaining questions.

For youth, lead a "get to know you" activity, such as Two Truths and a Lie or another game from "Deep Fun." Invite questions. If you have extra time, you might invite youth to decorate a Coming of Age sign for the room.

Applications   10 minutes

Gather families back together. Thank everyone for their time. Hand out registration forms and ask that they be completed now if families are ready. Collect the forms and any applicable fees. If families are not yet ready to sign, give them a deadline for returning the forms.

Sample Mentor Information Form

Name: Gender:

Ages of your children, if you have any:

Occupation:

Interests and hobbies:

What do you like about youth?

What is your understanding of a mentoring relationship?

What do you hope to give and receive from this relationship?

Tell briefly about your spirituality.

How long have you identified as a Unitarian Universalist?

What else do you want youth to know about you?

—North Shore Unitarian Church, Vancouver, British Columbia, adapted

Sample Charts for Parent-Youth Orientation

Program Goals

As a participant in Coming of Age, you will:

- get to know yourself better

- begin to understand other people better

- be part of a meaningful community of youth, beyond labels and cliques

- make Unitarian Universalism relevant to your life

- understand your own religious beliefs more deeply and know how to explain them

- examine your values and how they relate to your actions

- learn how to live your beliefs and values every day

- experience multiple ways to connect with what is spiritual—those things that put you in touch with the miracle of life

- build a strong and supportive relationship with an adult mentor

- develop and practice stronger leadership skills

- get to know more people in the greater congregation, both younger and older

- understand the role worship plays in our community and be a full participant in worship services

- identify our UU rituals and know their histories

- increase your knowledge of the workings of the congregation and the wider UU world

- have a real sense of accomplishment and a growing sense of maturity at the completion of the program

Program Components

- Workshop activities
  - ~ games
  - ~ discussions
  - ~ journals and credos
  - ~ acting, drawing, movement
  - ~ youth-led worship
- Mentored relationships
- Community service
- Field trips
- Retreats and overnights
- Worship service of recognition

Subject Areas

- *Community building:* creating a trusting and bonded group

- *Unitarian Universalist values:* identifying what Unitarian Universalists, including you, value most

- *Community service:* putting our values into action by serving others

- *Social action:* learning about social change and making it happen

- *Spirituality:* learning practices, from prayer to martial arts, that balance us and put us in touch with the miracle of life

- *Theology:* clarifying our ideas about humanity and the divine

- *UU beliefs:* looking at religious claims and "what we set our heart to" in daily life

- *UU history:* interacting with the past to gain inspiration for the future

- *Leadership:* developing skills to run meetings, handle conflicts, and speak in front of crowds

- *Worship:* designing and leading worship services for the group and the congregation

- *Spiritual growth:* creating meaningful opportunities for growing in maturity and faith

Sample Application for Participants

Name _____   Date of birth _____

Address _____

Phone _____   School attending/grade this fall _____

Parents' names _____

Parents' address(es), if different from yours _____

Parents' phone numbers(s), if different from yours _____

Siblings and ages _____

Special needs or considerations _____

To me, Unitarian Universalism means:

I have attended Unitarian Universalist congregations for _____ years.

What is special about you that you would like to share? Interests? Hobbies? School?

What is your favorite book or kind of book?

What is your favorite movie or kind of movie?

What is your favorite kind of music or musical group?

Who are your heroes?

What do you look for in a friend?

What are your current beliefs about God and the sacred?

What do you wish to get out of the Coming of Age program?

Youth Commitment
I wish to enter the Coming of Age program. I understand it will not be easy, but I am willing to accept the challenge, knowing I will have adult help along the way. I am making a commitment to participate fully in all the activities of this program.

Signed _____ Date _____

Parent Commitment
I agree to support my youth in participation in the Coming of Age program and commit to help them attend all of the sessions.

Signed _____ Date _____

—First Parish Universalist Church, Stoughton, Massachusetts, adapted

Small Group Ministry for Parents

As young people come of age, their parents' support, acknowledgement, and openness can smooth the process. Their growing maturity also represents a transition for their parents, who can be helped through the experience by forums that enable them to support each other. One such forum is small group ministry.

Increasingly, small group ministry is an integral part of congregational life. These groups are composed of four to twelve people, with an ideal size of eight to ten. One person serves as the facilitator and assumes responsibility for running the meetings; if possible, choose a person who has relevant skills. Advise the volunteer of the additional commitment to participate in a facilitators' small group.

Small group sessions should be scheduled throughout your program. Meetings can take place in a parent's home or at the congregation's building. If meetings are held in private homes, take extra care to ensure confidentiality; no children or other family members should be within earshot of the gathering.

A broadly held expectation of participation—including stepparents, grandparents, guardians, and parents' cohabiting partners—will help the program succeed. Participants need not be active in the congregation to have an investment in supporting their child in the program. Small groups will also enable parents to participate in the spirit of generosity and service by performing a community service project. Each small group will determine its project during the fifth meeting.

To set up small groups, take the following steps:

- Estimate the number of participants and determine the number of groups needed.

- Publicize the existence of the small groups for parents of youth in the program.

- Find out which meeting times work best for potential participants.

- Ask co-parents whether they would prefer to be in a small group together or separately. This can be a particularly sensitive issue for divorced or separated couples. Married couples may prefer to be in separate groups for childcare reasons.

- Determine the meeting place and times for the various groups.

- Assign parents to small groups.

- Recruit one or more facilitators from among the parents for each small group.

Session 1
Parenting: How Is It Going?

Time   60 minutes

Materials

- chalice, candle, and matches

- cloth for altar or centering table

- name tags

- markers

- newsprint and easel
- Copies of Handout 1, Resources for Parenting Adolescents (see page 54)
- copies of books listed on Handout 1 (optional)

Preparation

- Arrange chairs in a circle, with the cloth, chalice, and candle at its center.
- Set out name tags and markers.
- Set out copies of Handout 1, Resources for Parenting Adolescents, along with any of the listed books you may have obtained.

Chalice Lighting   2 minutes

Share these words by M. Maureen Killoran:

> For every time we make a mistake and we decide to start again:
>
> We light this chalice.
>
> For every time we are lonely and we let someone be our friend:
>
> We light this chalice.
>
> For every time we are disappointed and we choose to hope:
>
> We light this chalice.

Establishing a Covenant   10 minutes

Explain that, just as youth in the program will covenant together about behavioral guidelines, so will this group. Ask participants what guidelines would make them able to express themselves comfortably, genuinely, and safely. Write every suggestion on a sheet of newsprint, treating this initial phase like a brainstorm. These are some common guidelines that groups covenant to include:

- One person speaks at a time; there is no interruption.
- Personal stories are kept confidential.
- Speakers monitor their own participation so that the voices of all can be heard.
- Meetings start and end on time.

- Participants remember that they speak only for themselves; diversity of experiences, opinions, and theologies is assumed.

After the group generates a list, invite participants to ask questions and make points that clarify the suggested guidelines. Then ask for consent. If anyone is uncomfortable with a certain guideline, ask how it might be rephrased.

Check-in   15 minutes

Invite participants to introduce themselves and share, one by one, how they are doing and how their relationship with their child is going. Participation is voluntary, and facilitators can set a time limit for sharing, e.g., two minutes per person. Some groups find it valuable to go around the circle twice: first for initial sharing, and a second time for participants to share ideas and responses sparked by others' check-ins. More time is allocated for check-in in this first session than in later sessions so parents can introduce themselves.

Words for Meditation   2 minutes

Share these words by Anne Hillman:

> We look with uncertainty
> Beyond the old choices for
> Clear-cut answers
> To a softer, more permeable aliveness
> Which is every moment
> At the brink of death;
> For something new is being born in us
> If we but let it.
> We stand at a new doorway,
> Awaiting that which comes . . .
> Daring to be human creatures
> Vulnerable to the beauty of existence.
> Learning to love.

Focus   20 minutes

Introduce the discussion by saying something like the following:

> Parenting is no easy task. Looking out for a child's physical, emotional, and spiritual well-being requires a high degree of responsibility and responsiveness. There is no

single authoritative way to do it, nor should there be one; there are many styles of healthy parenting. Different ages require different approaches as parent and child both mature. The relationship is dynamic, ever-changing. Just when you understand how to parent your four-year-old, your child turns five. Progressing through adolescence, your child is becoming, well, less of a child. Even so, your child still needs to be parented, perhaps more than ever. At this gathering, we will share with each other what this parenting relationship is like and how it feels to be in a parenting role.

These questions can be used to spark a discussion:

- What hopes, fears, challenges, and joys do we experience as we raise adolescents?

- What can we do with our time together to help one another?

- What are some of your challenges in parenting your child?

- Name some of your joys and some of your fears in parenting.

- What are some of your hopes in parenting?

- How can this program help?

Likes and Wishes   7 minutes

Participants are invited to "check out," sharing what they liked about the meeting and ideas for how it could have been improved. It helps to phrase these comments lovingly and constructively, with the good of the group in mind. Saying "I liked _____" and "I wish _____" helps to affirm good things that are already happening and to make space for more good things to happen at the next gathering.

Closing Words   2 minutes

Share this reading by Jeanne Nieuwejaar:

When I was an adolescent, the places I felt safest and most able to be myself were in my church communities. Perhaps this was in part because I had already learned a deep sense of connection to and trust in the church. Perhaps it was because these churches were designed as places of acceptance and love. Perhaps it was because the people there truly liked me and my peers just as we were, with all our annoying teenage traits.

The church school teacher who took us to visit neighboring churches when we were in the seventh grade took us out for coffee (lots of milk and sugar) and doughnuts after every visit and talked with us as though he really enjoyed it. The woman who taught our eighth-grade class was as old as the hills and as sweet as sunshine. She knew we found the class deadly dull and could barely wait to break away and go sit at the soda fountain in the drugstore next door—and she forgave us and loved us anyway.

Closing Ritual   2 minutes

Lead a simple closing ritual that will be repeated each week. Examples include holding hands in a circle, sharing a moment of silence, or singing a song.

Session 2
Looking Back

Time   45 minutes

Materials

- chalice, candle, and matches

- cloth for the altar or centering table

- name tags

- markers, including several dark-colored markers

- copies of Handout 1, Resources for Parenting Adolescents (see page 54)

- copies of books listed on Handout 1 (optional)

Preparation

- Arrange chairs in a circle, with the cloth, chalice, and candle at its center.

- Set out name tags and markers.

- Set out copies of Handout 1, Resources for Parenting Adolescents, along with any of the listed books you may have obtained.

- Place the newsprint and easel so that it is visible to everyone.

Chalice Lighting   2 minutes

Share these words by Samuel A. Trumbore:

> O light of life,
> Be kindled again in our hearts
> As we meet together this morning
> To celebrate the joy of human community
> Seeking a wholeness that extends beyond ourselves.

Check-in   10 minutes

Invite participants to introduce themselves and share, one by one, how they are doing and how their relationship with their child is going. Participation is voluntary, and facilitators can set a time limit for sharing, e.g., two minutes per person. Some groups find it valuable to go around the circle twice: first for initial sharing and a second time for participants to share ideas and responses sparked by others' check-ins.

Words for Meditation   2 minutes

Share these words by Hodding Carter:

> There are only two lasting bequests we can hope to give our children. One of these is roots; the other, wings.

Focus   20 minutes

Begin by saying something like the following:

> As we prepare to move on to a new stage in our relationship with our children, it is good to look back even as we look forward. Remembering our youth as children can help us know them better as young adults.

Remembering can also help us know what we want to keep the same and what we want to change in our relationship.

Invite parents to reflect on and discuss the following questions:

- What was your child like in your first years together? Five years later? What are some of your favorite memories from those times?

- What do you cherish about the relationship you have had with your child up to now?

- What would you change about the relationship?

Likes and Wishes   7 minutes

Participants are invited to "check out," sharing what they liked about the meeting and ideas for how it could have been improved. It helps to phrase these comments lovingly and constructively, with the good of the group in mind. Saying "I liked _____" and "I wish _____" helps to affirm good things that are already happening and to make space for more good things to happen at the next gathering.

Closing Words   2 minutes

Share "A Wish for Our Children" by Bob Kaufmann:

> We wish for you a storm or two that you may enjoy the calm.
>
> We wish for you tranquility in time of trial.
>
> We wish for you a cool breeze on a warm day, and pale white clouds that you may better appreciate the blueness of the sky.
>
> We wish you darkness that you may see the stars.
>
> We wish you anticipation of high adventure, and we wish you the courage to avoid battle.
>
> We wish you a sense of wonder—and poetry—and music.
>
> We wish you companionship that you may appreciate solitude.

We wish you a friend who will understand you, and understanding so that you may have a friend.

We wish you may become all that you wish to be, and more than you hope that you can be.

We wish you a flower to smell,

A hand to touch,

A voice to cheer,

A heart to gladden,

And we wish you someone to love, as we love you.

Closing Ritual   2 minutes

Repeat the simple closing ritual you used in Session 1 (see page 46).

Session 3
Knowing and Not Knowing

Time   60 minutes

Materials

- chalice, candle, and matches
- cloth for the altar or centering table
- name tags
- markers
- copies of Handout 1, Resources for Parenting Adolescents (page 54)
- copies of books listed on Handout 1 (optional)
- handout containing quotes for reading (see Preparation)

Preparation

- Arrange chairs in a circle, with the cloth, chalice, and candle at its center.
- Set out name tags and markers.

- Set out copies of Handout 1, Resources for Parenting Adolescents, along with any of the listed books you may have obtained.
- Copy the quotes from the Focus section (see page 49) so that participants can read them.

Chalice Lighting   2 minutes

Share these words by Jean L. Wahlstrom:

In this small flame dwell:

the beacon light of lanterns guiding travelers home;

the warmth of hearth fires tended through the generations;

the transforming energy of furnaces and the power and life of our sun.

May these blessings—

warmth and light and life-giving energy—

be kindled in each of us.

Check-in   10 minutes

Invite participants to introduce themselves and share, one by one, how they are doing and how their relationship with their child is going. Participation is voluntary, and facilitators can set a time limit for sharing, e.g., two minutes per person. Some groups find it valuable to go around the circle twice: first for initial sharing and a second time for participants to share ideas and responses sparked by others' check-ins.

Words for Meditation   2 minutes

Share these words by James Baldwin:

For nothing is fixed, forever and forever and forever, it is not fixed; the earth is always shifting, the light is always changing, the sea does not cease to grind down rock. Generations do not cease to be born, and we are responsible to them because we are the only witnesses they have. The sea rises, the light fails, lovers cling to each other, and children cling to us. The moment we cease to hold each other, the sea engulfs us and the light goes out.

Focus   20 minutes

Ask three volunteers to read these three quotes as focus for the meeting:

> As I listen to boys across America, I am struck by the depth, compassion, and cry in their voices. . . . Our sons are telling us that the tremendous pressure they experience every day has become unendurable: they constantly feel prone to flunking out of school, becoming addicted to drugs, falling into depression, and to "snapping" with such intensity that at any moment their rage could spill over into violence.
>
> —William Pollack

> Teenage girls live in a junk culture filled with inducements to consume, to be sexual, to be lookist and self-absorbed. They are pelted with media much worse than anything my generation experienced as girls. They are also offered drugs and alcohol at a much younger age.
>
> —Mary Pipher

> Gay youth face the double jeopardy of surviving adolescence and developing a positive identity as a lesbian, gay male, bisexual, or transgender in what is frequently a hostile and condemning environment. Contrary to popular belief, adolescence is not "the time of our lives." It is a difficult and complex period of development filled with anxiety and few clear guidelines for helping youth resolve the problems they face, often for the first time, and making the transition to adulthood.
>
> —LAMBDA GLBT Community Services

Reflect on the following questions:

- How much do you think you know about your child's inner life (deep feelings, self-image, identity, spirituality)? How do you respond to those things you know or do not know?

- How much do you think you know about your child's outer life (friendships, romantic interests, activities, schoolwork)? How do you respond to those things you know or do not know?

- Should parents know everything about their teenage children's lives? If so, why? If not, what kinds of things should parents not know?

Service Project Discussion   15 minutes

Explain that the group will have the opportunity to perform a community service together, either for the congregation or for the community at large, and that the goal for the project is to put their faith into action in a way that is bonding and meaningful. Discuss ideas for service projects that could be performed as a group. Decide when and how the ideas will be researched and carried out.

Likes and Wishes   7 minutes

Participants are invited to "check out," sharing what they liked about the meeting and ideas for how it could have been improved. It helps to phrase these comments lovingly and constructively, with the good of the group in mind. Saying "I liked _____" and "I wish _____" helps to affirm good things that are already happening and to make space for more good things to happen at the next gathering.

Closing Words   2 minutes

Share these words from Christopher Buice:

> A few summers ago my wife Suzanne and I took our son Christopher gem mining in the mountains of North Carolina. We mounded a pile of mud and dirt, got a sifter, and began sifting through the soil in search of treasure.
>
> Liberal religious education is like gem mining. In a Unitarian Universalist Sunday school we endeavor to teach our children discernment. The word *discernment* comes from the Latin word *discernere*, which means "to separate," "to distinguish," "to sort out." In other words, we try to teach our children

how to be gem miners. The process of gem mining is simple. You take some dirt, place it into a strainer, run creek water through it, and sift until you find a gem.

Liberal religious gem mining requires the ability to discern what is worth keeping and what should be sifted out and discarded. This can be difficult. Our children have to sift through lots of information in life. They learn values from television, popular music, the Internet, books, magazines, their friends, and many other sources. We can't even know all the messages they are exposed to on a regular basis.

We cannot shelter our children forever. But we can teach them the process of discernment and the art of gem mining. We can help to awaken the conscience so that they will be able to make responsible choices, to separate things of value from things that have no value. At some point we must open the door and lead our children into the world and speak the words to them that tradition says God spoke to the children of Israel: "I have set before you life and death, a blessing and a curse. Therefore choose life."

Closing Ritual   *2 minutes*

Repeat the simple closing ritual you used in Session 1 (see page 46).

Session 4
Preparing for Transition

Time   60 minutes

Materials

- chalice, candle, and matches
- cloth for the altar or centering table
- name tags
- markers
- copies of Handout 1, Resources for Parenting Adolescents (page 54)

- copies of books listed on Handout 1 (optional)
- handout containing quote for reading (see Preparation)
- copies of Handout 2, Ritual Addressed to a Teenager (page 55)

Preparation

- Arrange chairs in a circle, with the cloth, chalice, and candle at its center.
- Set out name tags and markers.
- Set out copies of Handout 1, Resources for Parenting Adolescents, along with any of the listed books you may have obtained.
- Copy the quote from the Focus section (see page 51) so that a participant can read it.

Chalice Lighting   2 minutes

Share these words by Susan L. Van Dreser:

> That we may remember,
> That we may know,
> That we may imagine and touch our joy:
> Let us kindle true light
> From the fire of our souls.

Check-in   10 minutes

Invite participants to introduce themselves and share, one by one, how they are doing and how their relationship with their child is going. Participation is voluntary, and facilitators can set a time limit for sharing, e.g., two minutes per person. Some groups find it valuable to go around the circle twice: first for initial sharing and a second time for participants to share ideas and responses sparked by others' check-ins.

Words for Meditation   2 minutes

Share these words by Jim Cohn:

> Releasing the separate one is a difficult knot.
> Finding yourself is something only you can do.
> Imagine yourself coming back ten years from today
> Through time, to help you where you must now be.

Focus   20 minutes

Invite a volunteer to read the following parable, "Of a Foolish Father," by Universalist minister Clinton Lee Scott:

> And there was a certain man that had a son whom he greatly loved. And he thought within himself saying, None is wise enough to instruct my son in the mysteries of the eternal: neither priest nor Levite shall tell him what is good and what is evil, lest his mind be corrupted with error. And he saith, This shall he do: he shall wait until he is a man, then he shall know of himself what to believe.
>
> But it was not as the father thought. For the son did grow and was strong. Keepeth he his eyes open for seeing, and his ears for hearing. And his teachers were neither priests nor Levites. Neither did he come to the Temple for instruction. But his teachers were them that speaketh into the air, and them that were seen in the pictures of Babylon, and messengers in bright colors that were brought into the household on the morning of the Sabbath day.
>
> And when the father was old he understood that the mind of his son had not been as an empty vessel that waiteth for a day to be filled, but that it was like unto a parched field that drinketh of that which falleth upon it.

Process the story with the following questions:

- Thinking of your early teenage self, identify some of the personal skills and responsibilities you needed to acquire in order to become an adult. Name them.

- In addition to these, are there additional personal skills and responsibilities that your child needs to become an adult?

- What inner resources do you possess that you would also like your child to possess? How can you give these to your child?

- What inner resources do they have already, and how can they come to recognize them?

Discussion and Planning   15 minutes

Ask parents to let their creativity come to light as they design a ritual to be used at the final group session. The ritual should be no more than twenty minutes in length and can include songs, dances, and meaningful symbols. Keep track of who volunteers to lead various elements of the ritual and who volunteers to bring materials. These examples can be shared to spark the group's creativity:

Ritual 1: Parents bring photos of their youth at a young age, a recent photo of their youth, and an object, picture, or other representation of their hopes for their youth ten years from now. The group builds three altars: one to the past, one to the present, and one to the future. Parents decorate the altars with their photos and representations, as well as candles, flowers, and other beautiful things. After building the altars, parents form a circle around the altar of the past and share a song or words about the past. They do the same at the altars of the present and of the future.

Ritual 2: This ritual takes place outdoors or in a room with a fireplace. The facilitator brings one big, beautiful flower per parent. Parents take some time to think about the biggest thing they want to let go of and the biggest thing they want to claim in their new relationship with their youth. They write these things down on small pieces of paper. The papers that name the things they want to let go are burned in a safe manner. Parents hand the papers with the things they want to keep to the parent on their right. The group then takes turns going around the circle. Readers face the person on their left, saying "[Name], I wish for you ..." and reads the words on their paper. The reader then hands the person a flower, saying "May it bloom in your life." This process repeats around the circle until everyone has had a turn.

Likes and Wishes   7 minutes

Participants are invited to "check out," sharing what they liked about the meeting and ideas for how it could have been improved. It helps to phrase these comments lovingly and constructively, with the good of the group in mind. Saying "I liked _____" and "I wish _____" helps to affirm good things that are already happening and to make space for more good things to happen at the next gathering.

Closing Words   2 minutes

Close with these words from Dawna Markova:

> As adults, we must ask more of our children than they know how to ask of themselves. What can we do to foster their open-hearted hopefulness, engage their need to collaborate, be an incentive to utilize their natural competency and compassion, . . . show them ways they can connect, reach out, weave themselves into the web of relationships that is called community.

Closing Ritual   2 minutes

Repeat the simple closing ritual you used in Session 1 (see page 46). Distribute Handout 2, Ritual Addressed to a Teenager. Explain that it is a ritual families can perform together at home to help mark a youth's coming of age.

Session 5
Walking Forward, Together

Time   60 minutes

Materials

- chalice, candle, and matches
- altar cloth
- name tags
- markers
- copies of Handout 1, Resources for Parenting Adolescents (page 54)
- copies of books listed on Handout 1 (optional)
- materials for ritual
- copies of *Singing the Living Tradition*

Preparation

- Arrange chairs in a circle, with the table, chalice, and candle at its center.
- Set out name tags and markers.
- Set out copies of Handout 1, Resources for Parenting Adolescents, along with any of the listed books you may have obtained.

Chalice Lighting   2 minutes

Share these words by Lindsay Bates:

> Receive, O Mystery, the words of our hearts.
>
> If prayer worked like magic—if I knew the words that would guarantee prayer's power—I know what I would pray:
>
>> Let life be always kind to our children.
>> Let sorrow not touch them.
>> Let them be free from fear.
>> Let them never suffer injustice,
>>   nor the persecutions of the righteous.
>> Let them not know the pain of failure—
>> of a project, a love, a hope, or a dream.
>> Let life be to them gentle and joyful and kind.
>
> If I knew the formula, that's what I'd pray.
>
> But prayer isn't magic, and life will be hard. So I pray for our children—with some hope for this prayer:
>
>> May their knowledge of sorrow be tempered with joy.
>> May their fear be well balanced by courage and strength.
>> May the sight of injustice spur them to just actions.
>> May their failures be teachers, that their spirits may grow.
>> May they be gentle and joyful and kind.
>> Then their lives will be magic, and life will be good.
>
> So may it be. Blessed be. Amen.

Check-in 10 minutes

Invite participants to introduce themselves and share, one by one, how they are doing and how their relationship with their child is going. Participation is voluntary and facilitators can set a time limit for sharing, e.g., two minutes per person. Some groups find it valuable to go around the circle twice: first for initial sharing and a second time for participants to share ideas and responses sparked by others' check-ins.

Words for Meditation 2 minutes

Share these word by Paul H. Bicknell:

> There are some heights to which we have not risen, and never will; there are some depths to which we have not fallen, and never will, we pray. Somewhere between there are places where we can reach up and reach out for the strength we need for our journey.
>
> This is such a place.
>
> Thus we pause for refreshment; thus we gather in thanksgiving.

Focus 15 minutes

Introduce the discussion by saying something like the following:

> Today we will prepare for the transition our youth are about to be recognized for—their coming of age. This process is not only a transition for our youth, however. It is also a transition for us. We as parents must decide what we will hold on to, and what we will let go of, as our children grow into a more mature adolescence.

Here are some questions to help parents reflect upon their feelings about their youth's transition:

- What is most difficult for you about your youth's coming of age?

- What makes you the most hopeful about your youth's coming of age?

- What is your vision for your relationship with your youth next year? In five years?

- What do you need to hold on to and what do you need to let go of to help this vision become reality?

Ritual 20 minutes

Perform the ritual that the group designed at the previous meeting.

Likes and Wishes 7 minutes

Participants are invited to "check out," sharing what they liked about the meeting and also sharing "wishes"—ways the meeting could have been improved.

Closing Words 2 minutes

Going around the circle, have each participant read a line from Reading 688, "Hold On to What Is Good," from *Singing the Living Tradition*.

Closing Ritual 2 minutes

Repeat the simple closing ritual you used in Session 1 (see page 46).

Resources for Parenting Adolescents

Books

How to Keep Being a Parent When Your Child Stops Being a Child: A Practical Guide to Parenting Adolescents by Nic Cooper and Rick McCoy. Canton, MI: Willow Creek Publishing, 1999.

Beyond the Big Talk: Every Parent's Guide to Raising Sexually Healthy Teens from Middle School to High School and Beyond by Debra Haffner. New York: Newmarket Press, 2001.

Everyday Blessings: The Inner Work of Mindful Parenting by Myla and Jon Kabat-Zinn. New York: Hyperion, 1997.

Nurturing Children and Youth: A Developmental Guidebook by Tracey Hurd. Boston: Skinner House Books, 2005.

Parenting with Spirit: 30 Ways to Nurture Your Child's Spirit and Enrich Your Family's Life by Jane Bartlett. New York: Marlowe and Company, 2004.

"Why Are All the Black Kids Sitting Together in the Cafeteria?" and Other Conversations about Race by Beverly Daniel Tatum. New York: Basic Books, 1997.

Websites

www.aamft.org
The American Association for Marriage and Family Therapy is a professional organization of therapists that provides its members with the resources they need to nurture healthy family relationships. The website includes books, articles and other information on family problems, as well as a list of therapists searchable by city.

www.hsph.harvard.edu/chc/parenting/report.pdf
"Raising Teens: A Synthesis of Research and a Foundation for Action" by A. Rae Simpson, Ph.D., copyright 2001. From the Project on the Parenting of Adolescents at the Center for Health Communication of the Harvard School of Public Health.

www.search-institute.org/families
The Search Institute focuses on strengthening youth and families by building the developmental assets that enable youth to thrive. The family page contains practical resources for those who do the work of parenting.

Ritual Addressed to a Teenager

This ritual can help the transition from childhood to a new phase of life: adolescence.

Intention: To put behind the old in a safe and gentle way and to consider and prepare for the new.

Preparation: Perhaps you can arrange to spend time in your room with three large boxes, one for that which you have outgrown and no longer need (certain toys, games, books, or mementos), one for those things you have outgrown but with emotional value (a teddy bear or a jersey from a winning Little League game), and one for the things that are currently relevant to your life (particular records or books, jewelry, favorite art).

Think about what it would mean to give away childish items to another, younger child. These would be the things in box one. Think about what it means to not give up certain items associated with childhood, and having that be okay. These are the things to put in box two. Think about how the things for box three symbolize how you see yourself now.

As you put objects in their appropriate boxes—which you may decorate in ways that represent how you feel about yourself at these different stages of your life—you may find yourself feeling sadness, pride, anger, fear, or joy. Let these feelings happen; perhaps write about your experience in a journal. Have someone you trust with you if the feelings seem too much to handle alone. Every transition brings up emotions, often conflicting ones. Working them through is an important part of your change, of your sense of who you are and of who you are becoming.

To help develop this sense of who you can be, plan to add items to box three that represent what might be important to how you would like to see yourself and have others see you. Ask your family members to think about something you might like and/or need to help you in your growth. It might be a tangible gift, such as a razor or a thesaurus, or something such as guitar lessons or a certificate for a week with a half-hour extended curfew.

Manifestation: Invite your family to meet in your room at a designated time. Clean and arrange the room in a way that reflects your identity. Greet your family members and seat them around the room. Talk with them—as much as you feel comfortable—about what is in each of the three boxes and about your process in putting the boxes together. Particular focus should be on the third box, the "present and future" box. The family should listen intently and try to discover how willing they are to support your choices. As you present the contents of the third box, each family member should be prepared to offer a gift in harmony with your needs, which may also benefit you in who you feel you are becoming as you grow toward adulthood. A gift honoring a precious part of yourself of which you may be unaware, but that others may recognize and nourish, would also be appropriate. Then form a circle, in which everyone holds hands and pledges to honor each other's struggles and growth and offers to help make this time as easy as possible. After the circle, there can be a sharing of food or drink, made more relevant if you prepare it.

Grounding: You should designate a time to give away the things in the first box to a younger child who would benefit from them. It would be useful to check the things in the second box on a monthly basis to see how much energy they still hold and what you can pass on to someone else. It is important for the family to honor the use of the things in the third box and for all family members to remember and honor their pledge. To help you in each of these grounding steps, you may find writing in your journal helpful, as well as speaking to your family about some of the changes you feel happening in you. Thanking them for their gifts, and letting them know how using them helps you in your transition, can keep you in touch with your process and also honors an adult mode of communication in your new life.

Like all beginning rituals, this one represents an initiation of the Self, a movement toward individuation that is yours alone, through which you must pass alone. For that reason, the support of and connection with others is truly important to help you with your solitary struggles and movements. Your efforts may remind you and those around you of the beginning of something even larger than adolescence. You are in fact recreating in your life the labor and birthing of existence, the mythic emergence of something out of nothing, and the dawning of a new consciousness.

—Renee Beck and Sidney Barbara Metrick, *The Art of Ritual*

WORKSHOPS

This section contains detailed descriptions of workshops, organized in nine units, to use when meeting with youth. Each unit has a theme that is explored and expanded upon in the workshops for that unit. Use as few or as many workshops as your program will allow.

The sequence is flexible, though the order in which the handbook presents them does follow a certain logic. Earlier units generally include topics that need to be presented at the beginning of the program, and some units build on themes presented in earlier units. For example, the unit on theology appears after participants have had an opportunity to examine their own beliefs. The unit on credos appears early to give participants the maximum amount of time to prepare.

Within units, you will find that some workshops refer to activities that are part of earlier workshops. Be aware of this possibility if you are skipping or changing the order of workshops within a unit.

Be sure to read the introduction to each unit. It describes the nature of the workshops in that unit, noting those that might need advance preparation or special materials or have unique scheduling considerations.

The average workshop length is sixty minutes, but it is recommended that you allot at least ninety minutes for each regular meeting. If your group will meet simultaneously with worship services or religious education programs that last sixty minutes, consider running Coming of Age for those sixty minutes, plus another thirty minutes afterward. Families waiting to pick up youth after program meetings can indulge in congregational fellowship after the services.

Meeting for longer than sixty minutes allows increased time for bonding and time for at least one workshop and often additional activities, which could include check-in, worship, journaling, and *Unitarian Universalist Pocket Guide* and mentor discussions. If your program's major components are building blocks, think of these additional activities as cementers; they can be inserted as needed and will serve to increase group cohesion and solidify many of the values inherent in the program. See Leader Resource 34, Sample Program Outlines (page 252), for specific ideas on scheduling.

Check-in

Check-in is a tradition in many Unitarian Universalist youth groups. It provides a structured opportunity for people to share how they are doing, mention important things that are happening in their lives, and respond to one another. This sharing fosters caring, empathy, and compassion.

Group members take turns, either going around in a circle or by raising their hands to be the next one to speak; a participant who does not feel like speaking has the right to pass. Check-ins are understood as confidential, but it's acceptable to articulate boundaries on that confidentiality. For example, you might want to let the group know that leaders reserve the right to discuss reports of violent behavior or other areas of grave concern with the minister and religious educator.

Adult leaders and mentors typically also share during check-in, but it is important to keep boundaries on that sharing. It is not appropriate for adults to unload all of their emotions the way they might do with their peers. Their check-ins should be truthful, but not therapeutic. The goal in adults' sharing is to create community with and among the youth. See Leaders and Mentors (page 13) for additional guidance on boundaries.

Check-in is structured into some workshops, and you can add it to others if it is particularly successful in your group and you have the time. Some groups check in at every workshop. Be aware, however, that check-in can become so long that it leaves little time for other activities. If it seems to be taking over your workshops, you might need to provide other opportunities for youth to socialize. If you do not yet have a youth group for this age, this could be the perfect opportunity to form one. Youth whose need to share is filled outside the workshops will be better able to focus on the activities provided to deepen their Unitarian Universalist faith.

Worship

Worshiping together is the cornerstone of our Unitarian Universalist faith. Unit 4, Spirituality (see page 112), contains workshops on the nature and practice of worship. In Services of Recognition (see page 242) you will find tools to help you plan a year-end worship service to recognize the Coming of Age participants. Even if youth attend the congregation's main worship service together as part of Workshop 13, Attending Worship (see page 118), they will benefit from additional worship opportunities. Consider adding a regular spiritual component to your workshops by including a monthly fifteen-minute worship service. Recruit youth to plan and lead these services. This provides them an opportunity to deepen their understanding by practicing what they have learned about conducting worship in a safe and nurturing environment.

Journaling

A few workshops provide the opportunity for youth to reflect on various subjects by writing in a journal. If your program meets for ninety min-

utes or more, you can dedicate additional time for extended journaling. Journal writing allows youth space for creativity and spiritual growth. It also helps them grow in self-understanding as they respond to and personalize the messages they hear in Coming of Age. Ralph Waldo Emerson, one of our movement's most famous journal writers, found journaling important not just to record the happenings of one's life, but also "for the habit of rendering an account of yourself to yourself."

Participants will vary in their learning styles and needs. One youth might process information best in small group discussions, while another might prefer personal reflection. Journaling can be particularly useful for that second youth.

Finally, journaling leads naturally to the process of credo writing. When youth sit down to write their credos, they are able to draw upon all they have written in their journals rather than starting from scratch.

Decide if you will supply a journal for every youth or if they will bring their own. Include pens or pencils as part of your basic supplies for all workshops. Keeping journals at the meeting space ensures that they will always be on hand. Take care to make sure the journals are secured and kept confidential, though youth can be invited to share their writing if they so choose. If you do decide to let them take journals home, remind them via e-mail or a phone call to bring them to the next workshop when they will be needed.

Encourage all youth to try journaling, but do not be surprised if some choose not to participate; some youth enjoy this practice, but it does not work for everyone.

At the end of every unit you will find a leader resource that includes prompts for extended journaling. Read the prompts aloud and/or write them on newsprint and invite youth to respond in their journals.

The Unitarian Universalist Pocket Guide

Creating space in your program for youth to read, reflect on, and discuss chapters of the *Unitarian Universalist Pocket Guide* helps to cement such topics as Unitarian Universalist history and how we share our faith, among others. The *Pocket Guide* is also a great resource for those new to Unitarian Universalism. Use the suggested prompts found in the leader resources at the end of most units, or create your own. Participants could discuss the readings as a group, or you could ask youth to reflect upon the readings in their journals.

These tips can help you use this cementer:

- Before the first discussion, check that every youth has access to a copy of the *UU Pocket Guide*. Since readings will happen outside of meeting times, families may want to purchase a copy to keep at home; consider also having a few available for check-out. Suggest that families read the selections together. This can help youth for whom the vocabulary might be difficult or those who simply do not enjoy reading. Families may find that the time dedicated to reading together provides a useful entry into discussions about their faith.

- Read the chapters to be discussed in advance of the meeting.

- Remind youth of the reading assignments in the prior workshop and again a couple of days before the workshop at which a chapter will be discussed.

- If getting youth to do the reading outside of meetings proves difficult, use group time to read the chapters, or selected portions, out loud. Ask for volunteers to read. Be ready to support youth with learning differences who may volunteer to read, and to assist all youth with difficult words.

Mentor Discussions

Some workshops include questions or ideas youth might want to talk about with their mentors. These discussions allow youth to go to greater depths of reflection than can happen in class. How they take place will depend in large part on how you structure the mentoring aspect of your program. If a workshop provides questions for mentor discussion, it is a good idea to give mentors a copy of the questions, too. Suggested mentor discussions are not frequent activities; however, the few that are included serve to remind the mentor and youth that their time together is not only social, but also a time for spiritual and faith exploration and development. If your group particularly enjoys mentor discussions, feel free to add more to your schedule. Inviting mentors to more regular meetings is one way to increase this activity. If prompts are needed for additional discussions, consider using Leader Resource 10, Prompts for Credo Development (page 81) and the relevant leader resources at the end of every workshop unit.

Use the workshops in the following eight units to fill the spaces in your program design for regular meetings. Some are written to last longer than sixty minutes, but you can delete activities, if needed, to fit your time frame. If your meetings will be longer, add check-ins, worship, journaling, *UU Pocket Guide* discussions and/or mentor discussions. If you are planning an overnight, retreat (see Retreats and Rites of Passage, page 226), or if your group meets for longer than ninety minutes, combine several workshops with the cementers described above.

Community Building

We are all longing to go home to some place we have never been—a place half-remembered and half-envisioned we can only catch glimpses of from time to time. Community. Somewhere, there are people to whom we can speak with passion without having the words catch in our throats. Somewhere a circle of hands will open to receive us, eyes will light up as we enter, voices will celebrate with us whenever we come into our own power. Community means strength that joins our strength to do the work that needs to be done. Arms to hold us when we falter. A circle of healing. A circle of friends. Someplace where we can be free.

—Starhawk

For many youth, the trusting and supportive atmosphere is what they remember most strongly about their Coming of Age program. Community building can help satisfy not only a social hunger to belong, but also a spiritual hunger to be authentically known and accepted. In this light, community building is not peripheral; intentional games, trust-building activities, and recreational retreats are central to the content of successful programs. The vision of the Tapestry of Faith Lifespan Curricula of the Unitarian Universalist Association begins with the idea that participants in UU religious education will "know that they are lovable beings of infinite worth." Intentional community building can help make that aspect of the vision a reality.

The Youth Office of the Unitarian Universalist Association recognized that the key element in establishing solid youth groups is intentional building of community between the members. In the early 1990s they published the flyer "Five Steps to Building Community," which is reprinted here as Leader Resource 7 (see page 69). A model borrowed from Denny Rydberg, author of *Building Community in Youth Groups*, the five steps turn the intricate process of community building into simple directions for transforming an assortment of individuals into a solid, bonded group.

The first workshop in this unit works well as the opening workshop in the program. It contains activities to help the group establish a covenant and to explain the process of check-in. The second features a discussion on consequences of breaking the covenant and encourages all participants to help design an opening and closing ritual. The third workshop provides information on keeping the community healthy. All three workshops include games to help participants grow closer and have fun.

Use the workshops as written, or use individual activities to supplement other workshops or a retreat. The exceptions are the activities on covenant making and creating rituals, which need to happen early in the program. Note which activities the group enjoys the most so you can use them spontaneously during future sessions when you want to add a bit of fun.

Several activities call for some physical action. As needed, adjust or replace these activities to accommodate the special needs of participants who are challenged by the action involved. For group building to be successful, all activities must be accessible to all members of the group. The success of some activities depends upon the group's size, and a few are designated as particularly good for smaller groups.

If leaders see a major goal of their work with youth as the establishment of community, then they are able to make this aspect come alive in nearly every session. To incorporate community-building activities, use either of these strategies or combine them:

The Sleepover Strategy. Many Coming of Age programs can get off to a successful start with overnights or retreats. The typical activities—hiking, cooking, playing games, making crafts, worshipping, and even cleaning—provide significant time for interpersonal interaction, while shared sleeping quarters encourage camaraderie, story telling, and laughter. Further, there are ample opportunities for activities that are intentionally geared toward moving a group along in the five-step process of community building.

The Every-Meeting Strategy. Every gathering, whether it be youth and leaders only, youth and mentors, or even mentors only, is an opportunity for intentional community building. Many of the activities in this handbook build community, whether or not it is their primary purpose. When leaders see a major goal of their work with youth as the establishment of community, then they are able to make this aspect come alive in nearly every session.

The prospect of conflict within a group often concerns leaders. While it can be destructive if not handled effectively, it is not inherently bad; every conflict provides an opportunity for strengthening the community. Whether it involves youth only or youth and adults, conflict presents opportunities for participants to show that they care about each other, that they can accept diversity, and that they can abide by the covenants and consequences they established together. It helps community when conflict is addressed openly and calmly.

The following published resources address building community in youth groups:

Team-Building Activities for Every Group by Alanna Jones. Richland, Washington: Rec Room Publishing, 1999.

More Team-Building Activities for Every Group by Alanna Jones. Richland, Washington: Rec Room Publishing, 2002.

Quicksilver: Adventure Games, Initiative Problems, Trust Activities and a Guide to Effective Leadership by Karl Rohnke. Dubuque, Iowa: Kendall/Hunt Publishing, 1996.

Cowstails and Cobras II: A Guide to Games, Initiatives, Ropes Courses, and Adventure Curriculum by Karl Rohnke. Dubuque, Iowa: Kendall/Hunt Publishing, 1996 & 1989.

Growing Together: A Guide for Building Inspired, Diverse, and Productive Youth Communities by Greg Gale. Lincoln, Massachusetts: The Food Project, 2001.

The Youth Group Handbook. Boston: Unitarian Universalist Association, 2006. (Includes Deep Fun game compendium.)

Workshop 1
Covenant and Community Building

Time   60 minutes

Participant Goals

- learn the names of everyone

- start the year-long process of building bonds

- begin to see themselves as part of a cohesive group

- develop new friendships and strengthen old friendships within the context of the group

- covenant with each other about norms of group behavior

- have fun

Materials

- reusable badges, masking tape, or name tags
- markers
- a bag with enough edible treats for each participant to have several, or a roll of toilet paper (optional)
- copies of Handout 3, Sample Covenant (page 74)
- newsprint preprinted with the words from Handout 3, Sample Covenant (see Preparation)

Preparation

- Post a sheet of newsprint with the words from Handout 3, Sample Covenant.
- Arrange chairs in a circle.

Opening   5 minutes

Invite participants to make name tags as they enter. It is a good idea to ask participants to wear name tags for at least the first few sessions. There are a variety of methods for creating name tags, including the following:

- inviting youth to decorate reusable name badges
- writing names on masking tape
- writing names on sticker name tags that are used one time

Feel free to use any method that works for you and your group.

Syllable Clap   15 minutes

Before participants have introduced themselves to each other, have each member of the group clap out a beat corresponding to the number of syllables in their first name. For example, Marc claps once; Alison claps three times. If most first names have the same number of syllables, consider using last names.

Explain to the group that their task is now to find people with the same number of syllables in their names. They must do this without speaking:

Clapping and walking around the room are the only methods they may use.

Soon the group will be divided into syllable groups. Add anyone who is sitting alone to another group with a close number of syllables. Ask the syllable groups to spend five minutes introducing themselves to each other, sharing their full names, where they were born, and something they are proud of about themselves.

After five minutes, explain that their next assignment is to find out something that everyone in their group has in common that the average person would not guess: something besides number of syllables in their names or where they go to church! They will have three minutes to figure this out.

When their time is up, reconvene the whole group, and ask each syllable group to come forward and introduce themselves with the following:

- their number of syllables
- what they all have in common
- their names

Thank all groups for coming forward!

Alternate Activity

Tell All   15 minutes

This alternative is well suited for small groups.

Pass around the bag of treats, saying, "Take only a few, and don't eat them yet." Once everyone has their treats, announce that they have to share one thing about themselves for every treat they took. Encourage them to think of facts about themselves that most people in the group will not know.

This variation works well for retreats or overnights.

Announce that there is a toilet paper shortage. Pass around a roll and tell everyone to take all they will need for the rest of the retreat. After everyone has taken their paper, tell them they have to share one thing about themselves for every square of toilet paper they took.

Guided Check-in   10 minutes

Gather the group in a circle and explain that one ritual you will be doing pretty often in Coming of Age is called check-in. Say something like the following:

> During check-in, each member of the group is invited to say something about how they're doing, about what happened to them during the week, etc. Sometimes check-ins will be open, which means that anyone can talk about anything; sometimes they will be specific, which means that there will be a question to answer.
>
> We'll go around the circle and take turns. Once the first person is done, the person to the right can begin. Each person will share without comments from others. If you don't want to talk in check-in, it is fine to just say "I pass" and no one will think worse of you. Today we'll do a specific check-in, with the question "What do you want out of Coming of Age?"

Ask for a volunteer to begin, or you can start. Depending on the size of your group, set a time limit for each person's sharing. Once the sharing is complete, you are encouraged to make observations about themes and common desires that you heard from participants.

Spill the Basket   15 minutes

This game is played like musical chairs and requires a relatively high degree of physical mobility.

Set up a circle with one chair for each participant, minus one. Ask the group to sit. You (the leader) will be "it" first. Explain that whoever is "it" does not have a chair, but stands in the center and picks something that he/she might have in common with other members of the group. "It" then turns this into a phrase that starts with "I like people who . . ." For example, "it" could say, "I like people who are wearing red" or "I like people who are interested in politics."

Then, everyone to whom the statement applies must jump out of their chairs and find another chair. They cannot move to either of the chairs next to their original chair. The person remaining after all the chairs are taken becomes "it."

Variation for a group that already knows each other well:

Choose slightly more meaningful categories, and have everyone to whom they apply come to the center of the circle, hold hands, and give themselves a cheer before they rush to find another seat.

Covenant Making   10 minutes

Say something like the following:

> Throughout Coming of Age, we're going to get to know one another better and we're going to be sharing personal information about ourselves. To create a good, solid community, it is helpful for us as a group to talk about how we will treat each other. Is anyone familiar with the idea of making a covenant?

After soliciting responses from participants, continue as follows:

> A covenant is a promise we make to one another as a group. In your experience, what are good promises for groups to make with one another? [Allow time for responses.] For example, "listening to each other" is a good promise. In Coming of Age, we make a covenant about how we treat others, how we expect to be treated, and how we treat ourselves.

Distribute Handout 3, Sample Covenant, and explain that it is a sample covenant that youth and adults in the program can hold themselves to. Ask the group to take turns reading the items aloud. Ask if they have anything they'd like to add to the covenant. Explain that to add an item, the whole group has to agree to it; if an item is proposed and everyone doesn't agree, it can be rephrased so that everyone can accept it. (For example, "Keep quiet unless you're supposed to talk" could be rephrased to "No side conversations during group discussion.") Add agreed-upon items to the posted sheet of newsprint. Ask also if there is anything they would like to cross out, and follow a similar procedure of consensus to determine whether it will be crossed out or left in. Acknowledge that the process the group just participated in works because the covenant is a "living" document: the group can revisit it later to add or subtract elements as needed.

Once all items listed on the newsprint are accepted, lead the group in formally affirming this covenant. Ask them to repeat after you: "I, [state your name], promise to do my best to follow this covenant during Coming of Age. I will also help my fellow participants uphold this promise to each other. In making this promise, we understand that we are setting the stage for a strong, healthy community. This year, may it be so!"

Closing Circle   5 minutes

Invite the group to hold hands in a circle. Explain as follows:

> We will be passing a squeeze around the circle. You will squeeze the hand of the person to your right, and that person will squeeze the hand of the person to their right, until the squeeze has gone around the whole circle. When a squeeze comes to you from the left, you squeeze the hand of the person to your right.

Try this a few times in different directions, or simultaneously send around a few squeezes. If the group gets really good at it, ask someone to step out of the circle and time how quickly a squeeze can travel around the circle.

Explain that this group is a community where everyone has an effect on each other, just like they did in the circle. Restate the idea that this is what being in a covenanted community is all about; everyone's actions affect everyone else's.

Express how good it has been to meet together today before you send everyone on their way.

Workshop 2
The Community Building Continues!

Time   60 minutes

Participant Goals

* continue the process of building bonds

* see themselves as part of a cohesive group

* develop new friendships and strengthen old friendships within the context of the group

* develop a covenant about consequences for violating group behavioral norms

* create opening and closing rituals for the program

* have fun

Materials

* chalice, candle, and matches

* cloth for the altar or centering table

* small table

* name tags

* markers

* newsprint and easel

* bell or chime

* multiple copies of *Singing the Living Tradition* and *Singing the Journey*

* covenant from Workshop 1 (see Preparation)

* two rattles: soda cans taped up with small rocks inside

* two blindfolds

* butcher paper; various art supplies such as magazines, paints, crayons, markers, colored pencils, scissors, glue; and tape, if posting mural on the wall (optional)

* CD or tape of music (optional)

Preparation

- Arrange chairs in a circle, with the table, chalice, and candle at its center.

- Set out name tags and markers.

- Prepare sign-up sheets showing each session of the Coming of Age Program, in case you decide to have sign-ups for openings and closings.

- Rewrite the group's covenant on a new sheet of newsprint.

Opening   10 minutes

Invite participants to join the circle and light the chalice while you or your fellow leader reads a chalice lighting from *Singing the Living Tradition*.

Ask if anyone has ever taken part in an activity that opens with a chalice lighting. Explain as follows:

> Chalice lighting is a ritual that many Unitarian Universalist worship services open with. This Coming of Age group needs an opening ritual. Having opening and closing rituals will help all present know when we are starting and ending. It will also mark this time as special and help us focus our attention on the here and now. These ceremonies need not be fancy. An opening ritual can be as simple as lighting a chalice; a closing, as simple as extinguishing it.

Invite ideas from the group. If your religious education program has a standard opening and closing, consider keeping it. Other suggestions for openings include ringing a chime, inviting a moment of centering silence, singing a short song, or offering a prayer or meditation. Possible closing rituals include standing in a circle for a short blessing, offering a reading and extinguishing the chalice, having a one word check-out, or singing a song. Use the hymnals *Singing the Living Tradition* and *Singing the Journey*, along with any other meditation manual available, for possible readings and/or songs.

After the group has decided what the rituals will be, decide what materials will be needed and who will be responsible for gathering them. Ask for volunteers to help so the activity truly belongs to the group and not just the leaders. If responsibility will rotate, post a sign-up sheet; weekly e-mail reminders would be helpful.

If lighting a chalice, be aware of the flame at all times. A lit chalice in the room during active activities presents potential danger, so decide on a practical time to extinguish it.

Pinwheel Interviews   15 minutes

Divide participants into two groups of equal numbers: Group A and Group B. If there is an odd number of participants, one of the leaders can step in and join one of the groups. Ask Group B to get in a circle. Then ask Group A to form a circle around Group B. When the circles have formed, invite those in Group B to turn around 180 degrees and face the Group A circle. Each person in the inside circle should then be facing someone in the outside circle, and vice versa.

Explain that you'll be asking a series of interview questions. Each person will have one minute to respond to the question during a discussion with the person across from them. A bell (or chime) will sound when it is time to switch. After both partners have answered the question, the people in Group A will move one person to their right, and a new question will be presented.

Here are some sample questions:

- What is your birth month, and what is good or not good about having a birthday in that month?

- What are your favorite and least favorite subjects in school, and why?

- Name a recent movie you really liked, and say three things about what made it so good.

- If you have siblings, tell your partner about them. If you don't, tell your partner about what it's like to be an only child.

- Talk about something you're excited about in the Coming of Age program.

- Name someone you admire, and tell why.

- What kind of music do you like, and what is a favorite song of yours?

Covenantal Consequences 15 minutes

Draw the group's attention back to the covenant established in the last meeting. Explain as follows: "To be really serious about having a successful Coming of Age program, we need to agree on consequences for people who break the promises of our covenant. Let's look at the covenant in silence for a minute or two and think of what the consequences should be if someone violates the covenant."

After this period of silence, go to the posted newsprint and ask for ideas, explaining that this is now a brainstorm, which means that every idea is first listed without discussion. During this and all brainstorming, encourage as wide a range of responses as possible by welcoming all contributions. Avoid the pitfall of praising some responses and questioning others. Clarifying what a speaker means is always appropriate, but using questions to advocate your own set of values (in this stage of the conversation) will only inhibit a full and honest exploration of youth's concerns and beliefs. Write down all ideas that are generated, even silly ones like "Off with their heads!" After the list is made, ask which ones seem reasonable. Put a star next to these on the newsprint. Of those that are reasonable, find out which ones have the most support from participants and leaders. Seek consensus on consequences. It is very important that the whole group agree and that the ideas come from them. This way the group will take ownership for its own covenant. It is valuable for leaders to maintain a positive and nonjudgmental tone during this discussion.

Note: There may be different consequences for breaking promises to the group than there are for breaking promises to oneself. There also may be a tiered system to responding to broken promises. For example, on the first offense, the leaders will chat with you; the second time, there will be a discussion with the whole group; and if problems continue, there may be temporary suspension from Coming of Age activities.

Rattler 15 minutes

Have the group form a loose standing circle and choose two people to be the rattlers, who will stand in the middle with scarves tied over their eyes. The rattlers are given rattles, and the object of the game is for one to locate and tag the other, using the sound of the rattles. When one rattles, the other must rattle back. The circle of people contains them safely. When a rattler is tagged, the round is over and they choose their replacements for the next round.

Be aware that not everyone is comfortable with their eyes covered. Remember the right to pass.

Alternate Activity

Group Mural 15 minutes

This activity is well suited to a small group or an enclosed space.

Put out various art supplies (magazines, paints, crayons, markers, colored pencils, scissors, glue) and a large sheet of butcher paper. Play music at a volume that allows conversation, and let participants work on the mural. Consider using a theme, such as "My Communities" or one of the Principles. Encourage people to make their corner of the project their own, but to interact with and respond to what others are doing. Display.

Closing Circle 5 minutes

Use the closing ritual designed by the group.

Workshop 3
Peace and Put-downs

Time 60 minutes

Participant Goals

- continue the process of building bonds

- create an accepting, cohesive community in which the gifts of each participant are recognized

- strengthen the bonds of understanding and trust with group leaders and mentors

- create community that challenges the social hierarchies and divisions that exist outside the group

Materials

- pieces of blank scrap paper for each youth
- pens or pencils
- newsprint with silhouette (see Preparation)
- markers in two different colors
- trash-talk sign (see Preparation)
- trashcan or wastebasket
- five copies of Leader Resource 8, Put-down Vignettes Script (page 71)
- copies of Handout 4, Keeping the Vultures at Bay (page 75)

Preparation

- Draw a faceless silhouette on a piece of newsprint, and post it on a wall.
- Create a sign with the words "Trash talk belongs in the trash can."

Opening   5 minutes

Use the opening ritual designed by the group.

Trash Talk   20 Minutes

This activity is adapted from one developed by the Institute for Peace and Justice. Using separate pieces of scrap paper, ask youth to write up to three of the meanest things they have ever said to someone else. They could write one word or phrase on each piece of paper or write all the statements on the same piece. Tell them to wad each piece of paper tightly into a separate ball.

Depending on the size of the group, line up all or some of the participants to throw their paper balls at the faceless silhouette. Have them go one person at a time and throw their paper words with all the intensity they used when they actually "hurled" their mean word(s) at someone. Make sure they get close to the silhouette and throw as hard as they can.

Ask students to write one word or draw one image on the silhouette to express how they think this person felt. Use one color marker for this portion. After everyone who wants to add some-

thing has had a turn, have one or two participants read aloud or describe what was written on the silhouette.

Next, ask students what they can do or say, after the fact, to support the person or make up for what was said. Using a different color marker, have them write the words expressing this on the silhouette. After everyone who wants to add something has had a turn, again have one or two students read aloud or describe what was written on the silhouette.

Ask participants what all the paper balls on the floor remind them of. Their answers may include a mess, trash, or trash talk. Show them the trash-talk sign and have them repeat the slogan several times: "Trash talk belongs in the trash can!" Decide with the students where to post the sign prominently in the room (perhaps on a trash can) and refer to it whenever trash talk is used in the future.

End the activity by asking the following questions:

- What were the reasons for the put-downs you threw at the target?
- What are some other reasons why kids use put-downs?
- Has anyone ever thrown a put-down at you? What was it? Can you guess why that person did it?
- How did it make you feel?
- What Unitarian Universalist Principles are related to what we are discussing?
- What does it mean to live your UU values in an environment (like school) where people are putting each other down?

Warding Off Your Vultures   25 minutes

Set up a "stage" area of the room with two or three chairs. Ask for volunteers to play five different parts in two short skits. Give each volunteer a copy of Leader Resource 8, Put-down Vignettes Script.

Ask the players to perform the skits, one after the other. After the skits are completed, invite discussion. Ask these questions:

- How did it feel to hear Gary and Celia talk this way to themselves?

- Do you have friends or family members who talk this way about themselves? If so, how does it feel to hear them say negative things about themselves?

- Why do you think people put themselves down?

- What do you think we can do to stop putting ourselves down?

If the following points have not been made already in the discussion, bring them up by saying something like this:

> One of the Principles that Unitarian Universalist congregations agree to affirm and promote is "the inherent worth and dignity of every person." When we talk about every person, we are also talking about ourselves. Yourself. Many people who treat others with respect do not treat themselves with the same respect. They might never call other people names or intentionally hurt other people's feelings, but every day they call themselves names and hurt their own feelings. Self-put-downs keep us from feeling worthy or dignified. We can honor the first Principle of Unitarian Universalism by respecting ourselves and treating ourselves as if we have worth and dignity. We can stop putting ourselves down.
>
> Know that there is nothing egotistical or self-centered about having positive self-worth. Some people think that if they stop putting themselves down, they'll become snobs. Actually, they won't become snobs—they'll just become happier.

Distribute Handout 4, Keeping the Vultures at Bay. Review the handout and highlight what youth can do to stop putting themselves down. Ask participants if there is anything else they would add to the list of suggestions.

Wrapping It Up 5 minutes

Ask the participants if everyone can agree that all Coming of Age events will be "Put-down–Free Zones" where they will affirm Unitarian Universalism's first Principle by honoring the worth and dignity of all.

If everyone agrees, discuss how they will be held accountable for it. For example, people can say "Ouch" if they hear someone else putting down themselves or another person, or anyone who voices a put-down can be asked to say two positive things about its target, including themselves.

Closing Circle 5 minutes

Use the closing ritual designed by the group.

Five Steps to Building Community

Step One: Bonding

The first step in building community is to break down cliques and barriers and to establish a relationship of trust among the individuals in the group. A problem-solving task or other activity that requires group members to work side by side can create communal bonds. As they discuss solutions and help one another accomplish the goal, group members transcend their diverse backgrounds. Cooperation is the goal. As each person's input is accepted and welcomed by others, group members begin to identify themselves as part of the team.

Step Two: Opening Up

When an individual can share nonthreatening areas of his/her life, an exciting step in group building has taken place. If one person perceives that another is genuinely interested in his/her story, then trust will develop between the two. Unfortunately, the reverse is also true. If a person perceives that others do not care enough to listen or trust, the foundation of community will not be established. The more sympathetically a group listens, the more secure an individual feels as a member of a group.

The exercises done in this step should be flexible, so that people can share to whatever degree they feel comfortable. Participants go away from these activities enthusiastic about the deepening friendships they are developing in their group. They realize that their personal imperfections and struggles are shared by the group. Individuals discover that their uniqueness is not strange but wonderful and the group accepts and loves them.

Step Three: Affirming

The act of encouraging each other through affirmation is crucial to the growing process of a group. When a young man's peers compliment him, he feels more confident in himself in relation to the group and can share deeper feelings. When friends tell a young woman that they appreciate her, she realizes that she is worthy of love and praise. Many reclusive youth become active members of the group when they realize others care about them. Participants in affirming interactions leave feeling warm and fuzzy about the group and themselves. This feeling is especially crucial at this stage of the community-building process. After opening up, people need positive feedback before they will consider sharing further. It is important to remember that adult leaders and advisors are an integral part of the community-building process and need affirmation just like everyone else.

Step Four: Stretching

Difficult situations naturally arise if the group is together long enough. These may include problems that arise in group members' lives, like divorce, illness, or drug abuse or those that affect the group directly, like division of the church, rules violation, and cliques at conferences. These situations are opportunities for stretching. However, since many youth groups are together for only a short period, you may not want to wait for a stretching experience to surface on its own. It is sometimes necessary to initiate one.

Stretching exercises reap many benefits. When people move beyond their normal comfort level, they experience the greatest potential for growth. Group members facing struggles together must actively care for each other. Individuals cannot merely say they care for each other in a stretching exercise; they must actively show it. They must create an atmosphere where people feel comfortable enough to expose their imperfections to the group. For example, if the group plans a trip to the hospital to visit terminally ill children, a popular member who appears to have his life together might admit his apprehensions about talking one-on-one with those less fortunate than he. When he sees that the group still likes him, he realizes that his facade of perfection is unnecessary. When self-critical members of the group discover that even seemingly perfect people have struggles, they will be less hard on themselves.

Through a simple stretching exercise, individuals also realize they can achieve much more as a group than they could as a collection of individuals. They realize the importance of each member to the entire group. Facing and overcoming programmed difficulties give young people the confidence that they can cope with the everyday problems they face. They learn that they can accomplish more than they thought possible if they believe in themselves.

Step Five: Deeper Sharing and Goal Setting

At this stage, individuals share deeply with one another and set goals. The youth group becomes a setting where young people can express their visions of the future and present struggles. The group will not laugh at or condemn its members if they admit they flunked a test, or that they dream of becoming a U.S. senator, or that they have a drinking problem.

When a group member shares a problem, the rest of the group gives support and encouragement by expressing sympathy. The group can help the individual talk through possible solutions and goals. The group holds the individual accountable for his/her decisions, remaining supportive throughout the process.

It is important to keep in mind that not all of a person's thoughts are appropriate to share in a group setting. A person should be discouraged from telling the entire youth group details

of her life that might hurt another member of the group. She should be encouraged to share these struggles with another member of the group or the advisor(s) on a one-to-one basis and, in these conversations, come up with an appropriate way to bring them to the group.

Taking a group through the five steps is essential to the communal group, but it is only the beginning of the exercises' benefits. Once they have built a sense of community, participants will be ready to risk sharing with their peers in a nonprogrammed way. They will also be ready to set and accomplish other goals with a united effort.

—Denny Rydberg. *Building Community in Youth Groups*, adapted by Jennifer Martin and Galen Moore, *www.uua.org/leaders/leaderslibrary*

Put-down Vignettes Script

Vignette 1: Narrator and Gary

Narrator: Gary is sixteen and a sophomore in high school. He has many friends at school and church, and people generally like him. Even people who don't know him very well think he's a nice guy. He's a decent student, getting mostly Bs on his report card and sometimes a few As. He sings tenor in the school's show choir and plays goalie on the varsity soccer team, which is quite an achievement. Most people, even his parents, think he's a pretty happy fellow, but they don't know what goes on inside Gary's head.

Gary: "You idiot! Jerk! LOSER!"

Narrator: Gary's very angry at somebody. What could anyone have done to deserve being called these names?

Gary: "You're so stupid. You missed that ball. You should have known that the Bruins forward always kicks to the right. What a total loser you are. And we might lose this whole game because of you."

Narrator: If the coach heard Gary say these mean things to another player, he'd take Gary aside and discipline him. But the coach didn't hear these things because Gary never said them out loud. Gary's victim didn't need to hear them out loud to feel the hurt they created because Gary's victim was his very own self. You see, Gary is an expert at putting himself down. He could say the meanest, cruelest, and most unfair things to himself, and there would be no coach to take him aside, no one to stop the words from inflicting pain. Let's visit Gary again, the next day, in math class. He's in the middle of taking a test.

Gary: "The Pythagorean formula . . . is . . . X plus Y squared . . . or wait! X squared plus Y squared . . . I studied but I can't remember! I am so STUPID in math! Look at Jessie—she's just plowing through this test . . . And Richie, he's already turned it in! If I can't even do this, I am never going to get into college. My parents will be so disappointed. What is wrong with me? Stupid. Stupid!"

Narrator: Gary continues to struggle with the test. He grows more and more frustrated, and his classmates can see that his face is turning redder and redder as he clutches his pencil and stares at the page. The reason Gary can't remember the Pythagorean formula is because the night before, when he should have been concentrating on studying for the test, he was continuing to put himself down as if he alone had made his soccer team lose the last game. No one on the team—except Gary—blamed Gary for the loss. They all thought the Bruins won because they were a highly ranked team with very skilled players. But Gary wouldn't listen to this—in his mind, he knew that if he weren't such a stupid idiot, his team would have won. His friends tried to tell him otherwise, but he wouldn't listen. He thought his friends were just making things up to make him feel better. You see, it's hard to reason with people when they put themselves down. It can seem like no matter what you say or what you do, those who put themselves down won't change their self-hurting, self-defeating ways. It turns out that the only person who can stop Gary's self-put-downs is Gary.

Vignette 2: Narrator, Celia and Celia's Mom

Narrator: Let's examine the case of Celia. Celia is a couple of years younger than Gary. She's in middle school, and she is very self-conscious. Last year Celia had to get braces, and just about the same time, some pimples started to appear on her face. She's growing taller each year and occasionally knocks into things because she's not quite used to her new size. And as if all of this wasn't awkward enough, just last week Celia auditioned for the school play and didn't get cast. She didn't even make it to the callback list, despite having gone to drama camp for three summers! Celia is watching TV with her mom and younger brother. They are watching a sitcom, but Celia is frowning.

Celia: "Wow, that actress is so pretty. I bet she got cast in her school plays. I'm sure Mrs. Cranston didn't cast me because of my ugly face. Jennie got the lead and she's only had one acting class—but she's thin and pretty and blonde. God! I wish I wasn't so gross looking."

Narrator: Gross looking. If only Celia knew how many people would disagree with that. Some people even think Celia is cute! During a commercial break, Celia goes into the bathroom and looks at herself in the full-length mirror. She sucks in her tummy and pushes her chest out.

Celia: Too much here, too little there. [She puts her hands on her cheeks and pushes them back.] If only I could get plastic surgery . . . Maybe then I could get into a play. But maybe not—I'm really not that good an actress. I mean, I did such a stupid job the last play I was in. And I tripped over my own feet in the final number.

Narrator: Celia returns to the living room and sits down in front of the TV. Her shoulders are slumped and her frown has deepened.

Celia's mom: What's wrong, sweetie?

Celia: Nothing.

Celia's mom: I can tell something's wrong. Do you want to talk about it?

Celia: No. I just want to be alone.

Narrator: Celia goes into her bedroom and shuts and locks the door. She looks in the mirror and starts to cry.

Extended Journaling for Unit 1

Encourage participants to reflect upon the topics covered in this unit in their journals. Pose the following questions to get them started:

- How do you like playing games?

- Do you feel individuals in the group know each other better after the first few sessions of Coming of Age? Why or why not?

- What can you do to add to the cohesion of the group?

Sample Covenant

How will I treat others?

- I will listen with an open mind and heart.

- I won't interrupt.

- I will keep personal information confidential.

- I won't put people down.

- I will respect people's personal space and their privacy.

- I will respect people's opinions, even when they differ from my own.

- I will try to get to know the real person beyond the stereotypes.

- I will assume that people in the group have good intentions, unless proven otherwise.

- I will do my best to be on time for Coming of Age meetings and programs.

How do I expect to be treated?

- I expect to be listened to.

- I expect to be treated with respect.

- I expect to be valued as a member of the community.

How will I treat myself?

- I will refrain from putting myself down.

- I will share my honest ideas and opinions.

- I will be kind to myself by eating a balanced diet and getting enough sleep.

- I will speak up for myself when I am hurt or uncomfortable.

- I will be open to the changes and growth that this year brings.

Keeping the Vultures at Bay

Self-put-downs are like vultures. Vultures are birds of prey, like eagles or hawks, but vultures do not hunt for strong or lively animals. Instead, they look for animals that are weak, helpless, or even dead. Then they swoop in and inflict their damage, increasing the pain and suffering of those creatures who are already hurt. Self-put-downs are like this. When we experience sadness, pain, and disappointment, we are already hurting. But then if we let the vulture of the self-put-down come in—telling us we're stupid, lazy, ugly or no good—the vulture inflicts more sadness, pain, and disappointment, and we are hurt very deeply. Because one vulture has picked on us, we are weaker and more helpless. However, it does not stop there: Vultures love weakness and helplessness. So after one visits, the vultures start to circle around us. More and more of them swoop down—"Idiot!" "Loser!" "Freak!"—and do their damage. Soon our sense of self-worth is lying on the ground in shreds and tatters.

Following these suggestions can help you make the vultures fly away:

- Remind yourself that you have inherent worth and dignity and are worthy of love and respect. Unitarian Universalism affirms this.

- Learn to tell the difference between a put-down that has some grain of helpfulness and a put-down that just makes you feel bad. If you put yourself down for being lazy about chores, there is probably something you can do about that: You can pay more attention to your chores. Labeling yourself as "lazy" never helps the matter. Put-downs like "I'm so stupid" are never helpful; they just hurt.

- Develop some good comebacks. This way, if you put yourself down, you can also reply with a more affirming statement. For example, if you put yourself down for being clumsy, you can say, "Actually, I have pretty good coordination. I am not perfect, but 95 percent of the time I do just fine." If you call yourself stupid, you can say to yourself, "I'm pretty smart about most things. Sometimes I mess up, but everybody does at some time or another. I'll learn from this experience so I can do better next time."

Vultures do not like it when we show understanding and compassion toward ourselves. Every time we follow the suggestions above, we make them fly farther and farther away from us. The stronger we get, the fewer vultures we have hovering around our heads.

—Sidney Simon, *Vulture: A Modern Allegory on the Art of Putting Oneself Down*

Credos

Follow your heart, but be quiet for a while first. Ask questions, then feel the answer. Learn to trust your heart.

—Anonymous

Credo statements have been highly valued elements of Coming of Age programs in a large number of Unitarian Universalist congregations. *Credo* is commonly translated from the Latin as "I believe," and participants' credo statements have often focused on what they believe religiously. In Unitarian Universalism, the ultimate source of religious authority is the individual and his/her conscience. Our congregations and our movement are formed by people and institutions of diverse beliefs. Therefore we have placed high value on the development of individualized beliefs among our young people. We have affirmed them in all their diversity: atheist, agnostic, theistic, pagan, Bible believing, and more.

If we dig a little deeper into its Latin roots, we discover that *credo* literally means "what I set my heart to." This definition opens up the credo-making process to something deeper than the affirmation and rejection of religious truth claims. Our personal credos are about what we ultimately value and what greater purpose we live for. Our credos are also deeply about what we have faith in, what ultimate meaning we bind our lives to.

The resources in this handbook seek to build on this tradition by offering several angles from which to approach credo development, and to help leaders recognize their group's developmental readiness for such an undertaking. It can be a challenge for youth, especially those in middle school, to author an individualized set of beliefs. Developmental psychologist Robert Kegan's work shows that teenagers often understand authority as residing outside themselves. The idea that they themselves have religious authority is hard to grasp. In adolescence most youth are intensely concerned with what others think and what their groups think, whether those groups are social, familial, or religious. Therefore it can be very hard for youth to come up with an individualized credo. And to come up with one that they feel comfortable sharing with their peers and their entire congregation—well, that adds another layer of stress to this whole undertaking during this intensely self-conscious phase in life!

For credo development to be meaningful, youth need to know early on in the program that credos will be expected at the end. They need to be given structured opportunities to think about and discuss their credos at several points, and they need practice in articulating their own ideas throughout the program. This unit contains several concrete suggestions for journal writing, reflection, and mentored discussion that will build up to writing a credo.

Credo writing takes time to unfold. An ideal program interweaves this process with all of the workshops and activities throughout the year. See

Leader Resource 34, Sample Program Outlines (page 252), for scheduling suggestions.

Preparation for writing a credo begins as soon as Coming of Age participants begin exploring their own identities, values, feelings, and beliefs, which in most programs means right away. Each week's session includes suggestions for group discussion, individual reflection, and mentor conversations that will help participants identify "what they set their heart to." Mentors can play an important role in credo development. To do so most effectively, they need to be informed about the questions they are encouraged to discuss with their mentees.

This unit includes plans for a "spiritual autobiography" that can help youth in developing their credos. Inviting participants to consider the turns their own lives have taken and what sources of strength they have sought in difficult times can lay excellent groundwork for exploring their values and beliefs. A session that describes the parameters for a credo and makes space for participants to begin drafting their credos is also included.

Leader Resource 10, Prompts for Credo Development (page 81), includes prompts related to individual workshops and a few general prompts. Participants can use these prompts during conversations with mentors or for journaling. Leaders can also use them if there is spare time during the associated workshop or to refer to during the credo-writing workshops.

Offering Workshop 4 fairly early within your program not only sets the stage for credo development but also engages youth in journaling, which you may wish to explore more thoroughly in future workshops.

Workshop 5 should be presented about two-thirds to three-quarters of the way through the Coming of Age program. Decide before this session how long you would like credos to be in words and in time. A three-hundred-word page (one page of double-spaced 12-point type) takes about two minutes to read. Some congregations with smaller numbers of Coming of Age participants are able to allow five minutes or more per participant. Others choose to limit credos' length to two minutes or less.

You are also encouraged to decide how much creativity you will allow in fulfilling the goals of the credo. Could someone write a song or do a skit? Are there youth with developmental or learning differences for whom traditional credos might be hard? If so, it would be valuable to talk with them and their parents in advance about creative ways they could fulfill the goals of the project. Perhaps they could collaborate with their mentors to create scripted dialogues, or perhaps they could create visual art projects—something that expresses their beliefs and values in a way that is congruent with their abilities and talents.

Workshop 6 should be presented from one to three weeks in advance of the presentation of credos. Leaders and mentors are encouraged to be both kind and firm during this session, praising youth and the work they have done on their credos while also challenging them to meet high standards.

Workshop 4
Your Autobiography

Time   60 minutes

Participant Goals

- reflect on the impact of various influences on their lives

- put what is important in their lives into words

Materials

- journals

- pens or pencils

Preparation

- Remind participants in advance that their journals will be required at this session.

Opening   5 minutes

Use the opening ritual designed by the group.

Spiritual Autobiography   35 minutes

Arrange the session in whichever way you feel works best for the group: Participants can write in their journals on their own or discuss the questions with other youth or their mentors before writing.

- What is the story of your name? Is there significance in the name you were given? What about your name do you like and identify with?

- Create a family tree that shows the different religions and cultures of your family. Include the present members and as many generations back as you can. Reflect on how the different religious and cultural identities in your family affect your own identity.

- Draw a line all the way across the page; the left end represents your birth, and the right represents today. Make marks for important personal events that have occurred between your birth and today, including both happy and sad things. When you have made a basic timeline of your life, think about how each event made you feel. What did you learn from it? Did it change your understanding of yourself? Did it change your views on life, on death, on people, on God, on religion?

- Who are the three or four people who have had the greatest impact on your life? Why?

- What communities, religious or not, have had a lasting influence on your development?

- Think of the important decisions in your life. Discuss what they meant to you, how they were made, and the results.

Discussion   15 minutes

Ask participants, "What was that activity like for you?" Follow up with questions about whether or not they had thought about these things before and whether they found it helpful to write them down.

Depending on the trust level of your group, decide whether to have them gather in small groups to share one thing they wrote about or simply engage in a large-group discussion about what the process was like.

Closing Circle   5 minutes

Use the closing ritual designed by the group.

Workshop 5
Writing Your Credo

Time   60 minutes

Participant Goals

- understand the term *credo*

- start developing a credo

- exercise Unitarian Universalism's fourth Principle: the free and responsible search for truth and meaning

- understand how Unitarian Universalism fits into their beliefs, ethics, and values

Materials

- journals

- pen and pencils

- Leader Resource 11, Sample Credos (page 83)

- copies of handout describing credo parameters (see Preparation)

Preparation

- Before the workshop, familiarize yourself with Leader Resource 10, Prompts for Credo Development (page 81).

- Prepare a handout for participants listing the parameters you have set for the credo statement and process, including length, format, rough draft deadline, and final draft deadline. You can also share expectations you have regarding credo content, delivery, and mentor involvement in the process.

- Remind participants in advance that their journals will be required at this session.

Opening   5 minutes

Use the opening ritual designed by the group.

What Is a Credo?   5 minutes

Ask participants what they already know about credos. Explain that this program defines a credo statement as a statement about "what you set your heart to." This encompasses several aspects:

- what people, movements, and ideas you identify with

- what you value most highly, not only by what you think but also by what you do

- what you believe and have faith in

Read aloud one or two sample credos from Leader Resource 11, Sample Credos.

Expectations for Credo   10 minutes

Say something like the following:

> A credo is a snapshot of your values, faith, identity, and belief at one point in time. As Unitarian Universalists, we understand that your religious ideas will evolve throughout your life. It is understood by all that your credo is simply an expression of where you are now and not for all time. As a Unitarian poet in the 1800s wrote, "Revelation is not sealed," meaning that religious revelations continue to happen.

Specify the minimum and maximum lengths you would like participants' credos to be, in time and words. Note the deadline for first and final drafts, and specify whether you would like the credos given to you on paper or in an electronic format.

Specify the parameters you have concerning creativity. For example, can a youth write a song for his/her credo? Can two youth create a dialogue-based credo together? Can someone do an art project?

Discuss the role of mentors in credo writing. Will mentors work with youth to draft their credos? Or will youth draft their credos on their own?

If you are considering including the reading of credos in a service of recognition, let participants know.

Distribute and review the handout you have prepared in advance describing the parameters and expectations for credos.

What Do You Set Your Heart To?   30 minutes

Ask participants to take some time to individually explore the question: "What do you value most in life?" They can brainstorm a list of responses in their journals, and if there is time they can write a longer response.

Then ask participants to look over their lists and identify what they are sure they'll always have and what might go away. For example, individual people are not necessarily permanent fixtures in their lives.

Ask them to make a separate list of the things they value most that can never go away, at least in their lifetimes. They can take items from their previous list and add more. These might be abstracts, like truth or enlightenment or love. They may also be such things as human community, life force, or an infinite God.

Explain that this second list will suggest guideposts for their credo writing, because it contains some things in which they have enduring faith. Ask participants to make notes about their lists, using the following questions as guidelines:

- How have you come to value this being/idea/concept?

- What do you think is the most important thing about it?

- What do you do in your life to support it, celebrate it, or participate in it?

- How is it related to Unitarian Universalism?

- How does it help create the kind of world you want to see?

Ask participants to keep these notes (or their journals) with them and to share their responses with their mentors for further discussion and clarification.

Making a Draft   5 minutes

Reiterate the due date for the first draft. Explain that by this date, all participants will be expected to have turned their notes into a statement that they can later present to the congregation. Point out that anecdotes, analogies, and real-life examples that illustrate what they have faith in help make credos interesting. Encourage participants to show their personalities—to write like they write, and speak like they speak. They are expected to be their genuine selves when they share their credos.

Ask participants what kinds of settings they find helpful for writing. Make suggestions about where and how they can work on their credos in the coming weeks, and encourage them to set up time to work with their mentors. Answer any questions and clarify expectations.

Closing Circle   5 minutes

Use the closing ritual designed by the group.

Workshop 6
Finalizing Your Credo

Time   60 minutes

Participant Goals

- finalize credo statements

- gain experience and confidence with public speaking—especially speaking words that are close to one's heart

Materials

- copies of Handout 5, Making Your Credo Great (page 88)

- journals

- pens and pencils

Preparation

- A few days in advance of this session, call participants to confirm that they are working on their credos. If they have not yet begun their drafts, strongly encourage them to begin and let their mentors know so that their mentors can work with them.

- Remind participants to bring copies of their credos to this session.

- Invite mentors to participate in this session.

Opening   5 minutes

Use the opening ritual designed by the group.

Making It Great   25 minutes

Thank participants for all the work they have done in creating first drafts of their credos. Affirm that it is not always an easy process to articulate one's faith, and congratulate them for all they have done so far.

Explain that today they will have the chance to further polish their credo statements. Distribute Handout 5, Making Your Credo Great. Ask participants and their mentors to review the handout together, discussing ways that the first drafts can be improved. Encourage youth to take notes for revisions.

Voluntary Sharing   20 minutes

Explain that it can be helpful to share credos with each other at this point. Some people might be seeking tips for improvement; others might feel proud of their drafts and want to share them as examples. Ask for a few youth volunteers to deliver their credos to the group.

After each volunteer has shared, ask the group to offer constructive feedback. Explain that constructive feedback has these qualities:

- It is positive, both about the credo and the person sharing it.

- It offers specific suggestions for improvement without putting down what has already been done.

- It focuses on helping people express themselves better, not on the substance of their opinions or beliefs.

Questions and Next Steps   5 minutes

Invite questions and concerns from participants and address them. Update the group on next steps: final credo due date, rehearsal dates, etc. Congratulate youth on their work.

Closing Circle   5 minutes

Use the closing ritual designed by the group.

Prompts for Credo Development

Unit 1: Community Building

Workshop 1: Covenant and Community Building

Write about a community (friends, family, church, team, etc.) where you feel included and safe. Write about a community where you feel excluded or unsafe. What is the difference?

What makes you feel included in a community? What makes you feel safe?

Workshop 3: Peace and Put-downs

Who do you think puts you down more often: yourself or other people? Describe a time when someone else put you down. How did you feel? How did you respond? Describe a time when you put yourself down. How did you feel? How did you respond?

When you or someone else puts you down, what helps you feel better?

Unit 3: Unitarian Universalist Beliefs

Workshop 7: Unitarian Universalist Values

What stories, movies, or TV shows mean the most to you? Why? Do they reflect your values? If so, how? Do they reflect UU values? If so, how?

Who are the people you cherish? Why do you cherish them? What does that say about what you value?

What idea, concept, object, or philosophy do you think is the most valuable in your life right now?

Workshop 8: Unity and Diversity

What religious beliefs do you share with your family? Are there religious beliefs that you and your family don't share? If so, what are those and why do you think you came to hold different beliefs than other members of your family?

Workshop 9: Good and Evil

What have you experienced or seen that you would label "evil"? What have you experienced or seen that you would label "good"?

Where do you think evil comes from? Where do you think good come from?

Workshop 10: Talking about Unitarian Universalism

Tell about a positive experience and a negative experience you have had in discussing your faith and/or congregation.

Unit 4: Spirituality

Workshop 11: The Web of Interdependence

Write about a time when you experienced wonder and amazement. Would you call this a spiritual experience? Why or why not? When do you feel most spiritual?

Workshop 12: Learning to Lead Worship

Think about a worship experience that was meaningful to you. What made it meaningful?

Workshop 14: Rituals of Our Faith

Where, besides your congregation, have you experienced rituals? School? Home? A club or organization? Do you have fond memories associated with these rituals?

Workshop 15: Introduction to Spiritual Practice

When you feel anxious, depressed, discouraged, or angry, what spiritual practices can help you get back to your better self?

Unit 5: Unitarian Universalist Theology

Workshop 21: Starting with Us

> When you think about your own nature, do you find it useful to look at yourself as a mixture of good and evil? Is there another way you prefer to evaluate yourself? Explain.

Workshop 22: Your God Project

> How have your ideas about God developed as you have grown and changed? What kind of path do you think you're on in terms of your relationship with the sacred?

Workshop 23: The God You Don't Believe In, the God You Do

> Have you ever had experiences where you felt a sense of transcending wonder and mystery? If so, describe those experiences and what that sense felt like.

> What are you coming to believe about God, spirit, and the universe as a whole?

Workshop 24: Life, Death and the Afterlife

> What do you think is the best way to respond to death? To the reality that you too will have to die one day?

Unit 6: Justice

Workshop 26: How UUs Make a Difference

> Are there social issues that you feel strongly about? If so, describe them. How are they related to your values and beliefs as a Unitarian Universalist? Beyond this program, what would you like to do to address those issues?

Unit 8: Leadership

Workshop 29: The Meaning and Practice of Leadership

> What are your personal talents and gifts?

> What kind of person do you want to become?

Community Service Project

> What tasks were you responsible for on the community service trip? How did it feel to be doing these tasks? How were your tasks related to Unitarian Universalist principles and values?

> Who do you think it's important to serve? How would you do it?

Group Trip

> Who are your spiritual heroes and heroines? Why?

General Prompts

> What makes your life worth living?

> What represents the "good life" to you?

> What makes you feel hopeful? What makes you feel fearful?

> Do you have a purpose you feel called toward in life?

Sample Credos

I believe in living life with integrity, character, honesty, compassion, grace, and commitment.

I believe that a person's life doesn't always begin with a purpose. Sometimes we are drawn into great deeds by the life that we choose, but at times that life chooses us. Being Unitarian Universalist allows us the chance to combine these two choices, to be people that choose to be chosen.

I believe that everyone has a gift; it is what we do with these gifts that make them special. Many people live a lifetime never knowing their potential. Finding your gift, and having the desire to share it with others, can lift the human spirit.

I believe in the inherent worth and dignity of every person and that you will touch the lives of many in living this belief. When I was little, if asked what I wanted to be when I grew up, I would answer, "A horse." At the time I thought that it was a valid reply, as I was open to the possibility, and have always had the desire to guide my own destiny. As I've grown older, I've continued asking why, and have felt a desire to pursue my own answers. It has led me to be an independent thinker, secure in my own authenticity.

I believe in making sure that my family feels the love that I have for them every day, and being the type of friend that lasts a lifetime. I am fortunate to have been born into my family. With each day I learn so much from them all, each one a fabulous person, each of whom I would be glad to call my friend if we were not related. They have given me a gift with their presence in my life. So, to my mom for your humor and unconditional love, my dad for your consistency and patience, and my sister Laiken for your laughter and sheer joy, I give you all my gratitude.

As we make our way forward, into this new period of our lives, we need to continue to listen with both our minds and our hearts, trust our instincts—they come from a place that is authentic—remain true to ourselves, remember the importance of joy, and the value of love. . . .

—Austin Gay, First Unitarian Church of Dallas

My project is a representation of my belief that everyone has a path that they are to follow during their life. Everyone must deal with hardships and difficult times throughout their life, but those struggles always teach us more about ourselves. The doors represent these different aspects we learn and grow from. The end of the path does not symbolize an ending, but a continuation of growth and development into a bigger, more whole you.

The first door is Learning. The book symbolizes the fact that everyone has something they can share with you and that you can learn from everyone around you. Being a part of the Com-

munity Unitarian Church for the past five years, I have had many teachers, and now a mentor, who have graciously shared their religious beliefs with me and influenced my own beliefs. They are the examples that I see every weekend of what UUs are. I am so glad that I have had the experience of being taught and listened to in the process of learning more about my religion and my life. When people share themselves and their feelings and beliefs with you, it's only natural to take parts from them and evaluate them so that they fit into your life and what you believe to be meaningful and important.

The second door is Compassion. It is a feeling that grows and blooms inside of you as life progresses and you experience new things. The heart symbolizes the love you feel and want to share with others, as you help them. Here at church, I feel like I have a home away from home. I feel connections with countless people here, and waking up on Sunday morning to bright, welcoming faces makes my day that much fuller and happier. My class has grown over the year from a small group of kids who see each other once a week because they have to, to a group of young adults with opinions and friendships that they look forward to sharing. Making the world a better place could not happen without change, and change would not be possible without compassion for what you want to transform. It's also important to always leave your heart open, even when others have shut their hearts to you, because otherwise, they will never know the love you feel for them.

The third door is Reflection. You cannot move forward in life and learning without first looking back on the past. Sometimes, looking at yourself in a mirror, for example, is not enough. You need to look to others for help because they have the ability to see both the flaws and strengths you possess that you might not be able to notice yourself. At my camp, Rowe, I have learned many things about myself from the close friends I have there. They bring out the best in me and help me notice the worst too. But they don't leave me at that; they help me change and become a better person. The countless midnight conversations and post-chapel hugs every year help me reflect on the person I was, am, and am becoming. The mirror symbolizes that there is only one you, but there are parts which you allow the whole world to see and then there are some other parts that are more personal, that you share with different people.

The fourth door is Unity. Unity means working together with everyone and developing a sense of harmony and balance with all that surrounds you. I work together with people every day. They may be my friends, parents, relatives, teachers, or mentors. Although we all share a common ground for the most part, everyone is different. Working with people who are different from you in respect toward beliefs, social status, or emotional attachment helps you to develop a sense of harmony and balance within yourself because it teaches you how to work with everyone. The two hands represent making connections with people who are different from you and experiencing growth through new relationships.

The fifth door is Acceptance. Everyone in the world deserves the same amount of respect despite the fact that we are all different. Being accepting of others is the first step in making the world a better place to live in. It's very difficult to feel like you are not accepted, but that only makes you strive for bigger and better things for yourself and others. And eventually, I think everyone will find that one special place where they will always be accepted, no questions asked. The globe behind this door symbolizes a sense of everything coming together and changing from a state of many little pieces scattered about into a whole being.

As a whole, this project symbolizes growth and metamorphosis. The doors are just parts of life that you deal with every day, and it all leads up to a real evaluation and declaration of what is important about life to you. The globe is just a symbol of being whole and well-rounded. It also symbolizes balance and harmony, which is what I feel that Unitarian Universalism is helping me to understand.

—Catie Eichberg, Community Unitarian Church of White Plains, New York

Hello and welcome to all of those new and old to this church. My name is Ian Wilson, and I have been a member of this church since my religious flower began to bud. But what does that mean, religious? To some it is a term used as a shroud or as protection, and that is the point of my essay: what is my religion now. My religious background is Jewish, Protestant, Huguenot, and Universalist. If I tried to explain in writing what my dad is, I would probably get carpal tunnel syndrome.

When I was asked to talk about religion, I first wanted to explain what it means to be a Unitarian Universalist because I find that very few actually know what it is.

What Is Unitarian Universalism to Me?

I grew up here in a place where the word *sanctuary* still lives; our beliefs, no matter how odd they seem to the general public, can be respected just as all other religions. Whenever I am asked about what religion I am and my answer is "I am a Unitarian Universalist," the response is either "Huh?" or as my friend Sam says, "Unitarian? That's not a religion; you have no beliefs." It is hard to respond to someone when they say that to you. Unitarian Universalism to me used to be two hours on Sundays and all the Twizzlers I could eat, but as the years have passed I have realized it is of course much deeper. Unitarian Universalism is freedom, Unitarian Universalism is choice, and most importantly, Unitarian Universalism is me, and everyone in this room. Unitarian Universalists believe in seven Principles that are the seven basics of human life, and they have helped me become the person I am, a person with very few bias beliefs and a person who will go out of his way to help someone even if I do not know them.

Unlike the older religions of the past many thousand years, we have not killed millions over a few miles of ground that is the cradle of the three main religions, or over the amount of prayers we do daily. All religions that are still feuding grew from the same beliefs. Our roots are also from the Jewish and Christian belief systems, but we do not fight because we have no holy lands. Our holy lands are here in our hearts, and in our minds.

We keep the ideal of a safe church when so many have become battlegrounds in the war against terror and in the anti-Muslim beliefs that have been spreading like wildfire across the U.S. since 9/11. Our church members come from all backgrounds: Asian, Muslim, Jewish, Christian, gay, lesbian. Everyone is welcome to worship here. I think that as time goes on and culture changes, there is a loss of meaning in religion. Our religion never developed as a competition for who was better in the face of God.

My Religious Beliefs

As soon as I could really understand the difference, I was told that I could believe and worship in whatever way I wanted as long as I could explain what it was. I visited many churches and synagogues in search of that "right feel" that people can get from their chosen faiths. I thought to finally look into the one place I still had not been: myself. My religious views have had many important factors in their development. My grandfather, who has been my mental and physical mentor, taught me U.S. history from his days as the captain of a destroyer in World War II, while teaching me how to row a boat, chop wood, and properly cast for fish. He would talk to me about how this country grew to be what it is, or how it is influenced by different presidents. I know that I wanted a religion that would not tell me what I had to believe or try to persuade me to believe with fear instead of with hope. In my view, no one can really say which religion God favors or what makes one religion better or more true.

It was friendship that made me choose to be UU. It was the fact that there were all of these people from different backgrounds but with similar belief structures as me that helped me want to stay here. When I am here, there is a sort of unconditional bond with the people that makes you feel like you are with a family and not just with a group.

I have learned the values of the seven Principles, and that has helped me reverse the stereotype of most physically big kids. That is, that I am not a bully. It is really difficult at school to be this big. Kids are always challenging me to fight or to fight for them. It has taught me the power of words. Unitarian Universalism has taught me that when someone I don't know is treating me badly, it is probably just that they are angry about something having nothing to do with me. So I just let it roll off of my shoulders. I have been able to grow like this by having a good understanding of the seven Principles of the UU beliefs. The seven formal beliefs of UU are all printed on a bookmark, but here are the seven principles of my own beliefs:

- to respect those you know and those you don't

- to always leave violence as a last resort

- that all people are equal and none are better than others

- that there is power in words

- to strive for excellence

- to never say no without thinking about it first

- to always give someone a chance and not to stereotype

Now I know that these are not as deep as the original seven, but these are the principles, or guidelines, that I live by.

My Religious Future

So here I am at my Coming of Age, the so-called climax of my religious experience, but where do I go from here? What is the path I will walk, and where will I be when I have a job, family, and as little hair as my dad? This church is my home away from home. I plan on going on to the youth group, where I can help make choices for this church that in turn has helped me make so many of mine. This church has done plenty of things for me that I cannot explain or understand, but there is one thing that I do know for sure. That is that there is a church of equals. I believe in a church of equals; this is a church of equals.

—Ian Wilson, Community Unitarian Church of White Plains, New York

Extended Journaling and
UU Pocket Guide Discussion for Unit 2

Journaling Prompts

Encourage participants to reflect upon the topics covered in this unit in their journals. Pose the following questions to get them started:

- What was this experience like for you?

- Were you able to identify beliefs of yours that have changed over time?

- What brought about those changes?

UU Pocket Guide Discussion

Ask participants to read "Sharing Our Faith" before the scheduled discussion or schedule time during your weekly meeting to read and discuss the chapter, using the following questions:

- How did you and/or your family come to Unitarian Universalism?

- Are you a lifelong Unitarian Universalist?

- What is your earliest memory of this congregation?

- Is there anything in the chapter that speaks to your experience as a Unitarian Universalist?

Making Your Credo Great

Once you have a first draft of your credo, you are ready to make it great with these tips for writing and delivery.

Writing

There are as many great kinds of writing as there are great kinds of people. Over the years we have found that the following tips help good credos become even better.

Use your genuine voice. Write in a way that expresses the way you talk, who you are, and your interests. The congregation is most interested in seeing the genuine you shine through. If you are funny, include a joke! If you are shy, say so. If you like using big fancy words, use them, and if you don't, don't.

Give brief examples. Listening to a list of beliefs is not very exciting. Instead, offer examples of how your beliefs are applied in real life. These examples can be from stories that inspire you or from your real-life experience. They can also be imaginary scenarios that illustrate what you value or what you would do in a particular situation. Because the credo is short, keep your examples brief: just a few sentences.

Use appropriate grammar. This does not mean that you need to strictly follow every grammatical rule. However, it is a time to use everything you learned about sentence structure and subject-verb agreement in English class. When your credo is free of grammatical mistakes, listeners will be able to focus on your *message* rather than your wording.

Read it out loud. Sometimes a sentence looks good on a page but sounds awkward when it is read out loud.

Delivery

When you deliver your credo, you can impress your audience by using these techniques:

Speak slowly and naturally. Many people speak fast when they speak in front of groups because they are a little nervous. Remind yourself to slow down. Speaking slowly in your natural voice will ensure that your listeners get to hear all the words that you so carefully assembled to form your credo. There is such a thing as speaking too slowly, but most Coming of Age participants are not guilty of it.

Make eye contact with the audience. Spend some time getting to know the text of your credo so that you do not need to stare at it as you read it. Practice looking up at least one time per sentence and making eye contact with the listeners. Try to make eye contact with people sitting in all different sections of the room. Remember, you are reading to the listeners, not to your sheet of paper, and they want to see your face. If you can memorize your whole credo so you do not have to look at any paper at all, you can have an even more effective presentation.

Speak into the microphone. As you step to the podium to deliver your credo, take a moment to adjust the microphone so that it will pick up your voice. Ideally, you will have the opportunity to test the microphone before the service starts.

UNIT THREE

Unitarian Universalist Beliefs

How is one to live a moral and compassionate existence when one is fully aware of the blood, the horror inherent in life, when one finds darkness not only in one's culture but within oneself? If there is a stage at which an individual life becomes truly adult, it must be when one grasps the irony in its unfolding and accepts responsibility for a life lived in the midst of such paradox.

—Barry Lopez

Youth come into a Coming of Age program with varying degrees of knowledge and experience of Unitarian Universalist beliefs. Before leading sessions about beliefs, it is valuable to assess what youth have covered in their religious education up to the point of beginning the program. Some congregations offer significant Unitarian Universalist identity curricula, such as *Traditions with a Wink*, to middle school students, while others offer curricula with a significant theological focus, such as *God Images* or *How Do I Know What to Believe?* Some youth might already be at a stage where they are comfortable talking about their personal beliefs in a large group; others may not yet be able to articulate what they believe.

The workshops in this unit will explore two different aspects of Unitarian Universalist belief. *Belief* is a word that American culture typically associates with "opinion" or "faith in things unproven." However, the original meaning of *believe* and the Anglo-Saxon word from which it is derived is "to hold dear, to prize." This meaning has particular relevance to Unitarian Universalists, who tend to reject dogmatic beliefs or beliefs formulated as creeds. But we are far from nonbelievers. We believe in those things we prize, those things we hold dear, those things that lead

us to deeper meaning and more profound purpose in life and in death. The workshop plans that follow explore belief from both the vantage point of faith in things unproven and the lens of what we hold dear.

The activities in this unit should be adapted to meet the needs of the youth in your congregation at their stage of learning about Unitarian Universalism. Begin with what they already know and take it from there. The activities start with those beliefs that we share. Only after establishing a common basis do the sessions proceed to explore the diversity of Unitarian Universalist beliefs and the personal religious choices participants can make.

Many Unitarian Universalist adults are rightly concerned about not imposing their beliefs, or their religion's beliefs, on young people. However, that concern can sometimes get in the way of exposing UU beliefs to young people at all. Exposure is not the same as imposition. Research suggests that early adolescents want to know how the groups that they belong to "think." They want to know what their religious groups stand for so that they can figure out their own places in them. Given knowledge of Unitarian Universalist tradition, they can further develop and cultivate their personal beliefs in the spirit of a "free and responsible search for truth and meaning."

In a speech to the 1998 General Assembly, theologian Rebecca Parker said, "Covenant making must begin with the question, 'What have we been given? What is the covenant we are already in?'" Some youth in the Coming of Age program were born Unitarian Universalist and dedicated in the sanctuary of the congregation. Others came into Unitarian Universalism as their parents sought a spiritual home in which to raise them. Perhaps a few came to Unitarian Universalism on their own, because their personalities and religious questions led them to this free religious community. Whichever way they entered Unitarian Universalist communities, they have entered into a covenant by being here. It is a covenant with all those who came before, shaping the community into its present form. Parker continues, "We have inherited who we are. It is important for us to remember this side of things—that we are first of all relational beings, shaped by history, by a community of faith. Our exercise of free choice is in the context of relational existence." Therefore, while Unitarian Universalism offers freedom, it also offers a tradition in which to ground that freedom.

Unitarian Universalists share many beliefs, but we are not required to adhere to a creed. Rather, we have covenants, shared agreements about what binds us together. The Principles and Purposes of the Unitarian Universalist Association are a covenant between congregations about what it means for a congregation to identify as Unitarian Universalist. Additionally, individuals in congregations join together to uphold their own congregational covenants, mission statements, and vision statements. Within each of these covenants, there is room for variety in religious beliefs and practices.

Because UU beliefs are fairly diverse, it can be challenging to create a summary of beliefs we generally share. Rev. William Schulz, former president of the Unitarian Universalist Association, wrote a chapter, "Our Faith," in the *UU Pocket Guide* that identified such beliefs, and Unitarian Universalist minister David O. Rankin created a compatible list that is printed on a wallet card used in this unit. Familiarize yourself with these materials before meeting with the group.

We draw on many sources to provide a spiritual basis for our collective and individual beliefs as Unitarian Universalists. These include, but are not limited to, the six Sources delineated in the Unitarian Universalist Association's Principles and Purposes document:

- direct experience of that transcending mystery and wonder, affirmed in all cultures, which moves us to a renewal of the spirit and an openness to the forces which create and uphold life

- words and deeds of prophetic women and men which challenge us to confront powers and structures of evil with justice, compassion, and the transforming power of love

- wisdom from the world's religions, which inspires us in our ethical and spiritual life

- Jewish and Christian teachings which call us to respond to God's love by loving our neighbors as ourselves

- humanist teachings which counsel us to heed the guidance of reason and the results of science, and warn us against idolatries of the mind and spirit

- spiritual teachings of earth-centered traditions which celebrate the sacred circle of life and instruct us to live in harmony with the rhythms of nature

Life experience, as well as the experiences of worship and religious education, inform individual Unitarian Universalists' choices of the sources that ground their personal ethics and spirituality. Those sources, in turn, combine with lived experience to inform individual beliefs about God, the world, and spiritual reality.

Unitarian Universalism enables individuals to decide for themselves about many religious and spiritual beliefs, including the following:

- the existence and nature of a deity or deities

- the existence of divine beings like angels, demons, and spirits

- life after death and/or reincarnation

- the power of prayer

- the nature of salvation

- the meaning of the life and death of Jesus

- the value of the Bible

- the existence of destiny or fate

- the nature of souls

It is valuable to draw a distinction between beliefs that people simply agree with and beliefs on which people stake their lives. For example, there might be a UU woman who believes in reincarnation because it makes sense to her, but it does not really affect the way she lives her life. This is a different kind of belief from that held by, say, a devout Hindu woman who also believes in reincarnation. For the latter, reincarnation is a fundamental belief that structures the way she worships and interacts with people and the goals she has for living. Believing can be about much more than simply agreeing with a notion. In this unit, you will challenge participants to think about what they truly believe: what they structure their lives around and what they want to devote their lives to.

Developmental theory, as well as experience, suggests that eighth- and ninth- grade adolescents are more oriented toward group values than individual values. They are often not ready to articulate individual values that go against the grain of the group. The first session of this unit, Workshop 7, is grounded in the here and now: in the everyday experiences of the participants in their families, congregation, and schools. It will serve as a basis for exploration of Unitarian Universalist Principles and youth's own values and actions.

Workshop 7
Unitarian Universalist Values

Time   90 minutes to 2 hours

Participant Goals

- better understand Unitarian Universalist values

- formulate a UU identity through examination of their personal values in relation to UU values

- explore obstacles that can keep them from acting on their values

Materials

- one rubber band per participant, plus one extra

- one set of values cards per participant, plus one extra (see Preparation)

- one copy of Handout 6, What Would You Do? (page 104), per participant

- listing of the Unitarian Universalist Principles (see Preparation)

- one copy of Leader Resource 13, Unitarian Universalist Value Choices (page 101)

- newsprint

- markers

- journals

- pens or pencils

Preparation

- Assign reading from the following chapters in *The Unitarian Universalist Pocket Guide:* "Unitarian Universalist Principles," "Preface," and "Our Faith."

- Photocopy Handout 6, What Would You Do? Decide if you will ask participants to write about the situations or perform skits. Choose the situations to discuss and copy one sheet for each participant. If you choose the skit option, make enough copies for each group member to have a sheet for their situation.

- Write the Unitarian Universalist Principles on newsprint.

- Photocopy Handout 7, Values Cards (page 108), on cardstock. Cut cardstock so there is one word per card. Create sets of values cards by stacking the cards into piles, each pile including each word. Put a rubber band around each set.

Defining Values   15 minutes

Deal one set of values cards to participants so that each participant has at least a few cards. Ask participants to take turns reading aloud the words on their cards and offering a definition of each word. Define any words that are not familiar, such as *empathy* or *interdependence*.

After the cards have been read, ask, "What is a value?" Guide participants toward this definition: "A value is a principle, standard, or quality considered worthwhile or desirable." Note that we demonstrate our values as we interact with others.

A Day in the Life   20 minutes

Distribute one set of values cards to each participant. Invite them to spend a few moments thinking about yesterday: how they spent their day, whom they talked to, etc.

Ask them to look over their values cards, pick out the values they demonstrated to themselves or others yesterday, and put those cards in a pile. Then ask them to think about today and add to the pile any additional values they demonstrated today.

Say, "Are there values left over that you didn't act on yesterday or today, but want to act on at other times? Put those values in a separate pile."

Once their values are sorted into piles, ask them to take out their journals and write down those values in two columns: one for "Yesterday and Today" and one for "Tomorrow."

Ask participants:

- Were you surprised to see how many values you lived out in the past two days?

- Was anyone surprised to see how few values they lived out?

- Did you identify any values you lived out that were not included on the cards?

- What were some of the things that got in the way of living out your values?

- What does how we spend our time say about our values?

Forced Choice   20 minutes

Introduce this activity by saying:

> In this activity, you'll decide what you think Unitarian Universalists value more, based on your own experience and your understanding of the Unitarian Universalist Principles. What you decide is not necessarily what you value more—it's what you think Unitarian Universalists generally value more. I will present you with several value choices. If you agree with value A, go to the left side of the room. If you agree with value B, go to the right side of the room. If you are puzzled, you can stand in the middle. And you can move if you hear a convincing argument. Any questions about this process?

When you have answered any questions, continue with Leader Resource 13, Unitarian Universalist Value Choices. Read the two values. After participants have grouped themselves, ask the three groups to discuss, within their groups, why they are standing where they are. Once they have discussed in their small groups, ask for a volunteer or two from each group to share their reasons.

Then ask, "Which of the Unitarian Universalist Principles relate to this value? Do all of your values relate to a UU Principle?" Participants may find that the same Principle, such as the inherent worth and dignity of every person, brought different people to different places in response to the value choices.

Ask, "How do you think your Unitarian Universalist community encourages you to live this value?" When the group has finished considering a number of value choices, and before energy and interest run out, ask participants to return to their circle. If there is interest, continue processing as a large group.

What Would a Unitarian Universalist Do?
30 to 60 minutes

The first part of this activity, responding to scenarios, can be conducted as a written exercise or as a series of skits.

Explain that in this activity, the group will consider real-life situations that Unitarian Universalist students have faced in middle school and high school. Participants will describe how they would respond in these situations and identify values and Unitarian Universalist Principles that could guide them in their responses. Distribute the situations you chose from Handout 6, What Would You Do?

Post the newsprint list of the Unitarian Universalist Principles. Explain that being Unitarian Universalist and having values does not mean acting perfectly or behaving like a saint, and that the situations they'll be considering might make them angry. Ask them to write about (or act out) how they would genuinely respond based on the values they hold.

If they are journaling, allow ten minutes for writing, then invite volunteers to read a scenario and describe how they would respond. If they are doing skits, allow ten minutes for planning and twenty minutes for presentations. After preparation is complete, have participants read a scenario and present each response in turn.

Here are several questions to spark discussion:

- What are the problems in this situation? What are the important feelings in it? Are there opposing values involved? What possible results do you want to avoid?

- How did it feel to put yourself in these situations?

- Have you had experiences like these? Was it hard to respond the way you think you should have? If so, why?

- How might you respond to the situation? How does your response relate to the important values you have identified? How does your response relate to Unitarian Universalist Principles?

- Consider the best and worst that can happen if you respond in various ways. Are you willing to risk possible negative outcomes in order to try for the best?

- Does living Unitarian Universalist Principles and values make you popular in school? Why or why not? What makes a person popular or unpopular at school?

- Do you feel tension between the values of your family and religious community and the values of your classmates in school?

- Living Unitarian Universalist Principles is a challenge. It takes effort to honor the inherent worth and dignity of every person and to uphold justice, equity, and compassion in human relations. What are some of the rewards for trying to live these values?

Ask participants to write their top three values in their journals and identify how they act on these values in the present and would like to act on them in the future. Have them write at least three ideas about how they could live each value in the world.

Invite participants to focus on one of their top values for the week. Explain that the assignment is to notice each time they hear the word, see the value manifested, feel it working in them, act on it, or encounter the value in any way.

Note: Make time to write in journals about these experiences the next time the group meets and/or you lead the group in discussion.

Closing Circle 5 minutes

Ask all participants to name one thing they can do in school to support Unitarian Universalist values.

Workshop 8
Unity and Diversity

Time 60 to 80 minutes

Participant Goals

- understand what makes Unitarian Universalism a unified religion despite its diversity in belief

- identify some of the shared beliefs held by Unitarian Universalists, beyond the seven Principles

- consider their own religious beliefs and how they fit into the Unitarian Universalist tradition and framework

- build closer relationships between youth and mentors through interviews about beliefs

- gain more knowledge and experience of covenant

Materials

- one ball of yarn for each ten participants, including mentors

- newsprint and easel

- markers

- masking tape

- one photocopy or wallet card of the "Principles and Purposes of the Unitarian Universalist Association of Congregations" per participant (see Preparation)

- one wallet card "What Do Unitarian Universalists Believe?" per participant (see Preparation)

- one copy of Handout 8, Charting Our Shared Beliefs (page 110), per participant, including mentors

Preparation

- This is a good session to conduct with mentors present. If they are to be included, request their presence well in advance.

- Order wallet cards "What Do Unitarian Universalists Believe?" well in advance of this session. They are available at *www.uua.org/bookstore* or by calling 800-215-9076. Order a few extra to use in Workshop 10.

- Order wallet cards "Principles and Purposes of the Unitarian Universalist Association of Congregations" from the UUA bookstore, as above. Order a few extra, also to use in Workshop 10.

- This session is more effective if participants have read the *Unitarian Universalist Pocket Guide*, especially the chapter "Our Faith," in advance. The reading assignment can be given at the meeting prior to this one.

- If needed, arrange for a larger meeting space so that mentors, youth, and leaders can all be present.

- Recognize that mentors may be more ready to talk in this session than youth are. It may be helpful to explain in advance that you'll alternate mentors and youth in the discussion periods. If the adults talk too much, then youth will not have the space to think of their own ideas.

Opening 5 minutes

Use the opening ritual designed by the group.

Introduction 5 minutes

If the group journaled about their top values in Workshop 7, devote a few minutes to participants who wish to share their journal entries.

Then explain, "Today we will consider some intriguing questions. How does a religion with so many different beliefs stay together? What makes Unitarian Universalism one religion instead of many different ones? Today we will explore what binds us together."

Yarn Toss 10 minutes

This activity, adapted from *Growing Together* by Greg Gale, requires that youth be knowledgeable enough to state some of their religious beliefs.

If you do not think your group can do this comfortably, have them name things they like about Unitarian Universalism.

Follow these steps:

- Define *beliefs*: Say something like "Beliefs are ideas that we hold dear." These can be ideas about our world, ideas about morality, ideas about gods or goddesses, ideas about the meaning of life and death, and more.

- Offer some examples of beliefs: "I believe in the Golden Rule"; "I believe there is a higher power in the universe"; or "I believe in evolution."

- Divide into groups of ten or fewer, with mentors and youth mixed.

- Designate one person in each group to begin the activity by holding the ball of yarn, saying his/her name and stating a belief. Encourage participants to focus on what they *do* believe, rather than what they *do not* believe.

- Explain that others in the circle who share the same belief will call out. The first person will hold on to part of the loose yarn and throw the ball to someone who called out, stating that person's name and the belief that links them. That person says his/her name, repeats the shared belief, and then states another belief. For example, when Jimena catches the ball of yarn, she says, "I'm Jimena, and I believe in the Golden Rule. I also believe in evolution." Another person who believes in evolution calls out, and Jimena then tosses the ball to the third person. The game continue in this way until a web forms that includes every member of the group.

- Throwers always throw to an individual who has not yet received the yarn ball. It is up to the thrower to find a belief that the receiver shares.

- A person who states a belief not shared by any of the "un-yarned" people must think of a different belief that might be shared with at least one of them.

- The last person to receive the ball throws it back to the first person who threw it, again saying that person's name and a belief they share.

- When the "web" is complete, invite participants to tug at it to feel how strongly the whole group is connected.

- To undo the web, reverse the initial process. Alternatively, if time is short, just carefully lay the web on the floor and rewind the ball of yarn.

Say something like this: "Even though you are connected to only two people by the yarn, you are actually connected to the whole group through these two shared beliefs. What did it feel like to know that you are part of a community that has diverse beliefs, yet is bound together by beliefs that are shared?"

Principles and Purposes   5 minutes

Hand out the wallet cards "Principles and Purposes of the Unitarian Universalist Association of Congregations." Introduce the discussion of covenant by asking what participants know about the Principles and Purposes. If necessary, encourage discussion by asking whether they are a list of things that Unitarian Universalists believe. Wait for a few responses from youth and adults.

Share that the Principles and Purposes are not a statement of belief, but rather, they are a covenant. Share the following explanation from UU theologian Rebecca Parker:

> Covenant, most simply, means "to come together" as we are doing here . . . Covenant, more specially, means "to come together by making a promise" as when two people promise to love and care for one another. For example, marriage is a covenanted relationship. At the beginning of Coming of Age, we made a covenant together about group behavior. We promised to behave in certain ways toward each other.

Ask participants to look for the covenant in the statement of Principles and Purposes and to discover who the parties are to the covenant. Who are making promises to each other?

Explain that the Principles and Purposes describe the covenant between different congregations that call themselves Unitarian Universalist; that the seven Principles are what the congregations agree to "affirm and promote"; and that there is a lot of room for diversity of belief among our congregations and among the members of our congregations. Observe that in your group, there are also many diverse beliefs, but there are areas of unity within this diversity.

Beliefs Survey/Interview   20 to 40 minutes

Introduce this section by asking, "If the Principles and Purposes are not a statement of belief for individual Unitarian Universalists, are there beliefs that individual Unitarian Universalists hold in common?" Solicit a few responses.

Explain that the class will now have an opportunity to figure out some of their shared beliefs as mentors and youth interview each other. Distribute Handout 8, Charting Our Shared Beliefs, and instruct them to take notes as they are interviewing. After seven minutes have passed, signal that it is time for the pairs to switch roles.

Once youth and mentors have completed their interviews, ask them to draw circles around beliefs they hold in common and to compare their beliefs to the Principles. Do they think they could belong to a congregation that agrees to affirm and promote the Principles?

Optional: Set up newsprint and markers in the front of the room. Ask mentors and youth to read aloud the beliefs that they share. Take notes on newsprint. If more than one pair has the same shared belief, put one star next to that belief for each additional pair. Once all the beliefs are listed on newsprint, look for relationships between the different beliefs. For example, "People should be free" and "Democracy is best" would related beliefs.

Discussion   10 minutes

Lead a discussion with youth and mentors, based on the following questions:

- What was this process like for you? How did it feel? Were there any surprises?

- Did you discover unity where you thought there would be diversity, or diversity where you thought there would be unity?

- What do you think about the beliefs of our class? Are they similar to what you think most UUs believe? Different? How?

Explain that it is a challenge to democratically affirm a set of shared beliefs in a diverse religious movement. Pass out "What Do Unitarian Universalists Believe?" wallet cards, and describe it as one religious leader's effort at summarizing Unitarian Universalist beliefs.

After mentors and youth have had the opportunity to read the handout, ask if there are any clarifying questions or vocabulary that needs defining. Then ask whether participants think that this list of beliefs has much in common with their own group's list. Ask if there are any contradictions.

Invite participants to share any comments or insights they have concerning Unitarian Universalist beliefs, their unity, and their diversity. Let them know that the wallet cards are theirs to keep and suggest they put them in their wallets or purses or pockets.

Closing Circle   5 minutes

Use the closing ritual designed by the group.

Workshop 9
Good and Evil

Time   60 minutes

Participant Goals

- consider the nature of evil in the world

- become familiar with Unitarian Universalist ideas about evil

- understand that good and evil can be hard to distinguish from one another

Materials

- newsprint and easel

- markers

- masking tape

- copies of Handout 9, Why Do People Do Evil Things? (page 111)

- copies of the pamphlet *Unitarian Universalist Views of Evil* (see Preparation)

Preparation

- In advance of this class meeting, assign the UU World article "Confronting Evil," which can be found at *www.uuworld.org*. A portion of the article is included here as Handout 9, Why Do People Do Evil Things? Youth and mentors can be asked to read it together, or youth can read it on their own. A dictionary might prove helpful for looking up some of the more advanced words in the article.

- Order copies of the pamphlet *Unitarian Universalist Views of Evil* from the UUA Bookstore, (*www.uuabookstore.org*).

Opening   5 minutes

Use the opening ritual designed by the group.

What Is Evil?   15 minutes

Begin discussion by explaining that Lois Fahs Timmins, daughter of Sophia Lyon Fahs, a great UU educator, reflected back on her own religious education. She writes,

> We spent 95 percent of our time studying good people doing good things, and skipped very lightly over the bad parts of humanity. I was taught not to be judgmental, not to observe or report on the bad behavior of others. Consequently, because of my education, I grew up ignorant about bad human behavior, incompetent to observe it accurately, unskilled in how to respond to it, and ashamed of talking about evil.

Ask, "Why do you think it can be hard for UUs to talk about evil?" If necessary, guide youth toward possible answers, such as: "Because UUs like to believe there's good in everyone"; "Because we don't believe in the devil or hell"; "Because we don't think in black and white."

Ask, "What is evil?" and invite youth to offer definitions or examples. Write responses on newsprint. Explain that this is a brainstorm session, meaning that all responses are written down and it is not appropriate to argue if they do not agree with a particular response.

Why Do People Do Evil Things?   20 minutes

Review Handout 9, Why Do People Do Evil Things? and *Unitarian Universalist Views of Evil*. Ask participants which arguments resonate the most with them and why. Compare and contrast the statements on the handout to the results of the previous brainstorming.

Understanding Evil in the Everyday   15 minutes

Tell the group that in this exercise they will be asked to identify what they think is good, evil, or neutral in a given scenario.

Present the following scenario, pausing after each sentence to ask if the action is good, evil, or neutral.

- You decide that you want to give your little sister a gift.

- She loves soccer, so you decide to get her a soccer ball.

- You have been working hard doing extra chores around the house to earn money.

- You take the bus to the discount store, and there you buy the least expensive soccer ball you can find because you want to save money.

- Your cash goes into the cash register, and eventually into the bank account of the Mega Football Company, the manufacturer of the ball.

- Mega Football Company subcontracts their soccer ball manufacturing to small businesses in India, many of which use child slave labor to sew their soccer balls.

- The four-year-old girl who sewed your sister's soccer ball squats on a dirt floor with a needle and thread twelve hours a day and gets beaten every time she makes a mistake.

After the scenario has been presented, ask how it felt to go through this exercise. Then ask, "If we went through the exercise again, would you say it was evil to purchase the soccer ball? Why or why not?" (This is a tough question with many valid viewpoints. Some people would say, "No, it wasn't evil because you didn't know how the ball was made." Others might say, "Yes, buying the ball supported evil, so even though it was well-intentioned, it had the taint of evil.") Ask participants if they would like to share any personal experiences where the line between good and evil was not clear.

Use these questions as the basis for further discussion:

- Did this exercise make you feel that it is harder or easier to separate good from evil?

- What are some situations where it is hard to separate good from evil?

- In our society today, is it possible to live a purely good life?

- What can we do in our own lives to minimize evil acts and maximize good acts?

- What possible range of reactions do we experience when confronted with evil acts, both our own and the acts of others? Which of these reactions are most useful?

- What guideposts does Unitarian Universalism give us?

During the discussion, allow space for specific examples to illustrate answers.

Closing Circle 5 minutes

Use the closing ritual designed by the group.

Workshop 10
Talking about Unitarian Universalism

Time 60 minutes

Participant Goals

- boost the level of comfort when discussing Unitarian Universalism

- share experiences of discussing religion with peers

- increase knowledge of UU jargon

Materials

- extra wallet cards of "What Do Unitarian Universalists Believe?" and "The Principles and Purposes of the Unitarian Universalist Association of Congregations"

- a copy of Leader Resource 14, Unitarian Universalist Acronyms (page 102)

- one copy of the acronym worksheet per participant (see Preparation)

- pens or pencils

- journals

Preparation

- Create a worksheet for your group based on Leader Resource 14, Unitarian Universalist Acronyms, adding acronyms that are significant to your congregation or region. Put acronyms in the middle, what they stand for on the left, and definitions on the right. The Leader Resource has items matched correctly; mix them on your worksheet.

- Set up chairs in a circle.

Opening 5 minutes

Greet youth at the door. While shaking their hands, say "Salutations! Welcome to the Coming of Age workshop of the (fill in your full church name), a member of the Unitarian Universalist Association of Congregations."

All My Friends and Neighbors 15 minutes

Have participants sit in a circle with just enough chairs for everyone except the leader to sit. Stand in the center of the circle and explain the game as follows: "It" stands in the center and says, "I'm (say your name). "Everyone else should respond with "Hi, (repeat your name)!" "It" then says, "All my friends and neighbors (say something you are or like or do)." For example, "It" might say, "All my friends and neighbors like strawberry ice cream," or "All my friends and neighbors wear glasses." Whatever you say as "It" must be true for you. If it is also true for others sitting, they stand up and have to find another chair that is not to the immediate left or right of the seat they just vacated. "It" also tries for a seat. The one person left standing is now "It."

Play until at least everyone who wants to be "It" has a turn. Then pull another chair into the circle and start a discussion by saying something like: "It's fun to find out we have things in common with our friends. You and your friends probably talk a lot about the movies and foods you like and what you like to do during your free time. Do you ever discuss religion?" Pause for answers, and then ask what those conversations are like. Let youth share their experiences.

If you need more leading questions, use the following:

- Do you and your friends have the same ideas about God or the nature of the divine? About what happens after you die? About Jesus?

- Are your friends religiously diverse?

- Do your friends know you attend a Unitarian Universalist congregation?

- If so, what do they think about that?

- Have you invited friends to your congregation?

- Have you ever told anybody you are a Unitarian Universalist?

- Unitarian Universalism is not as well known as some religions, like Judaism and Catholicism. Did your friends already know about Unitarian Universalism?

- If not, did you explain it? How?

Wallet Cards and Elevator Speeches 20 minutes

Begin by saying, "It is not always easy to explain Unitarian Universalism, but being able to do so is useful because you might want to share your faith with friends. So let's talk about ways of talking about Unitarian Universalism." Ask if anyone still has the wallet cards used in Workshop 8 on them. If so, suggest they use them for the following exercise. The few extras you ordered can be shared during this activity.

Explain to the group that they will write "elevator speeches" explaining Unitarian Universalism. An elevator speech is short enough to be given between floors on an elevator ride. In reality, their explanations should be limited to no more than a paragraph. The goal is to describe what Unitarian Universalists believe, not what they do not believe. The speech can be couched in terms of what a youth believes and how those beliefs are captured within Unitarian Universalism. The speech may or may not include UU beliefs and values concerning God, the nature of good and evil, other religions, heaven and hell, or how we should live our lives. It should cover topics of importance to the youth. Some people erroneously think UUs can believe anything they want to, so it should talk about what holds us together as people of faith. Give participants seven minutes to work on this in their journals, and write your own speech as well.

After seven minutes, ask youth to get in pairs, listen to each other's speeches, and ask any questions brought up by the speech. The speech maker can choose whether to rewrite the speech to answer those questions. Let the pairs work for five minutes.

Reconvene the large group and ask for volunteers. Leaders might want to demonstrate their own elevator speeches before asking youth to volunteer. Conduct the demonstration as a role play where one youth meets another at lunch and asks where that youth goes to church. Continue until you run out of time or volunteers. As the last role play, a leader and a youth can demonstrate using the wallet cards as an elevator speech.

Know Your Shorthand   15 minutes

Say, "We just dealt with talking about Unitarian Universalism to a non-UU friend. Now let's switch focus and discuss talking about Unitarian Universalism with other Unitarian Universalists. In particular, let's talk about acronyms."

Explain that an acronym is a group of letters that stand for a group of words. It is an abbreviated way of saying something. Repeat the way you greeted everyone at the door, then repeat it again using acronyms. Distribute the worksheet you created using Leader Resource 14, Unitarian Universalist Acronyms, and instruct participants to match the acronym in the middle with what it stands for on the left and the definition on the right. They have five minutes to work individually.

After five minutes, ask if anyone needs to pair up with someone else to get help. If so, allow a few minutes for this to happen. Review the worksheet together.

Start a discussion with questions like the following:

* How are acronyms helpful? (Possible answers: They make it easier to say long phrases. They save time)

* How might they be harmful? (Possible answer: You can confuse them easily.)

A more important answer that youth might not think of is that acronyms create "insider" language. Point this out by saying something like this: "If you know the acronym, you belong to the group, and if not, you are an outsider. You're often not even aware that this is happening, unless you are the outsider! Then you may be painfully aware, but hesitant to ask for clarification because it makes it obvious that you're an outsider."

Ask youth if they have ever found themselves feeling like outsiders in situations where people were using insider language, and whether they spoke out at the time. Ask, "What can we can do about that in our congregations? Can we try to use fewer acronyms to be more welcoming to new people? Can we remember to explain the acronym the first time we use it so everyone starts off on equal footing? Can we agree to help each other do this? How can we remind each other with love?"

Remind participants that as they continue their involvement with Unitarian Universalism, they will encounter more insider language. Encourage them to ask for definitions of anything they do not understand. Point out that most people are not trying to shut them out and would be happy to explain.

Closing Circle   5 minutes

Use the closing ritual designed by the group.

Unitarian Universalist Value Choices

A

Accepting all viewpoints

Being kind

Creating happiness

Saving the world

Pursuing pleasure

Being independent

B

Taking a stand against some viewpoints

Being popular

Creating justice

Saving yourself

Being responsible

Being cooperative

Unitarian Universalist Acronyms

APF   Annual Program Fund

A major source of income for the UUA, in which each member congregation is asked to contribute a certain amount. The income generated helps provide services and programs back to the congregations.

AR/AO/MC   Antiracist, Antioppression, Multicultural

A common acronym because the UUA seeks to promote many programs of this nature.

BGLT   Bisexual, Gay, Lesbian, Transgender

Though often grouped together in discussions of oppression, *bisexual*, *gay*, and *lesbian* refer to affectional orientation, whereas *transgender* refers to one's gender identity. *Transgender* is an adjective, not a noun, so its correct use is "a transgender person."

DRE   Director of Religious Education

A common name for the coordinator of the religious education program. Other titles also exist for this position, such as [use your congregation's title here].

GA   General Assembly

Annual business meetings of the congregations belonging to the Unitarian Universalist Association.

MRE   Minister of Religious Education

A minister who specializes in religious education.

OWL   Our Whole Lives

The UUA's comprehensive lifespan sexuality program.

RE   Religious Education

A name often used to refer to the congregational programming that includes Sunday school and other classes that enrich the spiritual lives of members.

UUA   Unitarian Universalist Association of Congregations

The association of all member congregations. The headquarters is located at 25 Beacon Street in Boston and frequently referred to as "25."

UUSC   Unitarian Universalist Service Committee

An associate member organization of the UUA that works to promote and protect human rights around the world.

YAC   Youth/Adult Committees

Committee of youth and adults who work with youth that coordinate youth programming. Frequently found within youth groups at the congregational, district, regional, or continental level.

Extended Journaling and
UU Pocket Guide Discussion for Unit 3

Journaling Prompts

Encourage participants to reflect upon the topics covered in this unit in their journals. Pose the following questions to get them started:

- What are some of the values not discussed in these sessions that are important to you?

- Do you see your own values reflected in conversations with other Unitarian Universalists? Whether you do or do not, how does this make you feel?

UU Pocket Guide Discussion

Ask participants to read "Our Faith" before the scheduled discussion or schedule time during your weekly meeting to read and discuss the chapter, using the following questions:

- What do you think of the "faith affirmations"?

- William Schulz talks about Unitarian Universalism invoking "a global loyalty, an ecological ethic, and a deeper mercy." What are some ways our faith does this?

- Is there anything in the chapter that speaks to your experience as a Unitarian Universalist?

What Would You Do?

Situation A

You are in science class. You hear people in the class snickering and saying your name, and you realize that the boy sitting behind you has blown several spit wads into your hair. The teacher does not notice any of this.

What do you do?

What values or Unitarian Universalist Principles are connected to your actions?

Handout Six, page 1 of 4

Situation B

You're riding the bus home from school, sitting near your friend Katie, who is recovering from a brain tumor. The brain tumor kept her from growing, so she is very small and has not hit puberty yet. The treatment also made her lose her hair. Paul, a very popular star basketball player, is sitting near you on the bus. He is surrounded by his friends. He shouts, "Hey Katie, is that a wig?" You both ignore him. He continues. "Hey, little girl, are you ever gonna wear a bra? You ever gonna get your period? I'll buy you a tampon when you're forty!" Paul and his friends are all laughing hysterically. Katie is quiet, but you can see she is starting to shake and tears are forming in her eyes.

What do you do?

What values or Unitarian Universalist Principles are connected to your actions?

Situation C

You are studying World War II in history class, and you notice that your friend Chris has started to draw swastikas on the margins of her class notes. You think that maybe this is just because you are studying the Nazis. However, the next week and the week after, you see that Chris has drawn more swastikas in the margins of her notes and has put a big swastika on the cover of her notebook with a marker. When you ask her why she is doing this, she gets defensive and says, "Because it looks cool. I'm not a neo-Nazi or anything." You know that there are many students—including students of color and Jewish students—who have noticed her notebook.

What do you do?

What values or Unitarian Universalist Principles are connected to your actions?

Situation D

A group of your friends decides to start a new club. One member brings a catalog to school that features personalized leather jackets. Several of your friends like the idea of ordering personalized jackets for the club. The suggestion is made that all club members must wear the jackets. The jackets will cost more than $100, and you know that not all of your friends can afford them.

What do you do?

What values or Unitarian Universalist Principles are connected to your actions?

Values Cards

Tolerance	Respect
Cooperation	Happiness
Freedom	Honesty
Humility	Service
Justice	Empathy
Friendship	Courage
Fairness	Self-discipline
Peace	Love
Generosity	Responsibility

Handout Seven, page 1 of 2

Simplicity	Pluralism
Unity	Compassion
Sharing	Perseverance
Beauty	Kindness
Equity	Independence
Interdependence	Individuality
Nonviolence	Patience
Security	Prosperity
Popularity	Being "normal"

Charting Our Shared Beliefs

What are some of your beliefs about how humans should act?

What are some of your beliefs about the origins of the universe?

What do you believe about how the universe functions?

What are some of your beliefs about a higher power?

What are some of your beliefs concerning life, death, and the afterlife?

What do you think is sacred?

Which of these beliefs affect the way you act? How?

Why Do People Do Evil Things?

Most Unitarian Universalist ministers and theologians feel that there are no such things as absolute good and absolute evil. Most would also say that the label "evil" is better applied to acts rather than people. In this view, no person is evil, but his/her actions can be evil. The following is a sampling of comments upon the nature of evil from Unitarian Universalist ministers, taken from the article "Confronting Evil" by Warren Ross and the pamphlet Unitarian Universalist Views of Evil, *edited by Paul Rasor:*

Evil is a force within life. We perpetuate it—sometimes by choice, sometimes inadvertently; sometimes by our individual acts, sometimes by supporting oppressive social structures.
—Laurel Hallman

There is no intrinsic good or intrinsic evil. There is always some perspective from which you can demonstrate the good of what we label "evil."
—Bill Jones

Evil is the failure to understand the inherent worth and dignity of every person as part of the interdependent web of all existence.
—Thandeka

Evil comes into the world when our "good" comes into conflict with others' "good."
—Gordon McKeeman

Evil is always the assertion of someone's self-interest without regard to the whole.
—John Buehrens

I see evil as the willful separation from and lack of concern for the "common good."
—Abhi Janamanchi

We commit an evil act when we turn from the good that we know and do to another something we would not want them to do to us.
—Carolyn Owen-Towle

Evil begins with absolutism—the assurance of the righteousness of one truth at the expense of all others.
—Marjorie Bowens-Wheatley

People are born good, but people make choices, and along with our inherent goodness there is also an inherent capacity for evil.
—Rosemary Bray McNatt

Evil is best understood as the allure of that which weakens or destroys all that—in our right minds—we would cherish, encourage, and care for. Once we have succumbed to that allure, we literally cannot see the evil we ourselves are doing. That's what makes evil so potent. It is irrational and not subject to rational control.
—Alice Blair Wesley

Elaine Pagels' definition of evil is "violence committed against the innocent.". . . Yet it sidesteps some key questions: Who decides who is "innocent," and who defines what is "violence"?
—Nancy Palmer Jones

Evil is the capacity, within us and among us, to break sacred bonds with our own souls, with one another, and with the holy.
—Victoria Safford

UNIT FOUR

Spirituality

Deep in our innermost core we yearn to be connected with the mystery we call God, or nature, or the spirit. We yearn for that sense of oneness with each other and all creation, to know our place and our value. And, often, we yearn for someone to show us how to get there, to direct us on the right path that will lead us on the way to a deeper spirituality.

—Susan Manker-Seale

The following activities are designed to invite youth into an inclusive and expansive understanding of our relationship with the miracle of life, that which we call spirituality. This understanding does not require belief in a god or a particular spirit. The tradition of Unitarian Universalism upholds that no one needs a systematic understanding of God, the universe, and everything to be spiritually engaged.

Spirituality, as described in these activities, has several dimensions, including personal spiritual practice, such as meditation, service, or prayer, as well as spirituality through relationship with family, friends, significant others, and the web of life. Spirituality in this sense has three aspects: reflection, reaching out, and response. Reflection encompasses activities that help us be mindful of the miracle of life inside ourselves and beyond. Reaching out involves knowing how to ask for help, when to hold on, and when to let go. Response describes our personal reaction to the daily miracle of life, which can include a range of emotions from celebration to gratitude to sorrow. These three aspects are all commonly experienced in worship, which is the subject of three workshops in this unit.

Lama Surya Das says,

In this postmodern era, people don't just want a belief or understanding of divinity. They want a direct religious experience, some kind of special spiritual event. They want to be able to touch, feel, weigh, and know things for themselves, and they want to explore and understand themselves as well as the universe with all its mysteries. They feel the need to put together a spiritual life that involves their becoming intimate with themselves and with the divine, and to find ways to integrate spiritual values and practical, pragmatic practices into everything they do. They want to find a tailor-made spirituality that fits them and allows them to fulfill their spiritual potential, instead of just buying off-the-rack, ready-made dogma passed down by tradition or family.

You may wish to invite mentors to experience some spiritual practices along with youth. Mentors raised in other religious traditions may have difficulty dissociating the word *spirituality* with what their old traditions taught about it.

Although it is important to be sensitive to their concerns, youth's learning must be kept front and center; mentors who have difficulty with religious language can address those concerns in other forums.

It is unlikely that you will have enough time in your program to offer lessons on each form of spiritual practice outlined here, so choose those that you think will be most relevant to your youth and your congregational context. You may also have people in your community who can lead sessions on spiritual practices beyond those included here. Once you have decided which spiritual practices your program will offer, decide if you would like to invite a guest to lead a workshop and issue the invitation well in advance.

Workshop 11
The Web of Interdependence

Time   60 minutes

Participant Goals

- understand their connections to each other using the concept of interdependence

- realize that one definition of spirituality is our relationship to the known and unknown

Materials

- journals

- pens or pencils

- newsprint

- markers

- tape

- VIP badges (see Preparation)

Preparation

- Make five special badges that say "VIP – Very Interdependent Person." Be creative! These are rewards for one of the small groups in the Interdependence Brainstorm activity.

- Write "This is what we know about" on a sheet of newsprint. On a second sheet, write "What do we not know about?"

Opening   5 minutes

Use the opening ritual designed by the group.

The Human Machine   10 minutes

Ask participants if they can think of the name of a machine, real or imagined. Go with the first idea (unless it's offensive or completely unfeasible.) Announce, "Your task is to be the _____ machine. Each of you gets to be a part. You can use your whole body and your voice to imitate your part of the machine." Ask everyone to get in a line and go up, one by one, to build the machine. Explain that there should be no overall planning—the machine should simply be built by each person going up, seeing what part is needed, and acting out that part.

Once everyone is in place, give directions to the machine. First announce that the power is being revved up, then cooled down, and finally shut off. The machine should respond accordingly.

After everyone has taken their seats, ask questions like these: "What was that game like for you?" "How did it feel to be part of the machine?" "Did you notice how the part that you played was affected by the parts that other people played?" "Are there situations in your life that are like this machine—where the parts other people play affect yours?" (Some examples are team sports, friends, and families.)

Continue by saying, "Today we are going to explore our connections with other people, with earth and its creatures, with the universe, and with the divine. Just like in this game, where you each decided what part you would play when it was your turn, we each have some degree of independence. But like in the game, we're not totally independent: Our choices are affected by the whole system. In reality, we are interdependent. *Interdependence* means that we depend on others and others depend on us. The seventh Principle of the Unitarian Universalist Association talks about the interdependent web of all existence."

Interbeing   15 minutes

Invite participants to grab their journals and find a comfortable place to sit or lie down in the room. Explain that you are going to share a perspective on interdependence by Thich Nhat Hanh, a Vietnamese Buddhist monk. The reading will be followed by journaling and discussion. Invite participants to close their eyes if they choose to.

Read slowly:

If you are a poet, you will see clearly that there is a cloud floating in this sheet of paper. Without a cloud, there will be no rain; without rain, the trees cannot grow; and without trees, we cannot make paper. The cloud is essential for the paper to exist. If the cloud is not here, the sheet of paper cannot be here either. So we can say that the cloud and the paper inter-are. *Interbeing* is a word that is not in the dictionary yet, but if we combine the prefix *inter-* with the verb *to be*, we have a new verb, *inter-be*.

If we look into this sheet of paper even more deeply, we can see the sunshine in it. Without sunshine, the forest cannot grow. In fact, nothing can grow without sunshine. And so, we know that the sunshine is also in this sheet of paper. The paper and the sunshine inter-are. And if we continue to look, we can see the logger who cut the tree and brought it to the mill to be transformed into paper. And we see wheat. We know that the logger cannot exist without his daily bread, and therefore the wheat that became his bread is also in this sheet of paper. The logger's father and mother are in it, too. When we look in this way, we see that without all of these things, this sheet of paper cannot exist.

Looking even more deeply, we can see ourselves in this sheet of paper, too. This is not difficult to see, because when we look at a sheet of paper, it is part of our perception. Your mind is in here and mine is also. So we can say that everything is in here with this sheet of paper. We cannot point out one thing that is not here—time, space, the earth, the rain, the minerals in the soil, the sunshine, the cloud, the river, the heat. Everything coexists with this sheet of paper. That is why I think the word *inter-be* should be in the dictionary. "To be" is to inter-be. We cannot just be by ourselves alone. We have to inter-be with every other thing. This sheet of paper is, because everything else is.

Suppose we try to return one of the elements to its source. Suppose we return the sunshine to the sun. Do you think that this sheet of paper will be possible? No, without sunshine nothing can be. And if we return the logger to his mother, then we have no sheet of paper either. The fact is that this sheet of paper is made up only of non-paper elements. And if we return these non-paper elements to their sources, then there can be no paper at all. Without non-paper elements, like mind, logger, sunshine, and so on, there will be no paper. As thin as this sheet of paper is, it contains everything in the universe in it.

After the reading is finished, invite participants to quietly reflect on what they heard by writing or drawing in their journals. If they need prompts, frame the reflection with these questions:

- How did this reading speak to you?

- What does it mean to you that you are interbeing with this piece of paper, with other people, trees, and so much more?

Allow five to ten minutes for journaling. Call participants back to their regular seats, and ask a few volunteers to share some of their reflections.

Interdependence Brainstorm   25 minutes

Introduce the discussion by saying something like the following: "Interbeing is related to interdependence. While interbeing recognizes how, in essence, we are part of everything and everything is part of us, interdependence recognizes that we have a relationship with everything."

Divide the group into smaller groups of three or four participants. Give each group a marker and a large piece of newsprint. Ask each group to appoint someone to take notes.

Invite the groups to brainstorm for ten minutes on the question: "What and who are you dependent on for being here as you are in this very moment?" They can list people, things, events, plants, animals, technologies, ideas, political movements, and so on.

If participants seem frustrated, encourage them to think about different areas. For example, if they have been thinking only about their personal lives, encourage them to think of the history of politics and wars, or the history of Unitarian Universalism. If they have been thinking only about food and biological processes, encourage them to think of the technologies they have relied on to get them to this very moment.

When time is up, ask each group to count the number of items on its list. The group that has the longest list gets to stand up, take a bow, and receive their VIP badges.

Put up the sheet of newsprint that reads, "This is what we know about." Explain that science and reason have provided us with explanations of much of the natural world, but that understanding the mechanics of life does not make them any less "wonder-full" or awe inspiring. Then post the second sheet, "What do we not know about?" Point out that beyond what we know, there is much that we do not know for sure. For example, is there such a thing as fate? Is there a god behind all this? Are there many gods? Is there a loving spirit or force that we cannot see or feel or prove in the same way that we see and feel and prove other things? What lies behind the miracle of life and the interdependent web? Invite participants to identify what they consider things they know and things they do not know about.

Explain that our individual relationship to all this—both the known and the unknown, both the natural and the supernatural—can be called our "spirituality." Share these definitions of spirituality: "Spirituality is consciousness of infinite interrelatedness" (from Felix Adler, a founder of the Ethical Culture movement); spirituality, in its most basic sense, is about how we relate to the miracle of life (from UU minister Scott Alexander).

Ask participants to share any comments, questions, or ideas sparked by today's discussion.

Closing Circle 5 minutes

Use the closing ritual designed by the group.

Workshop 12
Learning to Lead Worship

Regular worship can build community, develop religious identity, and minister to the spiritual needs of the youth in your program. This workshop introduces circle worship and includes activities to help young people understand what is involved in planning and leading worship. Although participants are seated in a circle, the concept of circle worship goes beyond seating. Typically, it is led by laypeople who also sit in the circle and involves active participation by everyone present. Handout 10, Typical Elements of Circle/Youth Worship (page 135), describes this style of worship in detail and offers ideas for how to lead it.

Many Unitarian Universalist youth groups use circle worship at their meetings and conferences. In this program, circle worships offer an opportunity for youth to minister to each other and develop worship leadership skills. At the beginning of a Coming of Age session, circle worship can help center the group and ground it in its purpose; at the end of a session, it can help the group carry the week's learnings with them.

Time 60 minutes

Participant Goals

- experience worship that ministers to their spiritual and social needs

- develop skills and confidence in planning and leading worship

- grow in their capacity to take on responsibilities in a group

Materials

- chalice, candle, and matches

- a small table covered by a colorful cloth

- copies of Handouts 10 and 11, Typical Elements of Circle/Youth Worship and Typical Elements of a Traditional Worship Service (pages 135 and 137)

- worship resources, including hymnals and books of meditations

Preparation

- Recruit youth (and adults) to lead the components of this worship.

- Set up the altar cloth, chalice, candle, and matches in what you anticipate will be the center of a circle.

- Consider inviting guests to help instruct youth in worship planning. An older youth in the congregation who is experienced with circle worship and an adult youth advisor would be a great combination. Invite them to bring any sample Orders of Service they have previously used.

Opening   5 minutes

Use the opening ritual designed by the group.

Circle Worship Service   20 minutes

Let participants know that they will experience a style of worship called circle worship, which is sometimes called youth worship because many youth groups use this style. Mention that it is a style your group will be working with throughout the year and that participants will be invited to plan worships for future gatherings.

Gathering. Ask the group to stand in a corner of the room, and teach Hymn 389, "Gathered Here," as a round. Once they have sung it through once, invite participants to sing it again and take hands with each other, and guide them to walk while singing. Lead the group so it forms a circle, and walk around the circle once or twice while singing. Then invite everyone to take a seat on the floor.

Opening. Light the chalice and share these words:

> We light our chalice—this symbol of our faith tradition
>
> To celebrate and give thanks for the community we are forming in Coming of Age.
>
> May we learn, grow, and laugh together
>
> In the love, support, and freedom of our Unitarian Universalist congregation.

Song. Teach Song 1023, "Building Bridges," by the Women of Greenhorn Common in England, from *Singing the Journey.* If no one knows the tune, another song may be substituted.

Reading. Offer a few words about the process of coming of age, then offer this reading by Anne Hillman:

> We look with uncertainty
> Beyond the old choices for
> Clear-cut answers
> To a softer, more permeable aliveness
> Which is every moment
> At the brink of death;
> For something new is being born in us
> If we but let it.
> We stand at a new doorway,
> Awaiting that which comes . . .
> Daring to be human creatures.
> Vulnerable to the beauty of existence.
> Learning to love.

Centerpiece. Lead the group in a guided check-in with the questions: What new doorways are you excited about crossing? What new doorways cause a bit of anxiety? Participants can speak to one or both questions. Gently remind the group to listen to one another with respect. If it is their first time checking in together, outline the guidelines for check-in before proceeding. Close the check-in by asking for a moment of silence to reflect on the blessings of sharing what we have in common and what makes us unique.

Song. Teach and sing the simple song "Dear Friends" (words below), which can be sung as a round with "Building Bridges." If the song is unfamiliar, substitute another simple song, such as Hymn 16,"'Tis a Gift to Be Simple," from *Singing the Living Tradition*.

> Dear friends, dear friends,
> Let me tell you how I feel,
> You have given me such treasures,
> I love you so.

Closing. Close the worship with an affirmation such as "Amen," "Blessed be," or "Peace," or another affirmation that suits your group well. You may extinguish the chalice at this time.

What Is Youth Worship All About?   15 minutes

Consider inviting a guest to facilitate this activity if leaders are not experienced in planning and leading worship.

Ask youth if they have ever experienced UU worship like the service you just held, perhaps at a youth conference or camp, or at Children's Chapel with the religious educator. If some of them have, ask them to briefly tell the group how that service resembled the one they just participated in.

Distribute Handout 10, Typical Elements of Circle/Youth Worship. Ask volunteers to read through the elements and identify where each element was present in the worship service just conducted, if at all.

Ask youth if they have ever attended worship services with the congregation. If they have not, tell them you will be attending a service together in the future. Distribute Handout 11, Typical Elements of a Traditional Worship Service. Explain that the handout discusses typical segments of a congregational worship service and their purpose. Spend a few minutes reviewing the components listed, considering questions such as these: How do the two handouts compare? Can you match the activities of a typical circle worship service with those of a traditional worship service? Do some activities have the same purposes even if they have different forms?

Say in your own words,

> It would be easy to just prepare an outline for worship that says "chalice lighting, hymn, reading, homily, meditation, hymn, closing." However, as the two handouts demonstrate, different elements of worship, like hymns or meditations, serve different purposes. So, too, do different worship services. You might not want to design the same service for the first morning of summer camp for sixth graders as you would for midnight at the end of a weekend retreat of high school youth. For this reason, it is not enough to just know where to place the chalice lighting. Good worship design calls for an understanding of how the elements affect us and how they fit together.

If you or your guest brought Orders of Service from worship services you planned or led, share them and the experience with the group. Ask if there are any questions.

Planning Worship   15 minutes

If your group will be taking turns planning worship (in pairs or otherwise), ask people to sign up to lead worship at different group meetings and retreats. It is wise to have an adult leader partner with the groups to help them with this task, especially if your group is younger in age. Keep a record posted. You might also e-mail the schedule to youth, parents, mentors, and other Coming of Age leaders not present.

Invite participants and leaders to identify resources that worship planners can use to assemble readings, songs, and activities. These resources may include collections of readings, hymnals, people (such as the religious educator, music director, and minister), organizations (such as CUUPS or the youth group), and websites.

If you invited guests to lead this workshop, they might share examples from their own experiences planning circle worship.

Closing Circle   5 minutes

Use the closing ritual designed by the group.

Workshop 13
Attending Worship

Time variable

Participant Goals

- worship with the congregation

- analyze ways to help lead worship

Preparation

- Pick a place for youth to meet ten minutes before the start of your congregation's traditional worship service. Notify all youth, families, and mentors of the plan.

For the Service

Have youth and leaders sit together; mentors are welcome to join. Let the youth know that they should focus on the service more than usual because you will be discussing it later as a group. Save copies of the Order of Service, if one is provided.

After the Service

If time permits, gather participants, including mentors, and ask for questions and reflections about the worship service. These questions can help stimulate discussion: Did they notice anything they had not seen before? How many youth had previously attended a non-intergenerational UU worship service before? Was today's service in any way different from an intergenerational service?

Identify places within the service where the laity was active, noting that strong lay leadership in worship is a UU tradition shared by some, but not most, religious traditions. Mention that some UU congregations have no ordained ministers and are entirely lay-led and that, as youth and adults, there are many opportunities for them to provide leadership in the worship service. Ask if anyone, youth or mentor, has already done so, and let them know that in a future workshop, youth will learn about leading worship.

Workshop 14
Rituals of Our Faith

Conduct this workshop after participants have attended the congregational worship service as a group.

Time 60 minutes

Participant Goals

- identify rituals in UU worship services

- recognize other rituals of the congregation

- analyze the role ritual plays in worship

- appreciate the role worship plays in congregational life

Materials

- copies of Order of Service from your congregation's worship service

- newsprint

- markers

- tape

- calendar

- ritual props such as a chalice, hymnbook, or the rug children sit on during Time for All Ages (optional)

Preparation

- Write the following definitions on separate pieces of newsprint and post them around the room: "The prescribed order of a religious ceremony"; "A detailed method or procedure faithfully or regularly followed"; "The body of ceremonies used in a place of worship."

- Arrange to visit religious education classes for the ritual field trip (see page 119).

Today's Topic 5 minutes

Indicate the newsprint on the walls. Explain that these are definitions for a word that is the topic of today's workshop. Ask who can guess the word. If no one guesses correctly, say you will come back to the definitions later. If at any time during the workshop someone can name the word being defined (*ritual*), write it on the newsprint.

Opening   5 minutes

Use the opening ritual designed by the group.

Rituals of the Worship Service   10 minutes

Remind the group that virtually every workshop opens with the ceremony they designed. Ask if there are other activities that the Coming of Age workshops include every time or almost every time. If no one suggests it, mention your closing ceremony. Participants might also mention worship or check-in.

Pass out copies of an Order of Service from the congregational worship service. Ask for a volunteer to write the responses of the group on newsprint. Invite youth to look at the Order of Service and identify acts that are regularly repeated. These will be different at each congregation, but might include lighting the chalice, a responsive reading of the congregation's mission statement, the offertory, and Time for All Ages. To make this more active, ask for a volunteer to pantomime these parts of the service; other participants can call out rituals as they identify them.

Tell participants that these acts are rituals of your congregation's worship service, and ask if they fit the definitions on the wall. Say something like the following:

Not all Unitarian Universalist congregations use the same rituals, but most do have a few rituals they perform regularly in their worship service. Unlike most other religions, Unitarian Universalism doesn't require congregations to include any ritual in their worship service. The most common ritual of our faith—lighting the chalice—is not required, but has been accepted by many congregations because they find it meaningful. The chalice was a symbol originally used by the Unitarian Service Committee. Many of you are familiar with the committee, which is now the Unitarian Universalist Service Committee, from experiences with Guest at Your Table. The committee's work so inspired many UUs that the chalice became our symbol, too, and lighting it on

Sunday mornings provides a connection with thousands of Unitarian Universalists in the world who are also lighting their chalices. Chalice lighting is also a ritual we can easily perform at home to remind us of our shared faith.

Ritual Field Trip   15 minutes

Share with participants that Unitarian Universalism is a living faith and, as such, we are not afraid to change, add, or subtract rituals as needed. Offer the adoption of chalice lighting as a good example, and note that as people change, so do their needs.

Tell participants that they are going to take a ritual mini field trip around the religious education program. Visit the other ages in your religious education program, including adults, if possible. Share with the class being visited that your group is discussing rituals today. Invite each class to demonstrate a ritual they perform when they meet, then have the Coming of Age group demonstrate their opening ritual. Thank the host class and move on until you run out of time or have visited all the other classes.

Ask participants to share with the group any memories they have of rituals in earlier religious education classrooms, either in this congregation or elsewhere. Some participants might remember using rituals witnessed during the mini field trip. Ask why different groups use different rituals, and who created the rituals the groups used. Lead in to the next activity by telling the group that the purpose of rituals is perhaps the most important question.

What and Why   10 minutes

Hold a conversation with participants on the purpose of ritual and worship. Below are a few questions and possible answers. The answers are to inform the leader's conversation, not to be read to the group. Ask the questions and give youth a chance to contribute their answers before sharing your answers.

Q: What purpose does ritual serve?
A: Ritual is about giving concentrated thought and intention toward specific

actions. The thoughts and intentions give the actions a meaning they might not have otherwise. Concentrating on the actions takes us out of ourselves and brings us together as a body of people, all focusing upon the same action. For example, a wedding or civil union is not just about the legal contract that joins the couple. It is a ritual that allows the couple to be recognized by the larger community as having been transformed.

Q: What do rituals contribute to the worship service?

A: Rituals allow the congregation to act together as one body during worship. They focus us on that which we find sacred and worthy of our repeated attention. When a congregation repeats a doxology or mission statement, they are both reminding themselves of their beliefs and reasons for being together and affirming their dedication to those words.

Q: Why do people worship?

A: Ralph Waldo Emerson writes that "a person will worship something, have no doubt about that. We may think our tribute is paid in secret in the dark recesses of our hearts, but it will out. That which dominates our imaginations and our thoughts will determine our lives, and our character. Therefore, it behooves us to be careful what we worship, for what we are worshipping we are becoming."

The act of worship is about "shaping that which is of worth." Emerson's words are true: Everyone finds worth in something. During worship, participants join together in community to identify what is of worth to them (individually, as a congregation, and as residents of the world community) and how this worthiness shapes their lives (spiritually, ethically, and as a faith community).

Sometimes people talk about "within, among, and beyond." Different experiences in worship take us deep within (meditation), ask us to join among (Joys and Concerns,

prayers for the congregation), and help us live our Unitarian Universalist values in the world (through social justice actions, community service, inviting our friends to attend worship with us). At home, we can indulge in a personal spiritual practice, but our faith grows wider and deeper when developed in community.

Rituals of the Worship Year   10 minutes

Introduce the discussion by saying something like the following:

The rituals of the worship year vary by congregation. Many congregations celebrate Water, Bread, and/or Flower Communion services during the year. Many celebrate earth-centered holidays, such as Sanheim and Mabon. Others include Blessing of the Animals, Child and Teacher Dedications, holiday intergenerational services at Easter and Christmas, and Coming of Age and Bridging ceremonies. Though the rituals may vary, your congregation will also be home to weddings or civil unions and funerals or memorial services. There are also rituals that take place outside of the worship service, such as yearly retreats, Seders, Sunday potlucks and Halloween parties. Knowing the rhythm of the congregational year gives us all a sense of belonging.

On a sheet of newsprint, create a list of congregational rituals. Encourage participants to create as large a list as possible. You can do this as a group or divide into teams. Provide a calendar and perhaps even props to help spark their memories. Allow time for youth to share memories with each other.

Closing Circle   5 minutes

Use the closing ritual designed by the group.

Workshop 15
Introduction to Spiritual Practice

Scott Alexander, a Unitarian Universalist minister, describes spiritual practice as "any regular, intentional activity that serves to significantly deepen the quality and content of your relationship with the miracle of life." Spiritual practice comes in many forms, ranging from prayer to meditation to dance to community service. The purpose of introducing spiritual practice in this program is to awaken youth to the possibility of intentional spiritual development. We do learn and grow spiritually, whether or not we intend to. However, bringing intention to this growth fosters a richer experience: one characterized by more meaning, depth, compassion, self-understanding, and fulfillment. Spiritual practices can also help us cope with our emotions, both positive and negative. For example, anger, confusion, and feelings of alienation can be directly addressed through meditation.

Some of the following activities require more advance preparation than the average workshop. If you invite someone to teach a spiritual practice to the group, find teachers that are respectful of Unitarian Universalism and can present spiritual practices that are compatible with UU beliefs. Look for experienced teachers; some practitioners, even serious ones, may not have the skills necessary to teach youth about their spiritual practice. You may need to offer an honorarium to attract such a person.

Some spiritual practices, particularly movement-oriented ones, may require that your group meet somewhere other than its regular meeting room. A field trip to a tai chi center or a dance studio might be in order. Traveling to visit another group might also help youth take the time more seriously than they would have otherwise.

Everyday Spiritual Practice: Simple Pathways for Enriching Your Life, edited by Scott W. Alexander, presents essays on more than thirty possibilities for Unitarian Universalist spiritual practice.

Time   60 minutes

Participant Goals

- understand the purpose of spiritual practices
- appreciate the breadth of possible spiritual practices
- hear personal accounts of how spiritual practices enrich the lives of practitioners
- meet members of the congregation
- discover new spiritual practices

Materials

- newsprint
- markers
- tape

Preparation

- At least two weeks in advance, invite four to six people to be panelists. Panelists must be willing to talk for up to five minutes about their spiritual practices and to answer questions from participants. A panel composed of UUs offers the youth the added advantage of learning about different ways of being Unitarian Universalist and spiritual. Your congregation's minister(s) and religious educator could add a valuable perspective as panelists.

- In the week before this workshop, stay in touch with panel members, confirm workshop time and place, and answer any questions they may have.

- Determine who will moderate the panel. You can ask a youth or do it yourself. The moderator will introduce the panelists, keep time, and facilitate the question and answer time. Having a youth moderate the panel can help keep all youth more focused and involved. It can also help ensure that the panel focuses on youth's concerns.

Opening   5 minutes

Use the opening ritual designed by the group.

Spirituality Words and Images   10 minutes

Ask participants, "What words and images come to mind when you hear the word *spirituality*?" Possible responses include people praying; someone studying scripture; devotion; meditation. Generate a list on newsprint. Then ask, "What words and images come to mind when you think of Unitarian Universalist spirituality?" Generate a list on a second sheet of newsprint. When each list is complete, hang them side by side on a wall and ask participants to compare the two lists. What are some of the key differences? Similarities?

Depending on your congregation's theological orientation, it is likely that the group's ideas about Unitarian Universalist spirituality are less God-centered than their ideas about spirituality in general. Explain, "A common misconception is that you have to believe in God—or a specific kind of god—to have spirituality. In fact, spirituality need not be God-centered. Whatever you believe about God, or whether you believe in the existence of God, spirituality includes our relationship with the miracle of life."

What Is a Spiritual Practice?   5 minutes

Ask participants if they have ever heard of the idea of "spiritual practice." If so, ask them to share what they know.

Explain:

> Spiritual practices are things that people do to create spiritual awareness and centeredness. For example, going to church can be a spiritual practice, because it helps people pay attention to the miracle of life. Yoga is another popular spiritual practice, because it makes people feel centered and connected to the life force. For some people, writing in their journals is a spiritual practice, because they pay attention to what is important or sacred in what they write.

Invite participants to name some other spiritual practices.

Panel Presentations   25 minutes

The moderator will briefly introduce each of the panelists and invite them to speak for up to five minutes about their own spiritual practices—those practices that help each of them connect with the miracle of life.

Ask listeners to take note of any questions that they have or ideas that come up for them. Let them know that there will be a time for discussion after the panel.

Discussion   10 minutes

After all the panelists have made a presentation, it is helpful if the moderator leads off with the first question or two. One interesting question is "What were your spiritual practices when you were a teenager?" You can follow up by asking, "If you could talk to your teenage self today, what would you say to that self about the spiritual life?"

Ask for questions and comments from the group. As needed, the moderator can help draw participants into discussion by asking them these questions:

- What were some ideas that you liked in the panelists' presentations?

- What do you think is the value of having a spiritual practice?

- What can get in the way of spiritual practice?

- Are there any practices that the panelists described that you would like to hear more about?

Conclude the discussion by thanking the panelists for their time.

Closing Circle   5 minutes

Use the closing ritual designed by the group.

Workshop 16
Prayer

Time   60 minutes

Participant Goals

- process feelings about and experiences with prayer

- create prayer beads and learn ways to use them

Materials

- newsprint

- markers

- per participant (including mentors and leaders, if applicable): 23 small beads (about ¼-inch diameter); 4 medium beads (½- to ¾-inch diameter); 1 large bead (¾- to 1-inch diameter). Have a variety of styles and colors and many extra beads, so that participants can create something that suits their style. Make sure the holes in the beads are big enough to fit the cord or string you choose.

- 12 to 18 inches of cord or string per participant. Choose sturdy cord or string that can hold the weight of the beads and ties well in a knot.

- one beading needle per participant, if you are using cord or string that gets frayed or is not stiff. Needles should fit through the beads' holes.

- one pair of scissors for every three to four participants (including left-handed scissors)

- copies of Handouts 12 and 13, How to Assemble Your Prayer Beads and How to Pray with Your Prayer Beads (pages 138 and 139)

Opening   5 minutes

Use the opening ritual designed by the group.

Changing Ideas of Prayer   25 minutes

Ask participants to form small groups of two or three (or mentor-youth groups) and give them five minutes to discuss these questions:

- How did you understand prayer when you were between five and eight years old?

- How did you think it worked (or did not work)?

- What kinds of postures did you associate with prayer?

- What kinds of words?

Then give them five minutes to discuss these new questions:

- If your ideas about prayer have changed since that time, how have they changed?

- What are some of your new ideas about how and why people pray?

Ask participants to return to the large group and share highlights of their group conversations, focusing on whether their old views were similar to each other's and the differences and similarities in their new views.

Ask the group, "What motivates people to pray?" Write responses on newsprint. Some possible answers include that they care about somebody who is in pain; they want something to happen; habit; they are required by their religion; or they think it helps their relationship with God.

Once the list has been generated, ask, "Which of the motivations we listed is compatible with Unitarian Universalism?" Circle or place a star next to those motivations that participants believe are compatible with our faith tradition.

Read aloud this statement about prayer from Arvid Straube, a Unitarian Universalist minister:

> The fact is that prayer is the most simple, natural thing in the world. The only problem with prayer is to take away all the attitudes and preconceptions that keep us from prayer. I've come to think that prayer is simply being in touch with the most honest, deepest desires of the heart . . . in quiet, and in as much trust as we can muster, with as much honesty as we can possibly find. That's all. Prayers pray themselves.

Continue in your own words:

> In other words, we do not have to bow or clasp our hands in a certain way. We do not have to recite special scripts, and we do not even have to believe in a higher power in order to pray. Prayer is one of the many ways that Unitarian Universalists can connect with their spirituality: their relationship with the miracle of life. Prayer has both

an inward and an outward focus, praying for ourselves and for others. The following activity provides a loose framework for experimenting with a Unitarian Universalist form of prayer.

Bead Making   25 minutes

Introduce the activity by saying something like the following: "Rev. Erik Walker Wikstrom, a Unitarian Universalist minister, designed a way of doing UU prayer with beads. Here is how he describes the activity that we are about to do."

> I decided to focus on the process of prayer, on its form rather than its content, on the "how" of prayer rather than the "why" or "to whom." Having looked at prayer practices in a variety of religious traditions, I found that a few types or forms of prayer kept coming up. Christianity calls them praise, thanksgiving, confession, contemplation, and intercession; these same forms can be found by other names in nearly all of the world's religions. By using these common prayer forms as the foundation of this practice, I believe that Christians, Buddhists, neo-pagans, atheists, and even eclectics can use it to create a prayer experience that makes sense within their own tradition(s) and understandings. The practice I developed makes use of prayer beads. Beads have been used as a tool for spiritual discipline in many religious traditions—the rosary of Catholicism and the 108-bead Malas of Buddhism are two well-known examples. Beads [help] provide focus and direction.

Ask participants to form into their mentor-youth groupings if mentors are present, or to form into small groups of two or three. Distribute beading supplies and Handouts 12 and 13, How to Assemble Your Prayer Beads and How to Pray with Your Prayer Beads. Encourage the groups to discuss prayer and spiritual practice as they are creating the prayer beads.

When all or most participants have finished making beads, demonstrate how the beads can be used by choosing options from Handout 13, How to Pray with Your Prayer Beads. Explain that they have the freedom to develop prayers and meditations that are meaningful to them. The beads can provide a structure. If you choose to, give the group an assignment for the week: to find a quiet time and space to use their prayer beads and then write about the experience in their journals.

If there is extra time, ask groups to continue their discussions about prayer and spiritual practice.

Closing Circle   5 minutes

Invite participants to gather in a circle and, in turn, respond to the question: "If you could make a one-word prayer for the world, what would it be?"

Workshop 17
Making an Altar

In this workshop, youth will construct an altar that can be used in rituals at home with their families or alone. Rituals can honor the spirituality and connection in a family. All families have rituals, though not necessarily spiritual in nature. Taking home a family altar allows for the possibility of creating new, spiritually fulfilling rituals for the family or the individual.

Time   75 minutes

Participant Goals

- craft family altars

- generate a list of ritual uses for the altar

- become more comfortable with using an altar

Materials

- newsprint and easel

- markers

- fabric and craft paints in a variety of colors

- brushes

- water cups

- 18" x 18" piece of attractive fabric (velvet, silk, etc.)

- 8" x 8" piece of luan plywood (a thin and flexible plywood made from mahogany)

- pencils

- CD player with meditative music CD

- protection for work surface

- journals

Opening   5 minutes

Use the opening activity designed by the group.

What Is An Altar?   5 minutes

Write the word *altar* on newsprint and ask if anyone can define it or give an example. Continue by saying something like the following:

> An altar is a sacred space where religious rites or rituals are performed. Your congregation might or might not have an altar or use the word *altar* for the focal point of worship. An altar or centering point could be as small as a table or a niche in the wall. You might have an altar in your home, or maybe you've visited homes or other houses of worship with altars. Altars are places where people have brought their feelings and expression of their faith since the beginning of time. Whether they be shrines, sacred spaces in nature, or rocky ledges on which sacrifices are offered, altars are centering places. People pray, meditate, rest, wonder, be in silence, cry, give thanks, share, calm, focus, reflect, repent, and think at altars. The single element necessary to create an altar is intention.

Sharing Our Own Rituals   10 minutes

Ask participants to form small groups of about three and spend three or four minutes talking about rituals in their own families. Ask each group to list some of the rituals they shared on newsprint, focusing on spiritual rituals. These might include graces, bedtime rituals, holiday traditions, and rituals surrounding life transitions (such as births, marriages, and deaths). Invite small groups to share their lists with the larger group.

Icons   5 minutes

Explain that an icon is an image or representation of something that has meaning, and that in religions, icons—or symbols—have sacred meaning. Ask participants what icon is associated with our Unitarian Universalist faith. Post a sheet of newsprint and ask for volunteers to draw faith-based icons that are in their family. Then invite participants to draw icons of other faiths that may not exist in their own family and, finally, icons that are not necessarily faith-based, but have important meaning or value in our culture. Examples may be yin and yang, a crucifix, "om," a peace sign, the Sun, the Moon, etc.

Creating an Altar   30 minutes

Invite participants to create a simple altar to take home. Explain that the basic altar will be plywood laid atop an altar cloth and that they will have time to decorate both the cloth and board, using any of the icons they just drew or other artwork that is meaningful to them. Give each participant a plywood board and ask them to follow these instructions:

- Trace the shape of the board lightly onto the fabric. It can be a square within a square or a diamond within a square. Put the fabric aside.

- Divide the board into four equal quadrants, drawing with a pencil.

- Paint each quadrant, including the edges, a different color. You can choose colors that will tie in with the altar cloth, although this is not required.

- Add highlights and accents with the fabric paints, or add designs with craft paints.

- You can choose to leave the four quadrants just colored or add letters to each one, symbolizing four different concepts, ideas, icons, or qualities. Examples are North, South, East, West; T, H, I, S (Thankfulness, Hopefulness, Improvement, Sorrow); or Autumn, Winter, Spring, Summer.

- While the board is drying, decorate the cloth outside the traced area. Aim for decoration that will connect you to the divine or make a spiritual connection to the universe.

Home Rituals for the Altar   5 minutes

While the paint dries, suggest the following as possible rituals using the altar:

- Family members bring objects found in their daily journey to the altar and place them in a quadrant of the altar board (thankfulness, hopefulness, improvement, sorrow).

- Keep a small bowl with stones in the center of the altar. Before a shared meal, each family member takes a stone from the bowl and places it on the altar, sharing something meaningful about that day.

- Place a tea light for each family member on the altar. At the beginning of a holiday, family members can light their candles and share a special memory.

- Place the altar on the dining room table. At the beginning of meals, place a small amount of food on the altar. Say grace. Afterward, everyone takes a small piece from the food on the altar and eats it in silence, reflecting upon the grace.

If youth choose to use what was made as a personal altar, they can place on it objects that hold great significance to them, such as small gifts from their best friends, photographs, attractive seashells and stones brought back from vacation, or religious icons (crosses, a chalice, or small statues of gods and goddesses).

Ask for any other suggestions. Remind participants that during these rituals, it is respectful to always give family members the right to pass.

Pass out the journals. Play meditative music while participants write down the ideas they may want to share with their families or any thoughts and feelings about rituals and altars that arose during the workshop.

Sharing Our Family Altars   10 minutes

When the altars are dry, ask youth to gather in a circle and carefully set up their cloths and altars in front of them. Indicate that care should also be given at home when setting up the altar. Remind them that the intention they put into the altar makes it sacred space.

Invite participants to share their altars and tell what is meaningful about them for their families. If they like, they can also share one way they hope it will be used at home.

You may want to conclude this activity with a short blessing, such as:

> Created in the intention of love and fellowship,
> May these altars be sacred spaces of the mind,
> Sacred spaces of the heart, and
> Sacred spaces of the soul
> To bless our homes and loved ones.
> Amen.

Participants may now take their altars home. Say something like: "We said earlier that the single most necessary element in creating an altar is intention. Intention is important, too, to retain the sacred nature of the altar. Find a location to place your altar that is out of the way enough so it will not inconvenience your family, yet conspicuous enough to be seen as a reminder to tend to your spiritual needs."

Closing Circle   5 minutes

Use the closing ritual designed by the group.

Workshop 18
Stillness, Silence and Meditation

Time   60 minutes

Participant Goals

- experience different methods of meditation as a spiritual practice

- reflect on the experience of meditation by journaling

Materials

- one pillow per participant
- chime, bell, or singing bowl
- journals
- pens or pencils
- hot water
- cups
- selection of caffeine-free teabags

Preparation

- Decide which meditation technique(s) participants will experience.

- If you are doing the walking meditation, scope out a suitable area. Peaceful settings, such as parks and forests, are suitable for a certain kind of experience; busy settings, such as city streets, will provide a different type of experience. Decide what the limits of participants' wanderings will be and how they will know that the activity has concluded. If they will be within earshot, a bell or chime can signal the end of the meditation. If they will be farther away, you can set a specific time for return and ask that participants keep an eye on their watches.

Opening   10 minutes

Explain that the opening today will be a brief period of silent meditation, and that you are going to open and close the period of silence with the ringing of a bell. Participants are to sit in silence, with their eyes closed, and to focus on the sound and feeling of their breath. Remind participants to breathe in and out deeply, through their bellies. Allow two to three minutes for silent breathing. When the time is complete, ring a chime.

Ask participants what the experience was like for them. Was it easy to focus on breathing or was it hard to be still and silent? What were some of the challenges?

Share with participants the following background on how breathing relates to meditation:

Nearly all forms of meditation involve paying more attention to your breathing than usual. Even though we breathe in and out more than 20,000 times per day, most of us go through our lives without being very conscious of our breath. Practitioners of meditation find that in becoming conscious of each in-breath and out-breath, they become more centered and peaceful. If they have practiced, they are able to quiet their minds as they focus on their breathing. In many ways, it is the opposite of how we normally think: Normally, we pay attention to our thoughts and ignore our breath.

Some Buddhist forms of meditation use this focus on the breath to help the practitioner focus on the present moment, simply being in the here and now. Other forms ask practitioners to sit and breathe in a certain way so they transcend the present moment and experience an elevated realm of pure consciousness.

Silence   10 minutes

Invite the group into a conversation on the difference between silence and being quiet, by saying something like: "Many of you have experienced moments of silence in UU worship services. Sometimes we acknowledge tragedies with public moments of silence at school or sporting events. You also just experienced some silent sitting meditation. Based on these experiences, what are some differences between silence and simply being quiet?" Possible responses include that silence is purposeful; everybody's quiet together in silence; you focus more on your thoughts when you are silent.

Point out that silence has a place in many religious and spiritual traditions, including Quaker Christianity, Buddhism, Hinduism, and Unitarian Universalism.

Ask participants to identify the times and places that they get to experience peaceful silence in their own lives. Considering the busy and media-filled pace of many young people's lives these days, they may not be able to come up with much. If they are not able to, that point is instructive in itself and can lead to a conversation on the next point. Ask what can get in the way of experiencing peaceful silence. Once participants have responded, explain that meditation practices have evolved to help us get past these obstacles so that we can experience peaceful silence. It's called meditation practice because it truly takes practice to sit still and quiet the mind!

Meditation 35 minutes

Choose one or two of these three techniques for participants to experience. If you have time in your schedule for additional workshops on meditation or time during future retreats, you may want to introduce participants to techniques you could not cover in this session.

Guided Meditation. Invite participants to find places on the floor where they can lie down without being directly next to another person. Make pillows available for participants who want them. In a relaxed voice, slowly read the following text by yoga instructor Kevin Durkin. Pause between sentences so that listeners can visualize each image and action.

> Lie on your back in a comfortable position. If your back or neck is sore or stiff, put a pillow under your knees or your neck. If you cannot lie on your back, you can sit in a chair. Have your back supported and sit up as straight as possible.
>
> Lie still until you feel a sense of quiet come over you. [Pause.] When you feel the sense of quiet come over you, listen to your breath. Listen to the sound the breath makes when it enters the nose. Trace the path of the breath down the throat and into the lungs. Feel the breath fill the lungs. Listen to the sound of the breath as it leaves the lungs and flows out the nose. Now count nine full breaths. Keep your mind on your breath. When the mind wanders away from the breath, just gently bring the mind back to the breath.

> Now feel the weight of your body. Let yourself feel the full weight of your body supported by the earth. Let yourself accept the support of the earth. Let the earth support you. Give the full weight of your body to the earth. Trust that the earth will support you. Let yourself trust the earth. The earth will support you. Become aware of your skin. Become aware of the skin that is in contact with the earth. Let that skin become warm and full and expansive. Become aware of the skin of the back of the heels; let the skin of the back of the heels become warm and full and expansive. Become aware of the skin of the back of the legs; let the skin of the back of the legs become warm and full and expansive. Become aware of the skin of the back; let the skin of the back become warm and full and expansive. Become aware of the skin of the back of the arms; let the skin of the back of the arms become warm and full and expansive. Become aware of the skin of the back of the skull; let the skin of the back of the skull become warm and full and expansive. Now let the warmth of the skin of the back of the body flow around and warm the front of the body until the whole body feels warm and full and expansive. Now feel the warmth of the skin of the face like the warm wax around a candle flame. Let the skin of the face feel like it is melting. Let the tongue float in the back of the throat. Let there be warmth deep in the inside of the ear. Let the eyeballs sink farther back in the sockets. And finally let the brain pull away from the forehead and sink further back in the skull.
>
> All things need rest. Even your brain needs rest. The way you rest your brain is to quiet your thoughts. So just watch your thoughts as if you were sitting on a riverbank and your thought is a leaf floating by. As your thought enters your mind, just watch your thought as if it were that leaf floating by. [Allow a few minutes of silent meditation.]

Now make a long slow exhalation. Make each inhalation and exhalation a little deeper with each breath you take. Watch your mind come back to the here and now. Do you feel like you are coming back from somewhere?

Start to wiggle your fingers and toes, then your arms and legs. Stretch and refresh yourself in any way that feels comfortable. Roll to your right side and gently let your eyes flutter open. When you feel ready come up to a seated position.

After the guided meditation is complete, ask participants to find their journals and move to a quiet space. Invite them to reflect on the following questions:

- What was the meditation like for you?

- What images came up in your mind?

- What do you feel like now?

Invite participants to come back and drink tea together after journaling. Invite any volunteers to share something about their experience meditating. Ask participants to reflect on the connection between this kind of meditation and our relationship with the miracle of life.

Mantra Meditation. Introduce the idea of mantra meditation by sharing these words from Kevin Durkin:

A mantra is a thought or intention expressed as sound. The verbal root *man* means "to think"; the suffix *tra* suggests instrumentality. Thus, *mantra* means to think with the sound of a musical instrument. A mantra can be a prayer or a hymn or an affirmation. A mantra is used as a device to achieve a worldly end.

The language of yoga is Sanskrit. The most well-known Sanskrit mantra is *om*. To the yogi, the sound of *om* is the sound of the divine. It is said that "the past, the present, and the future—everything is but the sound of *om*. And whatever else that transcends triple time of past, present, and future: that, too, is but the sound of *om*."

Explain that a mantra is practiced by repeating a simple sound over and over again. Invite participants to sit in their chairs in a comfortable and relaxed position. Read the following text in a slow and relaxed manner:

Sit comfortably with a straight back and a lifted chest. Close your eyes and take a deep breath. Repeat to yourself, either out loud or silently, the sound of om nine times. Now sit quietly and feel the vibration. Realize that for thousands of years yogis have felt this same vibration that you are feeling. They feel it like many people feel a prayer.

Mantras don't have to be in Sanskrit. You can make up your own mantra. In English we call it an affirmation. Is there something you want? For example, do you want to feel smarter? Try this the next time you have homework to do and it seems hard. Sit like you did when you chanted the *om* and repeat to yourself: "I am smart, I have always been smart, and I will always be smart."

Repeat this affirmation many times; nine, twelve, or twenty-four are good numbers to practice with. Now see how you feel. Do you feel confident that you are smart enough to do your homework?

Think of any thing that you want: to be better at a sport, to make a new friend, to eat better, or anything else, and make up your own affirmation. Repeat it over and over again and see how you feel. That is mantra meditation.

Walking Meditation. Explain to participants that you are going to invite them on a mindful walk. Ask them to walk around the room the way they normally walk. They don't need to walk in a circle or in any particular pattern—they can simply walk, as themselves, in whichever direction they please. Give them one minute to walk around the room this way.

Then ask them to continue walking, but to walk mindfully for a full minute. Explain that walking mindfully means walking a little slower than normal, paying attention to your breathing, and being very conscious of your surroundings. Ask, "Did you notice a difference?"

Tell participants that you will soon be going outside to do some walking meditation, but first you will give them some more specific instructions about what makes mindful walking be like a meditation.

Share the following passage from Thich Nhat Hanh, a Vietnamese Buddhist monk:

When we do walking meditation outside, we walk a little slower than our normal pace, and we coordinate our breathing with our steps. For example, we may take three steps with each in-breath and three steps with each out-breath. So we can say, "In, in, in. Out, out, out." "In" is to help us identify the in-breath. Every time we call something by its name, we make it more real, like saying the name of a friend.

If your lungs want four steps instead of three, please give them four steps. If they want only two steps, give them two. The lengths of your in-breath and out-breath do not have to be the same. For example, you can take three steps with each inhalation and four with each exhalation. If you feel happy, peaceful, and joyful while you are walking, you are practicing correctly.

Be aware of the contact between your feet and the earth. . . . We have caused a lot of damage to the earth. Now it is time for us to take good care of her. We bring our peace and calm to the surface of the earth and share the lesson of love. We walk in that spirit. From time to time, when we see something beautiful, we may want to stop and look at it—a tree, a flower, some children playing. As we look, we continue to follow our breathing, lest we lose the beautiful flower and get caught up in our thoughts. When we want to resume walking, we just start again. Each step we take will create a cool breeze, refreshing our body and mind. Every step makes a flower bloom under our feet. We can do it only if we do not think of the future or the past, if we know that life can only be found in the present moment.

Invite participants outdoors for a walking meditation. Tell them the boundaries of where they are permitted to walk and the time they will be expected to return. Allow up to fifteen minutes for mindful walking if it is the only technique you are experiencing. If you are experiencing more than one, adjust the time.

After participants return, offer them tea, then provide an opportunity for journal writing and reflection. Invite them to reflect on the following questions:

- What was the meditation like for you?

- What did you see, hear, or smell that you might otherwise have ignored?

- What images came up in your mind?

- What do you feel like now?

- What is the connection between this kind of meditation and our relationship with the miracle of life?

After journaling, invite participants to come back together. Invite any volunteers to share something about their experience meditating.

Closing Circle   5 minutes

Use the closing ritual designed by the group.

Workshop 19
Spirituality in Movement

Time   60 minutes

Participant Goals

- experience movement as a spiritual practice

- reflect on the experience

Materials

- Consult the instructor about what supplies are required. They may include yoga mats, towels, larger mats, music, etc.

Preparation

- A visiting instructor is recommended for this workshop. Find an instructor who teaches a movement-based spiritual practice such as yoga, dance improvisation, tai chi, Nia (a mix of global dance forms, martial arts, and yoga), or qigong.

- It is best to find a person to lead these activities who is experienced in teaching them. Some practitioners, even serious ones, may not have the skills necessary to teach complex movement. You may need to offer an honorarium to attract such a person.

- Determine whether your group's regular meeting space will work for this activity. If not, find an alternative place to meet.

- Ask youth to wear clothes that will give them a full range of movement for this session.

Opening   5 minutes

Use the opening ritual designed by the group.

Movement as Spiritual Practice   50 minutes

Leaders or visiting instructors should lead youth through one or more forms of movement. Leave time for participants to either discuss or journal about the experience and any similar experiences with movement.

Closing Circle   5 minutes

Use the closing ritual designed by the group.

Workshop 20
Connecting to the Natural World

Time   60 minutes

Participant Goals

- learn about Unitarian Universalist movements that have been closely associated with nature

- discover spiritual connections to the natural world

- appreciate nature's gift and make a gift for mentors

Materials

- one sharp stick

- seven stones of similar size

- chalk

- protective cloth

- one pottery base per participant, 8" in diameter

- sand

- materials for the rock sculptures, such as stones (If stones are not readily available on the congregational grounds, inexpensive gemstones and crystals—e.g., quartz, pyrite, amber, and onyx—or glass beads can be used.)

- one votive candle per participant (optional)

- glue or hot glue guns

- bell or chime

- journals

- pens or pencils

Preparation

- Locate three outdoor spaces or clearings large enough to hold everyone participating.

- The first space must have a large patch of dirt or sand to use for writing words. Locate a sharp stick to write with, and leave it there.

- If your congregation has pagan or earth-centered ceremonies, a place associated with these rituals would work as the second space. Check in advance with the group that uses it. If no such space is available, a fire pit, labyrinth, or garden will do. In this second space, locate seven stones of similar size. Place six in a circle, with the seventh in the center. On the seventh stone, use chalk to draw a web.

- The third space should be one that connects to the congregation's effort to be environmentally friendly. It can be where the recycling bins are located or, better yet, where coffee grounds get dumped.

- Select a space, preferably outside, where you will construct sculptures. Cover the space with a protective cloth to catch loose sand.

Opening   5 minutes

Use the opening ritual designed by the group.

Unitarian Universalist Views of the Natural World   15 minutes

Say in your own words: "Though we have been inside while experiencing most of our spiritual practices, we can also get in touch with the spiritual outside. So let's go outside today. Bring your journals with you."

Lead the group to the first place you found earlier. Invite participants to get comfortable. Ask which of the spiritual practices you have talked about can be done outdoors. Then ask why someone would want to observe spiritual practice outdoors. Mention that many UUs throughout our history have found their deepest spiritual connections in nature, where they feel part of the rhythms of the earth, their greatest link to other living things, and an incredible sense of beauty, awe, wonder, and mystery.

Write the word *transcendentalism* in the dirt or sand with a sharp stick, and offer this definition from *The American Heritage Dictionary*: "a literary and philosophical movement asserting the existence of an ideal spiritual reality that transcends the empirical and scientific and is knowable through intuition." Explain that several authors and philosophers who were instrumental in the transcendentalist movement in the mid-1800s found it easier to connect with this ideal spiritual reality in nature. They also did not believe in separating humans from or elevating us above other living entities. Ask if anyone can name some of the Unitarian Universalists who were influential in this movement. Possible names are Ralph Waldo Emerson, Henry David Thoreau, Margaret Fuller, and Theodore Parker.

Walk to the second space, where you earlier placed the circle of stones. Ask youth if the stones remind them of anything connected to Unitarian Universalist beliefs. If a hint is needed, ask participants to count the stones or note the one in the middle. The stones represent the Principles; the seventh stone in the middle symbolizes "respect for the interdependent web of all existence of which we are a part." It is placed in the center because the connectedness it calls for, if truly realized, could bring about the other Principles. Inform participants that this Principle was added to the first six in 1985. Talk as a group about what this Principle means to you.

Walk to the third space. Ask who can identify where you are standing, and give hints if needed. Say to the group that many Unitarian Universalists are concerned about damage to our environment. Brainstorm ways that individuals are trying to take better care of the earth. Examples include recycling, using cloth bags instead of plastic, and buying organic produce.

Say that many congregations are also trying to be more aware of the environment. Brainstorm ways your congregation and others are doing this, perhaps by building "green" sanctuaries, using compact fluorescent light bulbs, or working with environmental groups like the Sierra Club.

The Gifts of Nature   25 minutes

Invite participants to show their appreciation for their mentors by making a gift from nature. Show youth the pottery bases and explain that they can fill them with natural (but no longer living) objects to make an attractive sculpture. If possible, work on the sculptures outside.

Let each youth pick a base and fill it one-third full with sand. The rest of the base can be filled with stones, glass beads, inexpensive gemstones, twigs, shale, small pinecones or shells, or anything else they find outside that is not attached to something living. You might include a small votive candle. Encourage them to choose colors that complement the base. Use glue or a hot glue gun to keep the pieces in place. Remind youth to use as little glue as possible and to work carefully to keep the sculpture attractive.

Put sculptures aside to dry.

Your Spiritual Connection to Nature 10 minutes

Gather the group, and tell them that they will have time to interact with nature as they please. Suggest that participants take their journals. If they are confined to a certain area, let them know the boundaries. Tell them that you will ring a bell or chime to let them know when time is up in about seven minutes.

After seven minutes, call everyone back together. Invite participants to share any observations. Remind youth that people from all cultures have honored the earth and celebrated their connection to it. Note that there are many ways nature can be part of a spiritual practice, from gardening to recycling to creating art from natural products to hiking.

Closing Circle 5 minutes

Use the closing ritual designed by the group.

Extended Journaling and
UU Pocket Guide Discussion for Unit 4

Journaling Prompts

Encourage participants to reflect upon the topics covered in this unit in their journals. Pose the following questions to get them started:

- Write about your feelings during the various spiritual practices you experienced.

- Does your family have any spiritual practices? How were these practices developed? Do you participate?

UU Pocket Guide Discussion

Ask participants to read "Our Worship" before the scheduled discussion or schedule time during your weekly meeting to read and discuss the chapter, using the following questions:

- Which elements of worship mentioned in this article have you experienced?

- Which do you enjoy the most and why?

- Is there anything in the chapter that speaks to your experience as a Unitarian Universalist?

Typical Elements of Circle/Youth Worship

Gathering: This can be done in many ways: asking people to gather outside the worship space and walk in holding hands and singing, or silently; allowing people to just filter into the room while music is playing and asking them to center themselves; etc. The goal of this component of worship is to create a sacred space.

Opening: This is usually done by lighting a chalice and saying a few words. The words can be simple, like "We light this chalice for love," or they can be a reading that has to do with the worship theme. This sets the tone for the worship.

Song: Songs are generally used to unite the group in a shared activity, and also to liven things up a bit. They are a way to make the worship a creation of the group, not something that can just be taken out of a box and run and then put back in the box. The best songs for circle/youth worship are usually short chants that are easily taught and sung without having to look at a book or a sheet of paper.

Reading: Readings are used to give participants a time to reflect and/or center themselves. Readings can be poetry, guided meditations, pieces of songs simply spoken, text taken from any book for children or adults, or written by anyone planning worship. The readings should have something to do with the theme of the worship.

Centerpiece: In regular Sunday morning worship services, the centerpiece is typically the sermon. In most circle/youth worship, the centerpiece is something participatory. It can be a sharing or a check-in; a dance that everyone takes part in, like a circle dance or a Sufi dance; a time to write, to breathe, or to laugh; or it can be a combination of all these. These are some examples of centerpieces:

- passing around the chalice and sharing a moment of awe from your past week

- passing around a bowl of water and having participants dip their hands, say what they are washing off (e.g., something bad in their life, like stress), and say what they are taking in (e.g., something good, like warmth)

- having participants form two concentric circles and rotate around each other so each member of the inner circle can hold hands and make eye contact with each member of the outer circle

There are also different ways to share, depending on the size of the group.

- Small- to medium-sized groups can go around the circle and give everyone a chance to share (or to pass).

- Medium- to large-sized groups can do a "popcorn-style" or "Quaker" sharing, where people share when they want to, if they want to.

- In very large groups, participants can share with the person next to them, so that everyone gets a chance to share in-depth, but it doesn't take an excessive amount of time. This method works particularly well with a whole congregation.

Reading: Symmetry is good in worship, so it works well to round out worships with another reading and/or song, not necessarily in that order.

Song: See above.

Closing: The closing brings everything together while officially marking the end of the worship. Closings are usually short. They can be brief readings (or writings), a few words like "This worship is ending, but may we continue to hold its spirit in our hearts," or even fewer words, like "Blessed be." These words can be followed by a closing song like "Go Now in Peace" (see *Singing the Living Tradition*) or by a group hug or a hug circle.

—Spirituality Development Conference Team, Young Religious Unitarian Universalists (YRUU)

Typical Elements of a Traditional Worship Service

Gathering: *call to worship, choral call/call with music.* This element marks the intentional gathering of religious community for the purpose of common worship.

Opening: *opening words, lighting the flame in the chalice, covenant, hymn.* This element indicates the opening of the sacred time we have chosen to spend with one another. The music and words heard, sung, and spoken here, the flowers and vestments, the flame of our heritage, the silences are lifted up and vested with special meaning. If we touch each other in greeting, it is sacramental touch. If we look upon each other in acknowledgment, it is sacramental seeing. If we partake of food, the elements are more than they would ordinarily be because we have declared ourselves to be a community and we intend to be changed by these things of which we partake.

Acknowledging: *family focus (story or special attention paid to children), welcome and announcements, joys and sorrows, greeting each other.* By this element, we open to putting ourselves in the stream of our history, and we acknowledge that we are part of the present company, its values and aspirations; its children are our children, its elders are our elders. We also address the bounty shared here and into the larger community, its needs and concerns touching us and requiring our response.

Giving: *offertory.* Here we participate in the life of the religious community by the gifts of our physical substance and by our willing presence.

Centering: *prayer or meditation, silence for reflection.* This element invites us to center down to be aware of what may arise from within us or enter our awareness from outside us. There might also be a responding song, such as "Spirit of Life."

Receiving: *readings, sermon, dance, poetry, visual art.* This element inspires, informs, deepens, declares the possibilities, encourages, comforts, disturbs. It may include congregational sharing, but never a talk-back in the sense of argumentation or disputation, for which there are more appropriate forums outside of worship.

Acknowledging: *song, responsive reading.* This is the congregational response to the end of the service. We who have gathered are about to disperse. It is good to be together. Let us rejoice in each good thing and in what we have done here.

Closing: *benediction.* This marks the end of the sacred time and is an invitation to take what has been shared, strengthened, quickened in this time and place and community out into the rest of life.

Dispersing/Postlude: Here we reenter the world, refreshed, enlivened, touched, changed, challenged, exalted. Doing this to music adds the dimension of moving into the ordinary to the rhythms of the sacred.

—Barbara Pescan

How to Assemble Your Prayer Beads

1. Tie a knot in the end of your string or cord.

2. Lace the cord through the large bead. This is your centering bead.

3. Add four small beads to the cord. These will be your warm-up beads.

4. Add the first medium-sized bead. This is for naming and thanking.

5. Lace on five more small beads. These are for breath prayer.

6. Add the second medium-sized bead for knowing.

7. Lace on another five small beads for another round of breath prayer.

8. Add the third medium-sized bead for listening.

9. Add five more small beads, again for breath prayer.

10. Lace on the fourth medium-sized bead. This one is for loving.

11. Add the last four small beads for cooldown.

12. Knot the ends of the string or cord together to form a loop.

How to Pray with Your Prayer Beads

Centering, Naming, Knowing, Listening, and Loving—this is the journey of this prayer practice. You will take the time to find a quiet place in your life, so you may focus upon the holy and the sacred miracle of life: seeing yourself within that reality as full and whole, tuning your sense to hear inner wisdom, and then turning your loving attention to the needs within and around you. Begin to work your way through the beads, holding one at a time. Start with the largest one.

Large Bead (Centering)

The large bead is for centering yourself in preparation for the journey. Breathe in and out several times, calming the body and quieting the mind. You might sit quietly with your breath, recite a breathing *gatha* or a chant, or sing a favorite hymn. When you feel ready, proceed to the next bead.

Breathing *gathas* are short poems like this one by Andrew Weiss. They are used in some Buddhist traditions to calm the mind and focus attention on the breath.

> Sitting in the present moment,
> I breathe mindfully.
> Each in-breath nourishes love,
> Each out-breath, compassion.
> Each thought, each feeling
> Creates the world.
> I hold joy and suffering
> Tenderly in each breath.
> Chasing after the world
> Brings chaos.
> Allowing it all to come to me
> Brings peace.

Chanting is a practice of people of many religious, spiritual, and ethnic traditions. Some chants are sung repeatedly with tunes; other chants are said repeatedly with a distinct rhythm but no special tune. It might be particularly meaningful for you to use a chant that is tied to your ethnic background or one that is drawn from a source of the Unitarian Universalist living tradition that is particularly meaningful for you (see Principles and Purposes of the Unitarian Universalist Association).

A contemporary pagan chant is:

> Earth my body, water my blood,
> Air my breath, and fire my spirit.

You can also try this contemporary Jewish chant, based on Psalm 121 and arranged by Rabbi Shefa Gold :

> *Esa eynai el he-harim me-ayin yovo ezri*
> *Esa eynai el he-harim me-ayin yovo ezri*
> My help comes from the One
> My help comes from the One
> My help comes from the One
> Creator of Heaven and Earth.

The Unitarian Universalist Association's hymnbook, *Singing the Living Tradition*, has several simple hymns that you can memorize for prayer. Your congregation might also have its own songs that you could use in centering. Here are some songs from the hymnbook that can work well:

   38 Morning Has Broken
123 Spirit of Life
352 Find a Stillness
348 Guide My Feet
391 Voice Still and Small
393 Jubilate Deo
394 Hava Nashira

Four Small Beads (Warm-up)

A set of four small beads separates the centering bead from the naming bead. These small beads provide your entry to this journey of prayer or, if you prefer a different metaphor, a warm-up period for this spiritual exercise.

Here you can meditate on ideas that come in fours:

- greeting the four directions (north, south, east, west), which many earth-based religions associate with various qualities

- acknowledging the four elements (earth, air, fire, water), which can help you connect with all that forms life

You can also check in with yourself, taking yourself back on a journey through your last twenty-four hours: all the places you were, the things you did, the feelings you felt. Each bead can signify a time of day, like sunrise, midday, sunset, and midnight. They could also represent body, mind, heart, and spirit.

First Medium-sized Bead (Naming and Thanking)

The first medium-sized bead is for naming the Holy. In the Islamic tradition, God has ninety-nine names, and there are Baha'i prayers that consist of nothing but lists of names and attributes for the Divine. The psalms in the Hebrew scriptures are full of ways of calling out to Yahweh. This is your chance to name the Sacred, to give voice to what you consider holy or where you have felt the Divine in your life. If you prefer not to imagine the Divine as a person, you could call up the attributes that you ascribe to the Sacred, or name whatever feeds your soul; this is your opportunity to give name to what you feel to be holy and sacred. Here are some names you might like:

> Source of all being
> Mother nature
> Interconnected web
> Sacred spirit
> Loving God
> Life force

You might also want to add descriptions to the name, for example, "Sacred spirit that dwells within, among, and beyond us" or "Loving God, to whom all hearts are open." Use a name that is meaningful to your own traditions, preferences, and spiritual inclinations.

This bead is also the place for you to lift up all for which you are thankful at this moment, all the blessings and miracles in your life, all the joy in your living. Take your time to "count your blessings," as the old phrase has it.

While you consider what you are thankful for, you are invited to contemplate how each thing affects your spirituality: your relationship with the miracle of life.

Here is an example of how the whole naming section of the prayer might sound: "Sacred spirit that dwells within, among, and beyond us, I am thankful this day for the gift of life. I give thanks for the kindness my family and teachers have shown me. I give thanks for my little brother and his jokes, because even though they annoy me sometimes, they also make me laugh. I give thanks for my soccer team—we really came together today at practice. And I give thanks for another day without bullying. Nobody picked on me and I didn't pick on anyone."

Five Small Beads (Breath Prayer)

Five small beads separate each of the medium-sized beads, providing a link between the stages of the journey. With each of these beads you may use a breath prayer, a two-line phrase that is said in rhythm with the in- and out-breaths.

Here are a few ideas for breath prayers:

- Breathing in I develop calm and self-control. Breathing out I find peace and joy.

- Breathing in I feel connection with all life. Breathing out I know I am not a stranger.

- Breathing in I know there is gladness. Breathing out I know there is peace.

You can also meditate on simple statements on each in-breath and out-breath without specifically mentioning breathing. For example:

- Great Mystery
  I seek to know.

- I feel love.
  I feel peace.

- Give me hope.
  Give me strength.

Second Medium-sized Bead   (Knowing)

The second medium-sized bead is for knowing yourself. Here you have an opportunity to reflect on your life as it is today, to recognize those places that call for reconciliation and atonement. It is not a time to list all the things you do not like about your physical appearance or to give yourself a hard time about things you cannot change. It is a time to look at yourself honestly and ask: "Did I stay true to myself today?" "Did I do my best?" "Was I kind?" "Did I get hurt?" "Did I hurt others?" "Did I stand by what I believe in?" As you consider these questions, you can draw on your spirituality to help you find acceptance, forgiveness, a way to make change, or whatever response is appropriate.

Five Small Beads   (Breath Prayer)

See above.

Third Medium-sized Bead   (Listening)

The third medium-sized bead calls you to sit back and listen. It is a place for experiencing what you name as divine. The Bible says, "Be still and know that I am God." Be still and listen to the Divine spark, the Buddha-nature, that is inherent in us all. You may meditate silently; gaze on an icon, statue, or mandala; or reflectively read scripture. Ralph Waldo Emerson writes, "There is guidance for each of us, and by lowly listening we shall hear the right word." In the silence, you may experience a feeling of peace, interconnection, or divine presence. You may also find that the silence helps your inner wisdom come out, helping you deal with some of the problems you considered when you meditated on the Knowing bead.

Five Small Beads   (Breath Prayer)

See above.

Final Medium-sized Bead   (Loving)

The final medium-sized bead is a reminder that a prayer practice that focuses only on the self is ultimately hollow, as is a life that is too self-centered. Here we lift up those we know, and those we don't, whose lives have pain and need. Hold them in your consciousness, bring them to your awareness. Someone once asked why people had to pray to God since God knows all things and should already know about the needs of everyone. The answer was that we do not pray so that God knows about people's needs; we pray to make sure we know. Either in silence or out loud, you can name those who are sick, in pain, or suffering in any way—emotional or physical. You can also name what you hope for them. Here's an example of a prayer for someone you know: "I pray for my cousin Rick, who is in the hospital. I hope he heals quickly, that he is in the care of good doctors and surrounded by people who love him." You can also pray for people you don't know personally: "I am thinking about the people who lost their homes and family members in the earthquake. They are in great pain, and I hope that they will be surrounded by love, compassion, and the material things they need." Having the chance to speak the name of someone in need and to state a hope for them can help you feel calmer and more caring toward them. It can also help you recognize your interconnected relationship with them through the interdependent web.

Four Small Beads   (Cooldown)

Four small beads separate the loving bead from the centering bead, mirroring the first four, providing a spiritual cooldown, and bringing you gently back to the everyday world. You can choose a cooldown that mirrors what you did with the four warm-up beads:

- You could bid farewell to the four directions (north, south, east, west) or the four elements (earth, air, fire, water).

- You could imagine your next twenty-four hours: all the places you expect to be, the things you'll do, the feelings you would like to feel. Each bead can signify a time of day, like sunrise, midday, sunset, and midnight.

- You could check in again with how you feel in body, mind, heart, and spirit.

Unitarian Universalist Theology

The gods we worship write their names on our faces, be sure of that. And a person will worship something—have no doubt about that, either. We may think that our tributes are paid in secret in the dark recesses of our hearts—but they will out. That which dominates will determine our life and character. Therefore, it behooves us to be careful what we worship, for what we are worshiping we are becoming.

—Ralph Waldo Emerson

The following are the "big questions" of theology summarized in personal terms:

- Who am I?

- Who or what is in charge?

- How do I know what I know?

- What happens after I die?

- What is my purpose? (Or what am I called to do?)

- How do I know what is right and what is wrong?

Theology is about much more than the "study of God." It is the study of the sacred within, among, and beyond us. It relates to our notions of humankind as much as to our concepts of the divine. In these workshops, participants explore questions of theology in ways that align with their personal experiences and religious traditions.

Though theology is about more than God, beliefs about God are certainly part of it. Unitarian Universalists have many different ways of looking at the concept of God. For some, the idea of "God" does not mean much. For others, God plays a role in their lives. Some profess that they don't believe in God. But even in that statement there is a question worth exploring: "Who is this God you don't believe in?"

This unit makes it clear that there is more than one acceptable vision of God. For young people to get in touch with their own theology, they must break down old "God" stereotypes and be introduced to genuine Unitarian Universalist ways of understanding ultimate reality. The workshops offer several options for participants to understand the holy and their path to it. They present metaphors, vocabulary, and ideas about human personality and its relationship to the search.

As a leader, it is valuable to remember where the youth in your program are developmentally. Some might be more ready than others to understand divinity abstractly. What you share with the youth in these lessons introduces ideas that they can draw on in the years to come, even if they do not completely grasp them yet.

Throughout the history of Unitarianism and Universalism, questions about the nature of God have always been deeply entwined with questions about the nature of human beings. The early Universalist minister Hosea Ballou took the "radical" position, saying "human beings are rewarded for good behavior, or punished for their misdeeds, in this life. At death they are transformed by the power of God's love as they enter eternity." Early Unitarian minister William Ellery Channing challenged the then-prevailing notion that humans are, by nature, totally depraved. Channing saw the good in human nature as reflective of the goodness of God. The influences of liberal Christianity and humanism within Unitarian Universalism have given our faith tradition a strong emphasis on the human potential for goodness.

A familiar context makes it easiest for youth to examine issues of human nature, so Workshop 21 starts with their own social experience. It then broadens outward, inviting reflection upon human nature in general. This session can be a good one to lead on retreats, when there is more time for discussion and movie watching.

One theological concept that religions strive to grapple with is death and the afterlife, the subject of Workshop 24. In mainstream American society, parents often attempt to shield young children from the realities of death by using euphemisms or reassurances, such as "Your grandma's in heaven watching over you." As children become young adults, they become able to understand that all life must end, but this understanding does not lessen the grief experienced with the death of a loved one. How Unitarian Universalism addresses this grief is a crucial part of a conversation about death.

As a leader of discussions concerning death, above all else show compassion for young people's feelings about the subject. Do not try to comfort youth with platitudes like "He's in a better place" or to encourage them to hide unpleasant emotions by "staying strong." A good discussion about death makes space for youth to be compassionate toward one another. Some have been through loss and tragedy; others have not. Because Workshop 24 might bring forward very strong emotions, it includes suggestions on providing additional support for youth. It can be very helpful to line up a list of resources for additional support, such as the congregation's minister or support groups for teenagers who have lost parents. The presence of a minister who is

familiar to most of the group may be useful during the discussion. It is important above all else to have group trust, and if the presence of outsiders would decrease that trust, do not invite them. Some participants may choose not to participate in discussions if they feel emotionally vulnerable. Be prepared to respect their needs and remember that passing is always allowed. An excellent resource for further conversations on death and grief is the Unitarian Universalist curriculum *Lessons of Loss*, available from Carol Galginaitis, 157 Lowell Rd., Wellesley, MA 02481, (781) 235-0851 or carolgal@comcast.net.

Workshop 21
Starting with Us

Time 75 minutes (plus optional 120 minutes for movie viewing and discussion)

Participant Goals

- analyze what motivates people to engage in good or bad behavior

- discuss cliques and how groups influence the behavior of individuals

- evaluate the Ten Commandments

- compose their own set of rules for ethical human behavior

Materials

- world map, large enough to be viewed by the whole class

- paper, pencils, and other optional art supplies

- Bible

- newsprint

- markers

- DVD of *Mean Girls*, directed by Mark Waters, 2004, and DVD player (optional)

Preparation

- Arrange for a DVD player if you are showing *Mean Girls*.

143

- Locate the Ten Commandments in the Bible (Exodus 20).

Opening   5 minutes

Use the opening ritual designed by the group.

Sinners and Saints   15 minutes

Invite participants to think of a time when they did something that they considered bad, even though other people might not have seen it that way. Lead a discussion in which youth share their motivations and feelings about this act, rather than talking about the act itself. Use the following questions:

- What led you to do something you knew was "bad"?

- Did other people's acceptance have anything to do with it?

- How do you know it was a bad thing?

Now invite participants to think of a time when they did something they believed was good, again regardless of other people's reactions. Use the following questions:

- What led you to do something you knew was "good"?

- Did other people's acceptance have anything to do with it?

- How do you know it was a good thing?

Explain that Jewish tradition talks about people having two tendencies, the inclination toward evil (*yetzer ha-ra*) and the inclination toward good (*yetzer ha-tov*). According to this tradition, we are all born with the inclination toward evil, but the inclination toward good doesn't take root until age twelve for girls and age thirteen for boys. Ask participants whether they agree with this approach, and ask what happens around the ages of twelve or thirteen that would make someone more capable of doing good.

Group Think   25 minutes

Explain that people don't always function as individuals. Ask, "For how many of you was the bad thing you thought of associated with the actions of a friend or a group of friends?"

Ask participants to draw maps of their schools, either individually or as a group of students who go to the same school. Ask them to indicate on the maps which groups of students hang out where, which areas they avoid, and which areas they spend the most time in. Discuss the following questions:

- Of these groups in school, who has money?

- Who has talents and special skills?

- Who badmouths whom?

- Who fights with whom?

- Who forms alliances with whom?

Display a world map, and ask whether citizens of the world sometimes act like the cliques in a high school. Ask participants to indicate who "hangs out" where, what they are like, and who does not get along with whom. Who has money? Who has talents and special skills? Who badmouths whom? Who fights with whom? Point out generalizations when they occur. For example, much of the world's wealth is concentrated in the United States and Europe, yet not everyone in the United States is rich. Can generalizations about the people of the world be damaging? Can generalizations about the groups in your school be harmful, too? How so?

Ask them to look at both maps, and consider:

- What would you change about the ways students interact at your school if you could?

- What would you change about the ways citizens of the world interact if you could?

Optional Activity

Mean Girls   120 minutes

Mean Girls can be an excellent vehicle for talking about how teenagers treat each other at school. After watching the movie, ask for comments. If needed, use these questions to start the conversation:

- Does anything like this happen in your school?

- Have you ever witnessed mean behavior? What, if anything, did you do?

- Have you ever been the target of meanness at school? What did you do? How did you feel?

- Are you ever mean to others in school?

- Do you think the way the main character is drawn into the group of mean girls is realistic?

- Have you ever felt like an outsider at school? What was that like?

Sin and Choice   25 minutes

Introduce the discussion by saying something like the following:

> Some religions see how we do bad things, and they call it "sin." Some types of Christianity and Judaism strongly emphasize human sin, understanding that by our very nature all humans sin. According to these religions, a sin comes about when our actions go against God's purposes. The disobedience of Adam and Eve, when they ate the fruit of the forbidden tree in the Garden of Eden, is referred to as the "original sin." Most Christian faiths believe that all humans are born sinful because of this act.
>
> Unitarians and Universalists do not believe that people are born in sin but that we each have the capacity to choose how we act. We all have the capacity to do both good and bad things. William Ellery Channing, in his Sunday School address, said children are born neither depraved (in original sin) nor holy, because virtue is a "free, voluntary effort of a being who knows the distinction of right and wrong, and who, if tempted, adheres to the right." He said we should "have faith in the child as capable of knowing and loving the good and the true, as having a conscience to take the side of

duty, as open to ingenuous motives for well doing, as created for knowledge, wisdom, piety, and disinterested love."
>
> Theist religions teach that God is a conscious being that has intentions for how people should and should not live. One famous list of these intentions is known as the Ten Commandments, delivered to Moses by God at Mt. Sinai, according to the Bible.

Ask what commandments participants can name, and write them down on newsprint. Fill in the others they do not name, referring to Exodus 20 from the Bible. Consider asking for volunteers to read them aloud while someone writes them on newsprint. Invite participants to discuss which commandments make the most and least sense to them.

Then invite participants to create their own Ten Commandments, either as a group or individually. Encourage them to think about their own lives, think about the maps of the school and the world, and to come up with the ten most important "rules" for ethical human behavior.

When lists are complete, invite participants to share them with the group.

Closing Circle   5 minutes

Use the closing ritual designed by the group.

Workshop 22
Your God Project

Time   75 minutes

Participant Goals

- chart their changing belief in the nature of the divine

- recognize that there are stages in faith development

- affirm their current stage of faith

- discover how Unitarian Universalism encompasses many, but not all, views of the sacred

Materials

- paper for drawing

- paper for writing

- markers, crayons, or pencils

- signs indicating the Seven Paths (see Preparation)

- copies of Handout 14, Seven Paths for the God Project (page 156)

Preparation

- Invite mentors to this session.

- Set out drawing materials.

- Make a sign for each of the seven paths listed in Handout 14, Seven Paths for the God Project. You need include only the name of the path since participants will have copies of the handout with the descriptions. Post the signs around the room.

Opening   5 minutes

Use the opening ritual designed by the group.

The God of Childhood, Last Year and Now
25 minutes

Present the idea that everyone has different "projects" in their lives: areas where they're continuously growing and gaining new understandings, like sports or home life or learning. Explain that Forrest Church, a Unitarian Universalist minister, suggests in his book *Lifecraft* that everyone has a "God project," meaning that everyone is gaining new understandings of what is sacred. Some people call the sacred "God"; others call it "goddess," "spirit of life," or "great mystery," or "the force of love." There are many names for the object of your God project. Another way of thinking of your God project is your ever-growing recognition of forces in the universe that are greater than our individual selves.

Throughout this workshop, encourage participants to define the word *god* for themselves or to use their personal term for the sacred.

Explain that participants will explore their own "God projects," starting with how they looked at God when they were young children. Mentors who are present may join in.

Ask participants to take three minutes to draw a picture of the God they thought of when they were five years old, whether or not they believed in God. It could be the God they believed in, or the God they didn't believe in. Explain that if this God does not have a particular form (like an old man or an earth goddess), they can make symbols for the characteristics they attributed to this God: for example, a brain for knowing everything, hugging arms for nurturing, a sun for illuminating life, or an ear for listening to people's worries.

Invite participants to move into groups of two or three and show their pictures to each other, looking for similarities and differences. Ask the groups to discuss their pictures for five minutes, offering time for each person to share. Give a two-minute warning.

Now ask participants to draw a symbolic picture of the God they did (or did not) believe in last year. After three minutes, invite participants to put this picture aside and draw the last picture: one that symbolizes what they believe in now, whether it is called "God" or "love" or "mystery" or whatever best describes the picture.

Invite participants to return to their small groups and discuss these pictures. Ask them to consider the similarities and differences between each other's pictures as well as the similarities and differences between their ideas at age five, their ideas last year, and their ideas now. Allow five to six minutes for this discussion.

Introduce the basic idea behind James Fowler's stages of faith: that people's ideas about God and religion change as they learn and grow, and that very few people have the same images of the sacred at age five as they do at twenty-five, fifty-five, or ninety-five. Share that each of us is, therefore, on a path of discovery and that as Unitarian Universalists, we are here to help each other and enrich our journeys along that path.

Seven Paths for the Journey   25 minutes

Explain that not only a person's age, but also their basic temperament and personality affect how they imagine God or ultimate reality. Share that in *Lifecraft*, Forrest Church talks about the "God project" and seven paths people might take to understand ultimate reality and live their lives in response to it.

Pass out Handout 14, Seven Paths for the God Project, and ask youth to take turns reading the descriptions aloud. If you have more time to devote to this activity, you can have youth draw descriptions out of a hat and think of creative and engaging ways to present these paths to the class.

Once each path has been described, ask participants to think about which path appeals to them the most. They do not need to decide which one they "are"; they simply need to figure out which they like the most. Anyone who thinks that none of the paths apply to them may create another path. Give any new paths names and descriptions and add sheets of newsprint on the wall to represent them. It is important that participants have the freedom to define their own paths and not feel they have been put in a box that is not authentic for them.

Ask participants to stand next to the sign that corresponds with the path they chose. There may be some paths that do not have anyone standing next to them, which is fine. Explain the assignment: They are to think about how the path they have chosen fits into Unitarian Universalism. They are to decide on three reasons their chosen path can be followed in Unitarian Universalism. They are to write these reasons down to share with the group.

At this point, ask if any volunteers want to write reasons for the paths that no one chose. Leaders can also fulfill this role.

Allow several minutes for small group discussion and writing.

Ask participants to present the reasons that they thought each path could be at home in Unitarian Universalism.

Discussion   15 minutes

Discuss the following questions:

- One of the gifts of Unitarian Universalism is freedom of belief. The result of freedom is diversity, a value we embrace as Unitarian Universalists. Do you think Unitarian Universalism is a home for all people on all paths?

- If so, how? If not, why?

Closing Circle   5 minutes

Use the closing ritual designed by the group.

Workshop 23
The God You Don't Believe In, the God You Do

Time   60 minutes

Participant Goals

- recognize God stereotypes

- discuss the many ways Unitarian Universalists view God or the divine

- examine the usefulness of the idea of God

- review list of concepts frequently associated with God and begin to develop these concepts into a personal theology

Materials

- newsprint and easel

- markers of many colors

- masking tape

- copies of *UU Views of God* (see Preparation)

- copies of Handout 15, Some Ways of Looking at God (page 157)

Preparation

- Order copies of the pamphlet *UU Views of God* well in advance of this session. It is available from the Unitarian Universalist Association Bookstore at 800-215-9076 or *www.uua.org/bookstore*. The text of the pamphlet is also online at *www.uua.org/pamphlets*.

Opening 5 minutes

Use the opening ritual designed by the group.

God Pictures 20 minutes

Share this story:

> A man walked up to a Unitarian Universalist minister after the service one Sunday and said, "You used the word *God* in your sermon today. But I didn't find it meaningful because I don't believe in God." The minister responded, "Hmm, that's interesting. Tell me about this God you don't believe in—because I probably don't believe in 'him' either!" Later on in the week, the two had a conversation. And the minister was right—she didn't believe in the all-powerful, all-knowing, all-seeing, all-good God that her parishioner rejected. Instead, she used the word *God* to mean the life force. And her parishioner agreed that there was a life force in the universe. But he said he'd rather call it "life force" than call it "God."

Say something like the following: "Today we'll be looking at two different kinds of gods: those we don't believe in and those we do. Not believing in God is an option, as is not finding the word *God* meaningful at all. But even if we don't believe that a God exists, we have beliefs about human existence and purpose. We'll explore the many different shapes that Unitarian Universalist beliefs about God, existence, and purpose can take."

Lead participants in coming up with a picture of what they imagine most Americans think of when they say "God." On a sheet of newsprint, draw their responses to the following questions as they brainstorm.

- What does this God look like? Draw a rough picture of God's physical attributes.

- Where does this God live? Draw God's surroundings.

- Who hangs out with this God? Draw a few of the beings that hang out with God.

- What does this God act like? How can we show that?

- How do good and evil fit into this picture? How about heaven and hell?

- Where is Jesus in all of this? Draw Jesus as part of God, etc. By now your picture is probably looking a little cluttered—that's OK!

- What about the Holy Spirit?

- Does this God know everything? Is this God all-good? Is this God all-loving? How can we show that?

- Is there anything else about this God we forgot? Anything we need to add?

When the picture is complete, say, "For many Unitarian Universalists, this total picture represents a God they do not believe in, even though parts of the picture might fit their beliefs. How does this picture mesh with your idea of God?" Solicit responses. Explain that many Americans who believe in God or gods—Christians, Muslims, Jews, Hindus, and people of other faiths—would not believe everything in this brainstorm either. Ask participants if they have spoken with friends of different religions about God and what they have heard. Unitarian Universalists are not the only people who look at God in different ways. Ask for comments on what it was like to complete this exercise.

What You Believe In 25 minutes

Now participants will be invited to consider what they *do* believe in, whether it's called "God" or something else.

Invite participants to reflect on and share with the group some of the valuable and meaningful ways they have heard people talk about God. For example, some participants might really admire their Christian friends' idea that God knows and loves them deeply.

Distribute Handout 15, Some Ways of Looking at God, and the pamphlet *UU Views of God*, published by the Unitarian Universalist Association. Review the terms on the handout with participants. Ask them to think about which terms appeal to them the most, and encourage them to explore their concepts of God with their mentor and minister. Explain that there is no need for them to decide today whether they are a theist, an atheist, etc.

Review the pamphlet *UU Views of God*. Consider asking for volunteers to read the introduction aloud. Ask for comments on the three ways the author, UU theologian Paul Rasor, says the concept of God can function for Unitarian Universalists. Share that "God" is a very flexible concept that means many different things to many different people. As Unitarian Universalists, our tradition invites us to decide what that concept means to us as individuals.

Emphasize participants' own roles in thinking about God by saying, "You can decide what you do and don't believe about the concept of God. If you do believe in God, what kind? And if you don't believe in God, what kind of deep meaning do you believe in?"

Choose whether to allow journaling time or discussion time to explore these questions.

Being Right 5 minutes

Explain that part of being Unitarian Universalist is understanding that humans are not perfect and we cannot come up with the one right answer about God, the universe, and everything else. Remind participants that their eventual task is to find a theology or religious philosophy that feels right to them, which is different from finding a theology that explains everything or a theology that makes sense to all people. Observe that we can know only pieces of the whole reality, and share this nineteenth-century poem by John Godfrey Saxe, based on a Hindu parable:

It was six men of Indostan
To learning much inclined,
Who went to see the Elephant
(Though all of them were blind),
That each by observation
Might satisfy his mind.

The First approached the Elephant,
And happening to fall
Against his broad and sturdy side,
At once began to bawl:
"God bless me! but the Elephant
Is very like a wall!"

The Second, feeling of the tusk
Cried, "Ho! what have we here,
So very round and smooth and sharp?
To me 'tis mighty clear
This wonder of an Elephant
Is very like a spear!"

The Third approached the animal,
And happening to take
The squirming trunk within his hands,
Thus boldly up he spake:
"I see," quoth he, "the Elephant
Is very like a snake!"

The Fourth reached out an eager hand,
And felt about the knee:
"What most this wondrous beast is like
Is mighty plain," quoth he;
"'Tis clear enough the Elephant
Is very like a tree!"

The Fifth, who chanced to touch the ear,
Said: "E'en the blindest man
Can tell what this resembles most;
Deny the fact who can,
This marvel of an Elephant
Is very like a fan!"

The Sixth no sooner had begun
About the beast to grope,
Than, seizing on the swinging tail
That fell within his scope.
"I see," quoth he, "the Elephant
Is very like a rope!"

And so these men of Indostan
Disputed loud and long,
Each in his own opinion
Exceeding stiff and strong,
Though each was partly in the right,
And all were in the wrong!

Moral:

So oft in theologic wars,
The disputants, I ween,
Rail on in utter ignorance
Of what each other mean,
And prate about an Elephant
Not one of them has seen.

Say something like the following: "The elephant is a metaphor for God, and the blind men are metaphors for different religions. Each religion has just a piece of the whole picture. We all have pieces of the truth—but just because they are pieces does not make them any less true! If everyone shares their different perspectives, then we come to a better understanding of what is real, meaningful, and valuable."

Closing Circle   5 minutes

Use the closing ritual designed by the group.

Workshop 24
Life, Death and the Afterlife

Time   90 to 120 minutes

Participant Goals

- connect with the universality of death

- view beliefs about death and the hereafter as part of their theology

- share personal experiences with the group

- understand how our faith helps us deal with death

Materials

- talking stick or object (optional)

- three types of candy for each participant: hard, soft, and chewy

- copies of Handouts 16 and 17, Grief and Mourning and Tools for Coping (pages 158 and 161)

Preparation

- Compile a list of resources for additional support, such as the congregation's minister or support groups for teenagers who have lost parents.

Opening   5 minutes

Use the opening ritual designed by the group.

Experiences with Death   30 to 60 minutes

You can either begin this activity with the Forced Choice exercise and continue with the sharing circle, or limit it to the sharing circle.

Forced Choice

Position one leader next to the light switch to turn it on and off at the appropriate times for this exercise. Make sure the room is clear of objects that people can trip over and fairly dark when the lights are out.

Designate one wall as the "agree" side and the opposite wall as "disagree." Explain that you will read a series of statements. Once each statement is read, the lights will go off and participants are to move to the side of the room that reflects whether they agree or disagree with the statement. Then the lights will come up. There will be no discussion or debate—the activity will be done in silence.

After you read a statement, turn off the lights to allow people to take their places. Then bring up the lights and ask participants to look around them, making eye contact with each other. After several seconds, move on to the next statement.

- I have known someone who has died.

- I have been to a funeral.

- Someone I love has died.

- I think about death pretty much every day at some point.

- I sometimes forget that I am going to die someday.

- Death scares me.

- I think it is possible that ghosts exist.

- I believe there is some kind of afterlife or place our souls go when our bodies die.

- It is possible that each of us has had a past life.

- Death is natural, but it feels unnatural when I think about it.

- I have seen a dead body.

- I think that mourning rituals, like wearing black, having a funeral, or sitting shiva, are important.

- I am grieving someone's death right now.

- If a good friend's parent died, I am not sure I would know how to react.

- I think the world would be a better place if no one ever died.

After people have taken their places in response to the last question, ask them to sit in a circle for discussion.

Sharing Circle

Explain that in the circle, each person will take a turn responding to the following five questions.

- What has been your experience with death?

- What makes it hard to cope with death?

- What helps you cope with death?

- How do you feel when you think about the fact that you will die someday?

- What do you believe happens to people after they die?

You may pass a talking stick for this activity. It can be any object that is passed around the circle to designate whose turn it is to speak. Make sure that it is clear that participants have the right to pass if they do not want to respond to a particular question. Leaders can share, too. After everyone has had the opportunity to speak once, you may find it helpful to pass the object around the circle once more in case anyone else wants to speak.

This also gives anyone who passed the first time another chance to share.

After Life   5 minutes

Introduce the discussion by saying something like the following: "Unitarian Universalists hold different beliefs about what happens after death. There is no one doctrine our faith asks us to accept about an afterlife. For many Unitarian Universalists, the more important question is how we can create 'heaven on earth,' making life on earth better."

Pose these questions to the group: If Unitarian Universalism does not offer people a vision of the afterlife, do you think our faith offers helpful ways to think about dying? If so, what are some of those ways? Some responses include that it helps us accept death as a natural part of life and it helps us value life on earth.

After discussing this question, ask, "What does Unitarian Universalism offer to people who have lost friends and loved ones?" Some responses include love, comfort, companionship in grief; a community to remember and celebrate the person who died; and a place in which to explore our own meanings of life, suffering, and death.

The Mustard Seed   10 minutes

Share this story from Buddhist tradition:

> Long ago, there was a young mother who had a two-year-old son. He delighted her and she loved him deeply. One day he became very ill, and even though the mother tried everything she could, he died the next week. Completely distraught and stricken by grief, she carried her dead son to a man she heard could heal him: the Buddha.
>
> When she saw the Buddha, she held out her son to him. Tears streamed down her face as she begged the Buddha to do all he could to heal him.
>
> The Buddha looked at her with compassionate eyes. He said, "Bring me a handful of mustard seed from a house where no one has lost a friend or family member to death." The young woman then set out on a

journey from house to house. At each door she inquired and was turned down. "No, I have lost my mother." "No, my daughter died." "No, I grieve for my uncle who died just last week." After a long day visiting everyone in her village, she was not able to come up with a single mustard seed. Every house had lost someone beloved.

She reflected on this, and realized that we all live and die. And although her sadness was intense, she realized she was not alone in her grief. Knowing this, she was finally able to bury her son. She returned to the Buddha, more compassionate and more enlightened, and became one of his most devoted students.

Ask for responses to this story.

Grieving Well   30 minutes

This activity discusses the natural process of grieving and how we can go with it and let others do the same. It points out that everyone has different ways of grieving and helps youth find resources to help them with grief.

Share that "a young person wrote the following letter to Go Ask Alice, an Internet site operated by Columbia University that gives advice on emotional and physical health" and read the following letter.

Dear Alice,

My mother just died and I just started my freshman year of high school. If this was on paper, you would see my teardrops covering it. I feel like I have no one to talk to. I see the school grief counselor once every three or four weeks, but I was wondering if there is anything else that I might be able to do to lessen my feelings of depression and the feeling that I've been abandoned.

Signed,
Lonely and Depressed

Ask participants to think for a little while, in silence, about what they might recommend to a friend who asked them this same question. Then lead a discussion, asking these questions:

- What are some of the things that people go through when they are grieving?

- Do people sometimes grieve even when no one has died? If so, what other situations can make someone grieve?

- What are some ways to be helpful to people who are grieving?

Participants will probably be able to name many of the things grieving people experience. If the following areas are not brought up by youth, mention some of these elements of the grief process, as identified by the Centre for Living with Dying: shock and surprise; emotional release; loneliness; physical distress with anxiety; panic and disorganization; guilt; hostility, projection, and anger; suffering in silence and depression; the gradual overcoming of grief; and readjustment to reality. In the discussion, affirm that "grief is a natural life experience we all go through in healing from the reality of loss and change. Each grief journey is unique. Reaching out to others for support and being kind to oneself can enable us to survive the pain." Share Handouts 16 and 17, Grief and Mourning and Tools for Coping.

The answer to the question, "Do people sometimes grieve even when no one has died?" is yes. Grief is present in many situations that include injury, acquired disability, divorce, custody loss, moving to a new community, imprisonment, a really difficult breakup, assault, trauma, and onset of mental illness, among others. Grief is a natural response to many kinds of losses and is experienced by both those directly affected by a situation and those who care about them.

As the group discusses ways to be helpful to people who are grieving, make points based on your own experience. You can emphasize some of the simple ways to be helpful to people who are grieving: being gentle and honest, allowing them to be sad, and offering to do simple things with them, like take a walk or make cookies. Share that it is important to take cues from the grieving person and to not force the person to express or suppress emotions. Emphasize that it can be a gift to grieving people to just be with them and accept their feelings and moods. Please mention, though, that grief is not an excuse to abuse someone. Let youth know that some grieving people can be hurtful to those who reach out to them and that if a grieving person is hurting them or someone them know with anger, violence, or neglect, they should get help.

In closing, share what Alice (of "Go Ask Alice") wrote back to the grieving ninth-grader:

Dear Lonely and Depressed,

You are experiencing normal feelings of grief. Grieving for a loved one, especially a mother, takes time, energy, and caring. Life has changed irrevocably. Your family structure has changed. You may feel that you are growing up faster than you had ever anticipated. You may feel as if there is no one to take care of you, and it is difficult and painful to feel abandoned.

During this time, it is especially important that you seek out and talk with people you feel close to. Often, people are happy to help; however, they may not know how. They also may be waiting for you to seek them out. You could choose someone, and ask [that person] to do something very specific: to listen to you, sit with you quietly, hug you, see a movie, or take a walk with you. Just sitting quietly or reading different books together can be comforting. Sometimes, exercise can make a difference. It is important to get your feelings out and take care of yourself more frequently than every three or four weeks. By the way, maybe you could talk with your school's grief counselor more often—at least for now.

Think about your family, friends, and neighbors. Who is already close to you? Who can you talk with? Who do you feel might understand? Your father? A sister or brother? An aunt or uncle? Cousins? A close family friend? A good friend's mother? A neighbor, or someone you feel close to or admire who lives nearby? Someone from synagogue, temple, or church could be understanding and helpful. Perhaps you can open up to a teacher.

There are also books you can read. Your school librarian or local bookstore will be able to steer you in the direction of books that are written for young adults about death. Death is a normal part of the life cycle, and something we all face sooner or later. There are also fiction books that deal with similar issues. Reading these kinds of books can help people experience, understand, and manage their feelings in a full and complete way.

You can also keep a grief and healing journal to compose your thoughts when you are happy, unhappy, or when you want to tell your mother something—just like you have done here. You can write her letters that express your feelings—this outlet will help you heal more quickly.

Finally, make an appointment with your pediatrician or family doctor, who can talk with you about your grieving process, assess your coping skills, and make a referral for counseling. You can also read Hope Edelman's book, *Motherless Daughters: The Legacy of Loss*. In addition, grief and loss groups are held at local community centers and churches. Alice will be thinking of you.

Alice

Ask for any closing comments or questions before ending the discussion.

Closing Circle 10 minutes

Gather in a circle. Pass out three kinds of candy: hard, soft, and chewy. Ask youth to take one of each kind, and as they do, ask them to think about today's workshop and name something that was hard for them, something that was soft and easy, and something that they are still chewing on.

Share these words from Rev. Forrest Church: "Religion is our human response to the dual reality of being alive and having to die."

Extended Journaling and
UU Pocket Guide Discussion for Unit 5

Journaling Prompts

Encourage participants to reflect upon the topics covered in this unit in their journals. Pose the following questions to get them started:

- What are some of the "big questions" not discussed that you wonder about?

- Have you ever had a discussion about theological questions that was particularly insightful for you? What made it so useful?

UU Pocket Guide Discussion

Ask participants to read "Our Ministry" before the scheduled discussion or schedule time during your weekly meeting to read and discuss the chapter, using the following questions:

- Describe a time when you interacted with a minister, either at this congregation or in another setting.

- Are ordained ministers the only people in our congregations who do "ministry"?

- Is there anything in the chapter that speaks to your experience as a Unitarian Universalist?

Seven Paths for the God Project

The Child

Children are not literal kids, but they are filled with childlike wonder. To them, everything in the universe is enchanted. God or the sacred is everywhere, and so is goodness.

The Lover

Lovers know God or the sacred by loving others and loving the earth. They are compassionate, caring, and concerned about suffering.

The Champion

whens the last time you felt p powr

Champions are passionate about righteousness. They serve God or the sacred by working for justice here on earth. They look at things globally and aren't always compassionate to the unjust.

The Servant

Servants rely on traditions and authority figures to know the sacred. They are devoted to scriptures, rituals, and authorized teachers.

The Dreamer

invented a story / im sur

Dreamers are storytellers and mythmakers. Their path to God is full of creativity and imagination, and they invent rather than discover God. They are hopeful, they think big, and their imaginations give meaning to life.

The Mystic

Mystics seek to feel God or the sacred firsthand, through prayer, meditation, or contemplation. They like quiet and solitude.

The Star Gazer

Star Gazers look at the universe and feel awe. They embrace science as a key to deeper spirituality and deeper fascination with life. They embrace earth and her creatures, recognizing that we are all children of the universe.

—Forrest Church, *Lifecraft*, adapted

Some Ways of Looking at God

Does God have to be. . .

All-powerful?
All-knowing?
All-seeing?
All-good?
A judge?
A trinity?
Male?
Elderly?

. . . in order to be "God"?

What is God like?

A Life Force?
A Mystery?
The Web of Existence?
The Biblical God?
Love?
Community?
Nature?
Found in Relationship?

Is God...

A word I use to name something important?
A concept that is meaningful to me?
Something I don't believe in?
A presence I feel?
Important to me?
Something I wonder about?

Is there a God? If so, how many?

Monotheism (from Greek, "monos" = one and "theos" = god). Belief in one god. Also called "theism."

Polytheism (from Greek, "polytheos" = of many gods). Belief that there are many gods and goddesses. In some forms of polytheism, the many deities are worshiped as different expressions of one god.

Atheism (from Greek, "a" = not and "theos" = god). Belief that there is no God.

Agnosticism (from Greek, "agnostos" = unknown). A view that it is impossible to know if God exists because human knowledge and experience are limited.

Where is God?

Biblical verses refer to God as residing in the heavens, dwelling in the Temple, or sitting on a throne. Many religious Christians and Jews would say that these passages aren't meant to be understood literally. The following terms describe different ways of locating God.

Immanentism (from Latin, "immanere" = to remain in). God is present in everything.

Transcendency (from Latin, "transcendere" = to surpass). God is over and beyond everything. God is superior to all creation.

Pantheism (from Greek, "pan" = all and "theos" = god). God is everything and everything is God.

Panentheism (from Greek, "pan" = all, "en" = in, and "theos" = god). God is in everything and also beyond everything.

Grief and Mourning

The death of someone close to us throws us into a sea of chaotic feelings. Sometimes the waves of emotions seem powerful enough to threaten our very survival; sometimes they feel relentless and never-ending; sometimes they quiet down, only to arise months or even years later when we least expect them.

Grief is not something we ever really "get over"—our loss remains a fact for a lifetime. Nothing about grief's journey is simple; there is no tidy progression of stages and its course is long and circular.

While there is no clear roadmap, there are some features common to almost everyone's experience. Some of the dimensions presented below may ebb and flow within a natural healing process. The walk down grief's road requires time, patience, attention, hard work, and lots of loving care.

Grief is the natural human response to any loss, not only death. An illness, a job change, divorce and separation, an unfulfilled dream, a move to a new location, or any other change can bring about a grief response. Grief is not a problem. It is a normal, healthy process of healing.

Shock and Surprise

Even if death is expected, you may feel numb or anesthetized for several weeks afterward. Your actions may be mechanical, and you may get things done (for example, handle all the funeral details) but you are not "all there." People around you may be saying "Isn't he strong?" or "She's handling this so well." The impact or reality of the death has not fully reached you. This period of shock is your psyche's way of protecting you by allowing reality in slowly. If the loss is sudden, unexpected, or violent, the period of numbness may be longer.

Emotional Release

As the period of shock wears off, reality can be acutely painful. As the full impact gradually dawns on you, conflict may arise about whether to show grief or not to show it. How much and for how long? You might try to keep up a good front or remain strong, even though you may feel like crying or screaming. If people are praising you for being so brave and not "falling apart," do you dare show them how you really feel? This is a time when emotional release is important and should be encouraged. Concealing painful feelings may prolong the grief process and increase physical and emotional distress. At this point, other mourners can help support your expression of grief.

Loneliness

Sometimes, even before the funeral, the feelings of loneliness, isolation and depression begin. The funeral is the focus for realizing that your loved one is really gone. Family and friends can be helpful and consoling, but after the funeral the prevailing attitude is "It's all over." The supportive people in your life may disappear. After the funeral you may suffer a second major loss: everyday contact with your loved one. For some, this might mean no home-cooked meals, coming home to an empty house, no welcome home greeting. For others, it may mean no one to cook for, no one to help with household chores, no one to hold and share the small everyday moments and rituals. If your child has died, there is no one to see come home from school, no one to share your future dreams with or to see grow up. If your loved one has been sick for a long time, you no longer have hospital visits to make. Your entire routine of daily living has been shattered. You are alone, suddenly overcome by an utter sense of depression and despair. It is important at this point to have people in your life who can validate the magnitude of your loss.

Physical Distress with Anxiety

Questions that may come up for you: What am I going to do? What's going to happen to me? How can I get along without her? Will I lose my friends? You may develop the same type of physical symptoms your loved one had. For example, if she had a heart attack, you may now have chest pains. Anxiety and stress may bring with it such physical symptoms as shortness of breath, insomnia, headaches, backaches, or an upset stomach. During the entire grief process, you need to take especially good care of your body; you are vulnerable and may need a lot more rest. You may want to see your physician for a physical examination.

Panic and Disorganization

You may have trouble concentrating on anything but the loss. You may feel something is wrong with you; you may replay thoughts such as: I can't get the images out of my mind; won't they ever stop? Sometimes I think I see her. Sometimes I feel his touch. Sometimes I hear his voice. I've got to do something. I can't sleep. I can't eat. All I do is think about her. Will it ever stop hurting? Will I ever stop dreaming about her? As a bereaved person, you need to know this does not mean you are going crazy. This is a normal part of the grieving process.

Guilt

When faced with real or imagined guilt, you may begin asking questions like: What did I do wrong? What if I'd stayed awake, hadn't gone to work, kissed her, showed I loved him? These questions may indicate guilt, regrets, or unfinished business, which need to be expressed. These feelings can be brought to the surface by sharing with a nonjudgmental listener, in a letter, or in a diary.

Partial or complete interruption of the grief process at this time can cause severe depression and/or suicidal feelings.

Hostility, Projection and Anger

In conjunction with or emerging from the feelings of guilt, you may experience hostility. Maybe you are hostile to people who you perceive contributed to your problem. Example: To the physician: Why didn't he do something? Why didn't he get there in time? Did he do everything he could? You may be experiencing anger at friends who draw away from you or seem to belittle your loss with well-meaning but clumsy remarks. You may be furious with God or fate for taking away your loved one. You may also be angry with your loved one for dying and abandoning you. Anger is a very normal, human emotion and it is important to find ways to release those feelings of "What I'm going through is so unfair." "Why did it have to happen to him? He was a good person." Talking about it and physical activity both help keep anger from burning inside.

Suffering in Silence and Depression

This is a time when you may suffer in silence. You might feel fatigued, worn out, and unable to get started in any activity. Your thought processes are involved with the loss—emptiness and loneliness—but you may no longer want to talk about it. You recognize that others expect you to stop grieving. Your tears, anger, frustration, or depression are poorly tolerated by others several weeks after the funeral. Except for the initial loss, this stage is the hardest. You, the bereaved person, feel all alone. You may have feelings of not wanting to go on, and then shock or guilt for having such thoughts. This is a period where you are re-creating meaning in life—and it takes time.

The Gradual Overcoming of Grief

Your adjustment to a new status in life gradually occurs with working through this grief period.

There can be a noticeable change as early as four weeks to three months, but often it is much longer. By the end of this phase, there is considerable brightening of mood, more activity, and the beginning of reestablishment with people.

Readjustment to Reality

Because traditional symbols of grief, such a black veil or clothing or armband, are out of style, many times it is easy for others to forget you are grieving. You are beginning to restructure your life without your loved one. You may want to take a vacation or a trip, or get involved in a new activity, or take up old activities you used to like. Occasionally, you may feel twinges of guilt as you begin to enjoy yourself or laugh freely again, as though you are somehow betraying the memory of your lost loved one. It is helpful to be aware of guilt feelings that get in the way of readjustment. It is also helpful to recognize that wedding anniversaries, holidays, birthdays, or the anniversary date of the death may cause a temporary flood of feelings or may bring back a very short version of the grief process. This is normal and does not mean that you will be in acute pain forever.

Remember . . .

Grief is a natural life experience we all go through in healing from the reality of loss and change. Each grief journey is unique. Reaching out to others for support and being kind to oneself can enable us to survive the pain.

—Centre for Living with Dying, *www.billwilson center.org/thecentre*

Tools for Coping

Here are some tips for dealing with the everyday feelings and realities of living when you are experiencing a major loss, illness, death, separation, or any life change.

- Be gentle with your own feeling process. Avoid self-judgment. Do not put "I should have" on yourself.

- Find a supportive person or persons you can trust. Share your honest feelings.

- Give yourself time for healing. Grief cannot be rushed. Plan so that you have specific time to focus on your loss and special time to escape from the pain of the reality of what you are facing.

- Try to maintain as regular a schedule as possible. Avoid unrealistic expectations or goals for yourself.

- Maintain an awareness of your body's need for nutrition and rest. If symptoms arise that are new or unusual, see a physician.

It can be very confusing to experience feelings of fear, anger, helplessness, sorrow, pain, emptiness, isolation, depression, or relief. Focus yourself by asking these questions:

- How do I feel right now? (Check body sensations, as well as thoughts and emotions.)

- What do I need right now? (Focus on immediate, attainable needs.)

- How can I meet (or get a supportive friend to help me meet) these needs right now?

Listening to your body is critical during this period, and listening is different from doing something for your body. Listening means honoring the message your body is sending you:

- Words or tears that are unexpressed will cause lumps in our throats.

- Anger that is held inside can give us upset stomachs, headaches, or tight necks and shoulders.

- Fear can be expressed by wringing hands, shakiness, or queasy stomachs.

- Guilt or resentment can feel like physical burdens we are carrying. ("I feel like I weigh a ton.")

- Sorrow or depression can feel like pressure or "breaking" in our hearts or chest areas. Breathing may be labored. We may heave great sighs.

Often combinations of feelings are felt. It is important to ask the part of the body that is feeling these sensations the following:

- If you could talk, what would you say?

- What would you need?

- What picture or symbol best expresses you right now? What do you look like?

- What is happening with you right now?

Writing a letter or drawing a picture about your illness, loss, or grief is a healing way to get your feelings from the inside to the outside. Writing to others with whom you feel at odds, to your body, or to institutions, the universe, your illness, God, or anybody enables you to process what your body longs to say. It also enables you to release anger, frustration, and isolation and move to a forgiving, life-affirming love for yourself and those who have touched your life.

Record a life evaluation:

- Who and what has been important in my life?

- Have I done what I wanted in my life?

- What do I need to do to be fulfilled?

- What activities would give me the most satisfaction right now?

- Is there anything or anyone with whom I feel incomplete or unfinished at this time? Is there anything I need to do about that for myself?

Realize that the world around you and your daily activities will be filled with land mines—moments of painful realizations of your loss and resentment at a world that marches on, apparently without noticing or caring. Verbalize these feelings. They are normal.

As a person facing grief or illness, you may be stigmatized. People may not know how to handle you or make you better. They may even be afraid of you because you represent fear and pain that could come into their lives. Allow yourself to be gently honest about your needs. Focus on taking care of yourself and surrounding yourself with caring people who will accept your process. You do not have to make it better for the world. This is a time to care for yourself as you would care for the most tender, vulnerable child who is hurting.

When you are left with an empty or breaking heart, do the following for yourself:

- Recognize the loss. Take time for nature's slow, sure, stuttering process of healing.

- Give yourself massive doses of restful relaxation and routine busyness.

- Know that powerful, overwhelming feelings will lessen with time.

- Be vulnerable, share your pain, and be humble enough to accept support.

- Surround yourself with life, plants, animals, and friends.

- Use mementos to help your mourning, not to live in the past.

- Avoid rebound relationships, big decisions, and anything addictive.

- Keep a diary and record successes, memories, and struggles.

- Prepare for change, new interests, new friends, solitude, creativity, and growth.

- Know that holidays and anniversaries can bring back the painful feelings you thought you had worked through.

- Recognize that forgiveness (of yourself and others) is a vital part of the healing process and that it cannot be rushed.

- Realize that any new death or loss-related crisis will bring up feelings about past losses.

Remember . . .

Grief is a spiral of feelings and experiences. It is not a straight line with a beginning and ending. The process of grief is healing the pain of loss and keeping the treasured memories and love within your heart.

—Centre for Living with Dying, *www.billwilson center.org/thecentre*, adapted

Justice

There is one inevitable criterion of judgment touching religious faith in doctrinal matters—can you reduce it to practice? If not, have none of it.

—Hosea Ballou

Most early adolescents experience an expanding sense of social awareness. They are newly able to think abstractly, grapple with ethics, and understand some of society's complexity beyond home, school, and congregation. In addition, they often have a sharply defined, even idealistic, sense of fairness. Although early adolescents can be self-absorbed, they are drawn to stories of heroic quests, and they prize books, movies, and video games in which good triumphs over evil.

Young people's dawning ethical sensibility and desire to make a difference in the world lead them to identify with those who seek to challenge unjust social structures. Nurturing adolescents' growing sense of social justice encourages their ongoing maturation—particularly their ability to empathize, their confidence in their own abilities, and their growing understanding of the responsibilities of adulthood.

People leading Unitarian Universalist social justice curricula sometimes confess to feeling like impostors. Your own social justice involvement and experience may be slight. You may be largely unaware of the issues, problems, and justice efforts present in your own communities. Know that lack of experience and knowledge may help rather than hinder you in leading adolescents. Youth appreciate a person who can lead them in their own process of discovery and sometimes claim more ownership in mutually discov-

ered answers than in answers imposed on them. Rather than playing the role of the all-knowing teacher, invite yourself to become a student as well, listening to the knowledge youth bring, asking questions, and seeking out community leaders from whom you can all learn.

These sessions will help participants understand the value and varieties of social engagement, including local efforts. If you choose to include a social action project as a building block of your program, participants will have a chance to design their own social action event, carry it out, and reflect on the experience (see Social Action Projects, page 207).

Workshop 25
Understanding Social Action

Time 60 minutes

Participant Goals

- recognize the differences between community service and social justice work

- understand the independent and combined value of various forms of social engagement

- develop a sense of empowerment in the face of complex and significant social problems

Materials

- newsprint
- markers
- masking tape
- Snurptown labels (see Preparation)
- copies of Handout 18, Snurptown and Contra-Viva Corporation (page 171)
- copies of Handout 19, Snurptown Map (page 172)
- paper
- pens or pencils
- knife
- cutting board
- large bowl
- small bowls or cups
- extra fruit for fruit salad (see Preparation)
- forks
- napkins

Preparation

- Ask youth in advance to each bring one piece of fruit to share.

- Bring several pieces of fruit, as some participants may forget. Consider bringing less common fruit, such as kiwifruit, star fruit, or prepitted litchi fruit, all of which are available at many supermarkets.

- Write the following labels on five pages of newsprint, two per page, at the top and in the middle of each vertical page: "Bigohl River," "Downstream Neighborhood," "City Hall," "Shopping Mall," "ContraViva Corp. Factory," "Boathouse," "Snurptown News," "UU Congregation," "Nowhere," "Other." Hang the sheets around the room.

Opening   5 minutes

Use the opening ritual designed by the group, either before or after the Standing Game.

Standing Game   5 minutes

You can play this game as soon as people arrive, without officially calling it a game. You need two people to start, and soon the whole class will be stumbling and giggling along.

Begin by sitting on the ground back-to-back with a partner, with feet flat, knees bent, and elbows linked. Then stand simultaneously, using the pressure of each other's backs for support. You will be standing smoothly after a few tries.

Onlookers will want to try with their own partners. As youth are mastering the two-person technique, suggest that three people try to stand together. Form groups of three with those who are ready. This will be more challenging than two, and four is even harder, but it can be done! Then see whether the whole class can stand together. One tip: A large group of people stand together best when they sit scrunched close together, then stand up quickly and at the same time.

After the game, say, "This goes to prove that it's challenging but worthwhile not to simply stand up for ourselves but to learn how to stand up with others."

Setting the Stage   5 minutes

Encourage people to take their piece of fruit to the table and find their seats. Explain to the group, "Today we will consider some intriguing questions. Do any of us have the power to make the world more fair? What ways work better than other ways? Today we will imagine all the different things we might do to make the world a better place, and try to decide which one of them is the best, or whether it might be better to do nothing at all."

Distribute copies of Handout 18, Snurptown and ContraViva Corporation. Ask for a volunteer to read the handout, which tells the story of ContraViva's arrival in Snurptown, and the jobs, pollution, and ecological destruction that resulted. As the volunteer reads, cut fruit for the fruit salad. After the volunteer finishes reading, explain that the class will try to find the best way to stop the damage that ContraViva Corporation is doing in Snurptown.

What We Can Do: Focusing   5 minutes

Pass out copies of Handout 19, Snurptown Map. Divide into small groups of two to four participants. Ask everyone to look at the town map and write down ideas for actions they might take at each location to affect ContraViva's pollution. During this time, finish cutting the fruit if necessary. Give the group a one-minute warning to let them know that the focusing time is about to end.

Brainstorming and Discussion   20 minutes

Ask for a volunteer to write responses on newsprint during brainstorming. Ask the group to share some of the ideas they wrote down. Remind them that during brainstorming, all ideas are accepted and written on the newsprint as closely as possible to how they are said; it is a time for creativity, not judging. After ten to twelve minutes of brainstorming, talk about the advantages and disadvantages of the proposed actions.

The following examples are provided to move discussion along if it becomes quiet.

Location: Bigohl River

Example: Organize a river cleanup to remove the globs of waste.
Advantages: Cleans up the river! Addresses the problem directly.
Disadvantages: Does nothing to change the long-term situation.

Example: Organize a rally or a vigil by the river, with signs posing questions like "Where have the frogs gone?" and "What is ContraViva doing to our river?"
Advantages: Draws attention to the location of the problem.
Disadvantages: Not very many people will get the message if it is directed at people already near the river. DDAPP. [Explain that DDAPP is an acronym for Doesn't Directly Address the Present Problem. It applies to an action that may be useful but works toward a future solution rather alleviating the present situation.]

Location: Downstream Neighborhood

Example: Go door-to-door educating people about the health risks posed by the river, and inviting them to sign up to learn more or get active in addressing the issue.
Advantages: Educates an affected population. Gathers motivated supporters.
Disadvantages: Time consuming for each contact. Since many people will not be home, will require producing printed materials, which requires time, energy, and money.

Location: City Hall

Example: E-mail, write, call, and visit legislators, lobbying them to enforce existing pollution laws or institute new ones.
Advantages: If successful, should eliminate the problem.
Disadvantages: Possibly DDAPP: legislation often moves slowly, which might not be immediately helpful. Legislators have a full agenda and may not pay attention unless you have a very large or powerful group of supporters. Legislators must balance your agenda with their own, as well as the agendas of other constituencies they serve (such as employees of ContraViva and their families, who may feel that the jobs ContraViva creates make it worth overlooking the pollution).

Location: Shopping Mall

Example: Hand out flyers to shoppers, informing them of situation.
Advantages: Reaches a large number of people quickly. Builds allies.
Disadvantages: DDAPP. Soliciting may be restricted. May encounter hostility (for example, from store owners and mall security). Since this is a general population (as opposed to the "Downstream Neighborhood,") many may have little interest in the issue.

Location: ContraViva Corporation Factory

Example: Stage a protest.
Advantages: Could draw significant attention to the problem and influence ContraViva to change.
Disadvantages: Treats ContraViva as the enemy rather than as a partner in solving the problem. If protesters have not already called multiple times for ContraViva to change, if they have not done their homework properly, or if they are undisciplined, the protest could tarnish the credibility of the reformers.

Location: Boathouse

Example: Inform boat enthusiasts of pollution problem and ask them to help.
Advantages: Builds power base.
Disadvantages: DDAPP.

Location: Snurptown News

Example: Send a news release to the Snurptown News, informing them of the problem, of an upcoming protest, or of the personal stories of people affected by the pollution.
Advantages: Draws tremendous community attention to the problem, thereby generating significant concern, even outrage.
Disadvantages: DDAPP. Requires skilled and sustained effort to create the release, which may or may not be picked up. Risks losing control of the message.

Location: UU Congregation

Example: Encourage the congregation to host public forums fostering calm, reasoned dialogue about the competing values of employment and environmental stewardship.
Advantages: Allows a rare public forum for reasoned discussion rather than swapping sound bites. Educates the community and congregation. Potentially builds power base.
Disadvantages: DDAPP. Brings controversy into the congregation, which will make some congregants uncomfortable.

Location: Nowhere

Advantages: No effort required. Focus just on enjoying one's own life, friends, and family!
Disadvantages: Does nothing to address the ongoing damage to the community. Does not improve the world beyond one's family and friendship circle. Does not express Unitarian Universalism's deepest values. Does not provide the experience of stretching toward one's potential.

Location: Other

These would be other places that the youth suggest an action be taken, such as at school, the state capital, local courts, the local Fishing Enthusiast's Club, a statewide animal rights and/or environmental organization, the Chamber of Commerce, neighboring congregations, or the cafeteria company that services ContraViva.

Analysis and Integration   15 minutes

After discussion, ask which proposal is the best one. As needed, lead the group in trying to decide. It should become clear that no one action is as useful as several. A river cleanup helps in the short term but not the long term; a rally outside of ContraViva helps in the long term, but only if the movement is large enough and publicized well enough to be noticed. Help the group talk about how each action is good, worthwhile, and important in itself, but they are even better when combined. Ask if anyone can describe what is similar between social action and the fruit salad they're all about to enjoy. (Possible answers include: Each of us brings only a little bit compared to the whole, but each little bit is important. Each part is wonderful on its own, and even better in combination.)

While enjoying the Social Action Fruit Salad, ask participants the following questions:

- Which action that we talked about would you be most interested to try in real life? Why?

- Have you ever participated in a social action similar to the Snurptown scenario before, and if so, what were the results?

- Read the quote at the beginning of this unit and ask participants what it means. If they need help, ask the following questions: Can you apply the quote to the situation in Snurptown? Does a lack of faith in getting positive results sometimes prevent us from taking a social action?

Closing Circle   5 minutes

Use the closing ritual designed by the group.

Workshop 26
How UUs Make a Difference

Time   90 minutes

Participant Goals

- build a bridge with the congregation's social action leaders and initiatives

- learn how congregation members are influenced by their religious beliefs to take action for peace and justice

- begin to understand what channels for social action are available in the local community

- explore their reactions to the influence of religious beliefs on taking action for peace and justice

- develop a sense of empowerment in the face of complex and significant social problems

Materials

- name tags for guests, participants, and leaders (optional)

- markers

- paper

- pens or pencils

- copies of Handout 20, Four Ways to Make a Difference (page 173)

- five copies of Handout 21, Questions for Guests (page 174)

- one 18" paper or cardboard circle for each five to six participants (a large bucket or trash can works well for tracing the pattern, and grocery bags can provide the paper)

Preparation

- If you have a small number of youth in the program, rather than having a panel you could ask youth to interview socially active people in the congregation about the relationship between their social action and their faith.

- If you will have a panel, at least one month prior to this session recruit four members of your congregation as guests. Allow yourself adequate time to find the most appropriate people for this activity. Look for people who are involved in local, district, or denominational projects. Ask your minister, board president, social responsibility chair, and/or church administrator for suggestions. You may also find people who are active not through your congregation but through their professions or through volunteer political or service activities. Appropriate guests may not be well known, but may be "quiet heroes." Avoid people considered to be abrasive. As much as possible, recruit guests who fit the following criteria:

  ~ They are or have recently been involved in activities of social education, social witness, and social action. (See Handout 20, Four Ways to Make a Difference, for an explanation of these terms.)

  ~ To a large extent, they are moved to act by their religious values and principles.

  ~ They can articulate why and how their religious values and principles motivate them to act as they do in these areas.

  ~ They are willing to meet with your group and talk openly about these topics.

  ~ They interact comfortably with early adolescents.

~ They represent the diversity of your congregation, community, and/or group. One
of the four should be an older adolescent
or, if none is available, a young adult.

• When you have recruited your guests, give
each a copy of Handout 20, *Four Ways to Make
a Difference* and Handout 21, *Questions for
Guests*. Ask them to be prepared to talk about
themselves in relation to these questions for
about five to seven minutes. Let each guest
know who the other guests will be. Finally, ask
the guests to arrive ten minutes before the
session begins.

• Call guests several days before the workshop
to confirm and answer any questions they may
have.

• Place a comfortable chair for each guest at the
front of your space. Arrange the chairs for the
participants and leader(s) in a semicircle facing the guest chairs.

• When your guests arrive, explain the plan for
the session. Invite them to take part in the activities, but to let the adolescents take the lead
in doings such as the opening game. Remind
them how long their presentations are to be.

Opening and Gathering   10 minutes

Greet participants as they arrive. If you are using
name tags, hand them out as people enter the
room. If you ask the guests to wear name tags,
be sure that you and the participants also wear
them.

Give participants and guests Handout 20,
Four Ways to Make a Difference, as they arrive,
and encourage them to look it over as they wait
for the rest of the group.

When the group has gathered, ask people to
take a seat in the semicircle. Direct guests to their
seats. Introduce the guests, or have them introduce themselves. Ask the young people to introduce themselves.

Give the group a brief overview of this session.

The Tiny Island   10 minutes

Divide the group (including guests) into groups
of five to six players. Give each group one of the
precut circles. Tell them, "Your group is boating
down the Bigohl River when your boat hits a blob
of unidentifiable goo and sinks. The river is so
polluted from the factory upstream that if you
spend more than a few seconds in the water, you
won't be able to swim. The only thing you have to
save you from drowning is a tiny island to cling to
until help arrives. How can you get everyone onto
the island with no one left touching the water?
You'll have a few minutes to come up with a plan.
Then I'll give a signal, and each group will try their
approach. You can say it's impossible if you want
to, but then you're sure to drown. Ready? Go!"

After a few minutes, tell them time is almost
up. Give the signal, and let the groups try their
methods. Go around the circle afterward to see
what different methods were used. Give the
methods descriptive names, such as the Starfish
or the Tortoise Back.

Making a Difference: Focusing   10 minutes

Gather the group in the semicircle and chairs, and
say something like, "Last session we talked about
ways people could make a difference in an imaginary place, Snurptown. But Unitarian Universalist
social engagement is not imaginary, it is real. Our
guests today are Unitarian Universalists from
our own congregation who are working for peace
and justice. Each of them will tell you something
about the real ways they are working to make the
world better. First, however, let's take a minute
to understand some ways we all can make a difference." Check to see if anyone needs a copy of
Handout 20, *Four Ways to Make a Difference*. Ask
for volunteers to read the bold title and italicized
first sentence of each way.

Exploring   30 minutes

Explain that each guest will speak and then there
will be time for questions and comments. Hand
out paper and pens or pencils, and invite the young
people to write down questions and comments.

Invite one of the guests to begin. Be aware of the time, and if necessary, politely remind the guest of the time limit. Follow the same procedure with each guest.

As the guests speak, jot down your own ideas or questions.

After the second guest has shared, invite everyone to take a quick stretch break. If youth seem restless and time allows, engage in briefly attempting one another's solutions to the Tiny Island game played earlier.

Integrating   20 minutes

After the remaining two speakers, invite questions and comments. Allow guests to respond to each other, but be sure that their interaction does not overwhelm youths' involvement. If participants run out of questions and comments, direct appropriate questions to the youth and/or guests.

With a few minutes remaining for this activity, ask participants to respond to the following question with a couple of words or a phrase: When you think about what you have heard today, what feels the most helpful [or important, or another adjective of your choice] to you?

Reflection   5 minutes

Talk about how in some ways, the earth is like a small island that we need to learn how to live on together, in cooperation and fairness. Thank the guests for all that they do to help us move toward a more just and peaceful way of living with one another and the earth. Thank them for their participation. Then encourage participants to spend some time in the coming week noticing what social issues exist in their communities.

Closing Circle   5 minutes

Use the closing ritual designed by the group.

Extended Journaling and
UU Pocket Guide Discussion for Unit 6

Journaling Prompts

Encourage participants to reflect upon the topics covered in this unit in their journals. Pose the following questions to get them started:

- Do you have a social justice hero or heroine?

- If you were leading your Coming of Age group in a workshop about this person, what would you say? What activities would you do?

UU Pocket Guide Discussion

Ask participants to read "Our Work for Social Justice and Diversity" before the scheduled discussion or schedule time during your weekly meeting to read and discuss the chapter, using the following questions:

- This chapter discusses a few areas of oppression where Unitarian Universalists are active. Have you experienced any work toward eradicating these particular oppressions in your congregation?

- What other areas of social justice involve members of your congregation?

- Is there anything in the chapter that speaks to your experience as a Unitarian Universalist?

Snurptown and ContraViva Corporation

Imagine that you live in beautiful Snurptown and have lived there your whole life. Almost every one of the hundred thousand people who live in Snurptown agree it is a great place—there's the mall for shopping, grassy parks for the outdoorsy types, a clear blue stream full of frogs and fish, and your favorite place to see your friends on Sundays, the Unitarian Universalist Congregation of Snurptown. Sometimes, though, you hear adults complain that there aren't enough good jobs in town and that it is hard to make enough money to pay the bills.

When ContraViva (CON-tra-VEE-vah) Corporation announces that it is going to build a new factory in Snurptown, right beside the Bigohl River, the townspeople are very happy. Dozens of local people are hired to build the factory. After the factory is complete, the townspeople throw a great celebration, and soon the factory hires hundreds of people to manufacture all kinds of ContraViva products.

But then something terrible happens. You and your friends begin to notice that the fish are washing up on the shore of the Bigohl River, the songs of the frogs are disappearing, and people who live downstream from the factory are getting sick. One day, while riding your bike past ContraViva's factory, you notice a big pipe dumping manufacturing waste into the river. No wonder the animals are dying and people are getting sick! As you watch, chunks and clumps of gross-looking goo plop into the river. The water swirling beneath the pipe has turned from glassy blue to a much more unnatural shade.

As you watch the pipe pour clump after chunk of gross goo into the river, a factory door bangs open and a businessman storms over to you. "Hey kid!" he says. "What are you doing watching our discharge system? You're lucky I'm not calling the police! You're on private property. I could have you arrested you for trespassing. I'm the president of ContraViva, and I'm telling you, you have no right to be here. If you don't like how we do our business, too bad. Get out of here, now. Now!"

You pedal away as fast as you can, glad the man didn't call the police. You're scared, but you're also angry at the way the man treated you and the way ContraViva is treating the river. It is good that ContraViva is providing jobs to the town, but not if it is going to ruin ecosystems, kill animals, and make people sick as a result. You decide that you want to do something. But what can you do? You're just one person. You can probably get some friends from your UU congregation to help, but even then, you won't be very many. What would make a difference? Should you do something at ContraViva? At the neighborhood where people are getting sick? At city hall? At the shopping mall? Somewhere else entirely? What's the best way to stop the harm that ContraViva Corporation is doing to the environment, animals, and people of Snurptown?

Snurptown Map

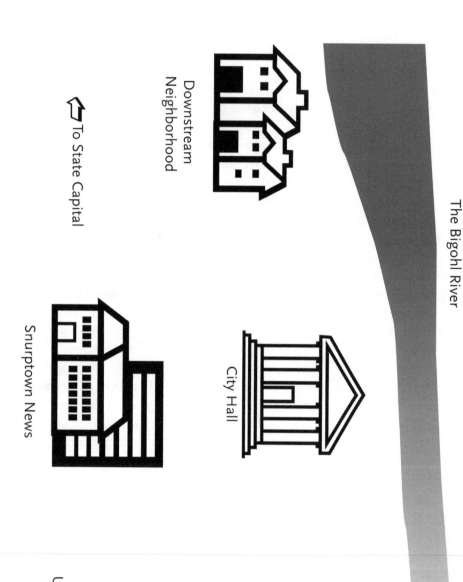
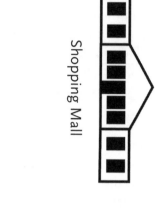

Downstream Neighborhood

To State Capital

Snurptown News

City Hall

The Bigohl River

Shopping Mall

Factory

UU Congregation of Snurptown

Boathouse

Four Ways to Make a Difference

Unitarian Universalists use four major methods to try to build a better world:

Social service: *We respond to immediate needs in our communities and across the world.* For example, we donate food and serve in food pantries, volunteer in animal sanctuaries, collect and donate money for worthy causes, participate in river and highway cleanups, and serve in shelters for homeless people. This work is also known as charitable assistance.

Social education: *We inform ourselves about social issues and their causes, then invite others to become more aware and knowledgeable about those issues.* This begins, for example, when we serve food to so many hungry people at a food pantry that we start to ask, "Why is there this level of hunger in our community?" We educate ourselves through, for example, study groups, lectures, videos, Sunday services, forums, and information compiled by our UUA Washington office and other trusted organizations. We go on to inform our community through, for example, hosting community-wide forums and discussions, conducting door-to-door information campaigns, and encouraging congregants to talk to friends and neighbors.

Social witness: *We act in ways that express clear moral statements about a social issue.* We witness to our values and convictions as a matter of personal integrity and because we believe others may respond to our individual and institutional expressions of sincere belief. Examples include marches, pickets, resolutions, street theater, worship services and sermons, signing on to petitions, writing letters to the editor, and sending press releases to the media.

Social action: *We apply ourselves in an organized way to directly influence the forces and structures that oppress and cause injustice.* In *The Prophetic Imperative: Social Gospel in Theory and Practice*, Rev. Richard Gilbert describes the difference between social action and social service: "Social action involves concentration on causes of injustice rather than symptoms." Examples include protests, vigils, rallies, and boycotts directed at institutions contributing to social problems; lobbying legislators and other decision makers by e-mail, phone, letter, or in person; personal lifestyle choices, such as vegetarianism or refusing to buy clothes produced in sweatshops; physical obstruction and other forms of civil disobedience.

All four of these ways of making a difference are invaluable. Which form is best or most appropriate depends on the situation; often, several forms in combination are more effective than any one practice would be alone. In the same way, individuals are often more effective when we join with others who also care about these issues. Organized groups that know how to use their power can have even more of an impact than individuals on decision makers and institutional structures in working to address local, state, national, and international social problems.

Questions for Guests

What are your core religious values and principles?

In what ways do these values and principles influence the way you act in terms of social justice?

What struggles have you gone through in acting for peace and justice?

What keeps you going with this work ?

Do you have advice about these concerns to share with youth in the Coming of Age program?

UNIT SEVEN

Unitarian Universalist History

History is the only laboratory we have in which to test the consequences of thought.

—Etienne Gilson

As in other units in the Coming of Age program, youth will bring their own experiences and knowledge to the topic of Unitarian Universalist history. The workshops in this unit invite participants to deepen their understanding of UU history by exploring some of its major themes and relating them to the beliefs, values, and Principles that brought them about.

In recent generations, UUs have become increasingly aware that our heritage is not only the history of men, but of women, too; not only the legacy of white people, but also of people with many other racial identities; not only the inheritance of people of privilege, but also of people with limited means and education; not only the story of heterosexuals, but also of gay, lesbian, bisexual, and transgender people. All of this, together, is our history.

In *Unitarian Universalism: A Narrative History*, minister and professor David Bumbaugh writes, "Unitarian Universalism is a peculiar religious tradition in that what binds it is not so much a shared theology, or even a shared response to the experience of the sacred, as it is a shared history." Like "the people of the Book" who are bound together by the narrative history of the Bible, Unitarian Universalists are also united by a common story. Yet Bumbaugh points out that this shared history is not so much the record of our direct biological ancestors, but more the affinity we hold toward those who have struggled against the rigid confines of orthodoxy in the past. He says,

> We are one people because of our inchoate understanding of the journey through time which we share. This is not to suggest that we are always accurate about the history we claim or that we always understand the motives, the behaviors, the attitudes of those who have preceded us, but rather that we are enraptured by a mythic sense of having shared a journey which began by rejecting conventional views and has been defined by a continuing struggle toward a personally satisfying understanding of the self, of the nature of the human venture, of the meaning of existence.

It is something of this journey that we are seeking to impart to those participating in a Coming of Age program—to instill an appreciation of the high price paid by our forebears for the free faith we hold today. An awareness of this heritage is also an invitation to recognize the agency each of us has to shape the world around us. Just as we claim that revelation is not sealed, so too we must remind ourselves that history is continually unfolding with each passing moment. As with the Unitarians and Universalists of the past, our times challenge us to live out our faith, recognizing that our actions today will be the history of tomorrow.

Workshop 27
Our Unitarian Universalist Story

Time   60 minutes

Participant Goals

- dramatize the life experiences in the lives of a few Unitarian Universalist ancestors

- analyze historical scenarios for common themes of shared Unitarian Universalist beliefs, values, and Principles

Materials

- three to six copies of Leader Resource 19, Our Unitarian Universalist Story Scenarios (see Preparation and page 179)

- props, costumes, or scripts for skits (optional, see Preparation)

Preparation

- Decide how many skits the group will perform and have enough copies of the scenarios for every youth who will be in a skit.

- Optional: Gather materials that can be used in your skits.

- Optional: If you have congregation members who enjoy doing drama with youth, invite them to assist you in this workshop. They can help obtain props and costumes and give tips during rehearsals.

- Optional: If you think your group will have difficulty creating skits, write scripts in advance of the session.

Opening   5 minutes

Use the opening ritual designed by the group.

Telling Our Story   40 minutes

Ask the group, "Is Unitarian Universalism a new religion?" Take a few responses before saying something like the following:

> Unitarian Universalism could be considered a new religion since it was just in 1961 that the American Unitarian Association and the

Universalist Church of America officially joined to become the Unitarian Universalist Association. However, neither Unitarianism nor Universalism is new. The origins of both can be traced back more than a thousand years. We cannot cover that much history in our short time together. The timeline in *The Unitarian Universalist Pocket Guide* gives you a good idea of many of the historical landmarks in our story. Next workshop, we'll have other resources you can use to find out more details of that history. Today, we're going to find out about a few people who were key players in what can be thought of as our Unitarian Universalist story.

> Sometimes when we think of history it seems to be only about dates and faraway places. The reality, though, is that there would be no history without people—real people like you and me—making decisions and taking action based upon their beliefs. If we examine the actions of several Unitarian Universalists in our story, do you think we can find common beliefs they might have shared? We'll see, because today we have scenarios of four players in that story. I am going to ask you to take the scenarios, apply your imagination, and create a skit of five minutes or less about the actions these players took. In your skit, make it very clear what beliefs you think might have fueled their actions. Your group will have fifteen minutes to create the scenario and rehearse.

Either to flesh out the scenarios or for your own interest, you can find more information in the following resources:

- King John Sigismund: *Unitarian Universalism: A Narrative History* by David E. Bumbaugh

- Judith Sargent Murray: *Judith Sargent Murray: A Brief Biography with Documents* by Sheila L. Skemp

- Martha and Waitstill Sharp: Unitarian Universalist Service Committee website at *www.uusc.org/info/history.html*

- Merging Youth Groups: *We Would Be One* by Wayne Arnason and Rebecca Scott

Divide the group into smaller groups of three to six participants, and give each group a different scenario from Leader Resource 19 (page 179). Let them use other available spaces for rehearsal. Walk around to each group to answer questions and give tips and encouragement. Give them five-minute and two-minute warnings before calling everyone back into the larger group to present their skits.

Discussion   10 minutes

Lead a discussion of the skits based on the following questions:

- What are some of the Unitarian Universalist beliefs, values, or Principles your character might have possessed? What makes you think so?

- Were there any reccurring themes in the skits?

- Did any of the skits involve incidents in our history that you were already aware of? What other historical events or people do you remember from other years in religious education? Do any of them connect with the skits you saw today?

- Are there any other comments about Unitarian Universalist history in general?

Closing Circle   5 minutes

Use the closing ritual designed by the group.

Workshop 28
The Local Story

Time   60 minutes

Participant Goals

- learn about the history of the congregation

- locate places where the congregation honors their history

- meet another congregational leader, the church historian

Materials

- copies of the scavenger hunt (see Preparation)

- pens or pencils

- treats or prizes (optional)

- copies of various issues of *UU World*

- copies of Handout 22, Unitarian Universalist History Resources (page 184)

Preparation

- Design a scavenger hunt that represents your congregation's history. Involve as many areas of the building as possible without putting youth in places where they will disturb others. Combine easier items with challenging ones, and create a list that will take participants at least fifteen minutes to complete. Next to each item note how youth should "collect" it: by bringing it with them, writing down where it is located, or recording what an item has written upon it. Suggested items include the following:

  ~ your congregation's vision and/or mission statement

  ~ your congregation's membership book

  ~ the inscription on the building's cornerstone or other memorial plaque

  ~ the name of your first minister or your current treasurer

  ~ items donated in years past by members

  ~ your Welcoming Congregation certificate

  ~ your church cemetery or memorial garden

- Invite the congregational historian or someone who is very knowledgeable about your congregation's history to speak to the group. This person can help put together the scavenger hunt or at least be given a copy of it the week before the workshop. The speaker should prepare a five- to seven-minute presentation that includes the items on the scavenger hunt, photographs, videos, written memorabilia and anecdotal stories youth might find interesting. Since your congregation's story is being examined as a piece of Unitarian Universalist history, any historical events or stories that connect the congregation to the wider UU world would be relevant. Try to find a presenter who can talk about past and present leaders and explain congregational polity, current governance, and how your congregation fits into the Unitarian Universalist Association.

- Find an article in an issue of *UU World* or online at *www.uua.org* about a congregation, group, or individual working to make the world a better place. It could be around the issue of gay marriage or immigrant rights or local school board elections. Flag the page so you can find it easily during the activity.

Opening   5 minutes

Use the opening ritual designed by the group.

Scavenger Hunt   25 minutes

Pass out the scavenger hunt sheet and pens or pencils. Explain to participants, including your guest, that they should find all the items on the sheet. Point out that the sheet specifies how to "collect" each item. Decide if participants will work individually or in teams, give them a time to come back, answer any questions, and begin the hunt.

Visit from the Church Historian   15 minutes

Introduce the speaker, and tell participants that they will hear about the history of their faith home, as well as how it fits into the larger story of Unitarian Universalism.

After the presentation, allow time for questions.

The Story Continues   10 minutes

Pass out Handout 22, Unitarian Universalist History Resources. Inform participants that these are resources for finding out more about Unitarian Universalist history. Pass out copies of different issues of *UU World*. Invite them to look through the magazine for a few minutes. Ask participants how this could be a resource. Some might correctly answer that they found an article about Unitarian Universalist history, but there is also another answer. Find the article you selected earlier. Point out to youth that this is history in the making, right here and now. Ask if anyone can find other articles that are history in the making. Say something like the following: "Our UU history gives us examples of brave humans who acted upon their convictions to change the world. May we, in our own way, be tomorrow's history."

Closing Circle   5 minutes

Use the closing ritual designed by the group.

Our Unitarian Universalist Story Scenarios

King John Sigismund

King John Sigismund followed in the footsteps of his mother, Queen Isabella, in establishing a state where religious tolerance was the law. In 1568, he convened public debates by representatives of the major religions that existed in Transylvania at the time. They were in conflict over whose religion was the truth. King Sigismund declared the earliest edict of complete religious tolerance and freedom. He said they were all free to practice their faith, and he established a list of state-recognized religions, which included his own religion: Unitarianism.

Judith Sargent Murray

In 1751, Judith Sargent was born in Massachusetts to a wealthy family that belonged to the local Congregational church. She wanted a formal education like her brother's, but instead was tutored only in the basics. She developed a love for reading and writing in her family library and wrote plays and essays. She converted to Universalism and helped establish the first Universalist congregation in her hometown, and she started the religious education program at the congregation where John Murray was minister. Her Sunday school lessons are believed to be the first religious education material by an American Universalist and the first writing of any kind by an American Universalist woman. After her first husband died, she married John Murray. A strong voice for women, she denounced the idea that they were inferior and called for more education and better treatment for women. She died in 1820.

Martha and Waitstill Sharp

In 1939, Martha and Reverend Waitstill Sharp, as representatives of the American Unitarian Association, left their family to travel to Czechoslovakia to see what they could do about citizens—artists, academics, and other anti-Nazi protestors—who were being persecuted by the Nazis. The Sharps helped many find jobs in the U.S. and thereby obtain exit visas. In 1940, the Unitarian Service Committee was organized in response to World War II, and the Sharps were sent to France for a relief and rescue mission. The relief took the form of a large shipment of milk to feed children, while the rescue involved facilitating the emigration of twenty-nine children and ten adults, who otherwise might have been shipped to concentration camps and/or killed. Communicating with their Unitarian Service Committee counterparts in the U.S., the Sharps located families to sponsor the children (many of whom came to the U.S. without their parents), convinced officials to process paperwork, and arranged transatlantic passage for the emigrants.

Merging Youth Groups

The American Unitarian Association and the Universalist Church of America had discussed the possibility of merger for many years. The two liberal faiths held many beliefs in common. They both had youth organizations—American Unitarian Youth (AUY) and Universalist Youth Fellowship—that met in a joint conference in 1951 and merged in 1953 to form Liberal Religious Youth (LRY). The governing bodies of the youth organizations debated, discussed, and voted on the merger, and LRY was formed with its own governing body, thereby establishing youth autonomy as a major theme in the Unitarian Universalist youth movement. During this time, Sam Wright, executive director of AUY, wrote "We Would Be One," Hymn 318 in *Singing the Living Tradition*, about the hopes and dreams that helped drive the merger.

Extended Journaling and
UU Pocket Guide Discussion for Unit 7

Journaling Prompts

Encourage participants to reflect upon the topics covered in this unit in their journals. Pose the following questions to get them started:

- If you could leave your mark on Unitarian Universalism, what would the history books say about you?

- What is to be gained by knowing our Unitarian Universalist story?

UU Pocket Guide Discussion

Ask participants to read "Important Dates in Unitarian Universalist History" before the scheduled discussion or schedule time during your weekly meeting to read and discuss the chapter, using the following questions:

- What themes can you identify in our faith's history?

- Are you surprised by how far back in history our roots go? Tell why or why not.

- What events in our faith's history are familiar to you?

Unitarian Universalist History Resources

Helpful short surveys of Unitarian Universalist history can be found in the opening pages of David Robinson's *The Unitarians and the Universalists*, as well as Harry Scholefield and Paul Sawyer's "Our Roots" found in *The Unitarian Universalist Pocket Guide*.

Sketches, paintings, and photographs are used to create a video history of Unitarian Universalism in *Unitarian Universalism: An Heretical History*, produced by the Unitarian Universalist Church of Rockford, Illinois.

There are also a number of incredibly helpful websites with extensive resources:

The Andover-Harvard Library's Unitarian Universalist Research Guide: *www.hds.harvard.edu/library/research/guides/uu/*

Starr King School for Ministry, online guide to Unitarian Universalist history: *www.sksm.edu/research/uu_history.php*

The Unitarian Universalist Historical Society: *www.uua.org/uuhs/index.html*

Dictionary of Unitarian Universalist Biography: *www.uus.org/uuhs/duub*

Unitarian Universalist Women's History Annotated Bibliography: *www.geocities.com/Wellesley/Garden/1101/history.html*

For more in-depth background, the following books are also valuable resources:

We Would Be One by Wayne Arnason and Rebecca Scott. Boston: Skinner House Books, 2005.

A Chosen Faith: An Introduction to Unitarian Universalism, 2nd edition, by John A. Buehrens and Forrest Church. Boston: Beacon Press, 1998.

The Unitarian Universalist Pocket Guide edited by William Sinkford. Boston: UUA, 2004.

Unitarian Universalism: A Narrative History by David Bumbaugh. Chicago: Meadville-Lombard Press, 2000.

Long Challenge: The Empowerment Controversy (1967–1977) by Victor H. Carpenter. Chicago: Meadville-Lombard Press, 2003.

Universalism in America: A Documentary History of a Liberal Faith edited by Ernest Cassara. Boston: Skinner House Books, 1997.

Historical Dictionary of Unitarian Universalism by Mark W. Harris. Oxford: The Scarecrow Press, Inc., 2004.

The Larger Faith: A Short History of American Universalism by Charles A. Howe. Boston: Skinner House Books, 1993.

Challenge of a Liberal Faith by George N. Marshall. Boston: Skinner House Books, 1988.

Black Pioneers in a White Denomination, 3rd edition by Mark D. Morrison-Reed. Boston: Skinner House Books, 1994.

The Epic of Unitarianism: Original Writings from the History of Liberal Religion compiled by David B. Parke. Boston: Skinner House Books, 1985.

The Unitarians and the Universalists by David Robinson. Westport, CT: Greenwood Press, 1985.

The Premise and the Promise: The Story of the Unitarian Universalist Association by Warren R. Ross. Boston: Skinner House Books, 2001.

Standing Before Us: Unitarian Universalist Women and Social Reform, 1776–1936, edited by Dorothy May Emerson. Boston: Skinner House Books, 2000.

A Stream of Light: A Short History of American Unitarianism edited by Conrad Wright. Boston: Skinner House Books, 1989.

Leadership

I don't know what the future may hold, but I know who holds the future.
—Ralph Abernathy

As young people grow into different roles within Unitarian Universalism, their leadership skills will be needed and solicited. There are many paths to leadership. Congregational, district, regional, and continental youth groups and organizations need chairpersons, secretaries, social action representatives, and other officers. Youth can serve on committees and, in some congregations, on the Board of Trustees. Youth can be service leaders and teachers in religious education classes.

One of the goals of Coming of Age is to help shape a new generation of Unitarian Universalist leaders. The workshops in this unit will help youth identify some of their strengths as leaders and where their interests may lie in congregational leadership.

As youth develop a strong Unitarian Universalist identity, they need to be encouraged to find their own niche in the workings of the congregation. The message you are sending, that youth are welcomed as and even expected to be congregational leaders, can be reinforced by making sure you provide opportunities for them to practice leadership within the program. With a little guidance, youth can lead worship, brainstorming sessions, check-in, and *UU Pocket Guide* discussions.

Workshop 29
The Meaning and Practice of Leadership

Time 90 minutes

Participant Goals

- identify their own leadership qualities

- prepare for possible leadership roles in the youth group and beyond

- determine what leadership means to them

- demonstrate different styles of leadership and the ways these styles complement and support each other

- play leadership roles that they may not typically play

- reflect on peace and conflict in the Unitarian Universalist youth setting and the larger society

- recognize that conflict is a healthy part of life

Materials

- newsprint sheet of leadership quotes (see Preparation)

- components for How You Lead activity: newsprint sheet, plus cut-out petals or flames or one index card per participant (see Preparation)

- newsprint

- markers

- masking tape

- construction paper or index cards

- "Strongly Agree" and "Strongly Disagree" signs (see Preparation)

- one copy of Leader Resource 21, Leadership Quotes, and Leader Resource 22, Leadership Role Characterizations for Actors (pages 191 and 192)

- copies of Handout 23, Leadership Role Characterizations for Audience, and Handout 24, A Youth Leader Is . . . (pages 194 and 195)

- pens or pencils

Preparation

- Write the leadership quotes from Leader Resource 21, Leadership Quotes, on newsprint and post around the room.

- On newsprint, draw a large picture for participants to affix their leadership qualities to, and cut out small pieces of construction paper that correspond with the drawing. For example, for a chalice, cut out one "flame" per participant; for a flower stem and center, cut out one "petal" per participant. If you prefer to keep it simple, write "Coming of Age" on the newsprint and distribute one index card per participant.

- Tear off small pieces of masking tape for taping up index cards/flames/petals.

- Cut a copy of Leader Resource 22, Leadership Role Characterizations for Actors, into six cards, with one leadership role per card.

- Create a masking tape continuum on the floor. Above one end, place a sign that says "Strongly Agree." Near the other end, place a sign that says "Strongly Disagree."

Opening   5 minutes

Use the opening ritual designed by the group.

Follow the Leader   10 minutes

Ask for a volunteer. Tell the group that this person is the leader and that everyone has to do what the leader does. If space permits, line the group up and let the line meander around, always following the leader. If not, the leader can stand in the front of the room facing participants. Switch leaders several times, asking for volunteers. Let everyone who wants a turn get one. Ask the group: Which was more fun, leading or following?

The Meaning of Leadership   10 minutes

Introduce the activity by saying that we all have times when we are followers and times when we are asked to be leaders. Ask participants to name some images that come to mind when they hear the word *leader*. Ask, "Where do we get these images?" Answers might include TV, movies, the government, etc.

Ask the group what characteristics come to mind when they think of a leader; possible answers include good planner, articulate, listens to others, etc. Take notes on newsprint.

Invite a different participant to read aloud each of the quotes about leadership that are posted throughout the room.

Ask, "Does this give you any different ideas about leadership?"

Leadership Role Play   20 minutes

Ask for six volunteers, and give each a different card from Leader Resource 22, Leadership Role Characterizations for Actors. Instruct them to read their descriptions to themselves and not to show them to anyone.

Have the volunteers form a circle on the floor. Tell them that they are having a mock business meeting to plan a youth group retreat. They have three tasks:

- to make a list of the things that need to be done for the retreat

- to choose an item from that list and discuss it

- to make decisions about that item, involving who, what, where, and when

Pass out Handout 23, Leadership Role Characterizations for Audience, and pens or pencils, and ask the other participants to refer to it during the role play. Tell them that their job is to figure out who is playing which role; they can write their guesses down during the role play and discuss them afterward. Explain that the volunteers will participate in the meeting by acting out their assigned roles.

After assigning the tasks, take an observer role. As the business meeting progresses, check to make sure that each volunteer is participating. Do not let the meeting drag on. Draw it to a close once all volunteers have had a chance to act out their characterizations.

When the role play is complete, ask the group to identify which volunteer played which role. Once that is determined, explain to the group that individual people can have many of these characteristics; that every person has a different leadership style that has its strengths and weaknesses; and that being a leader involves learning about and becoming comfortable with your own style of leadership, recognizing your strengths and weaknesses, and working with them.

Ask for questions and comments.

How You Lead   10 minutes

Pass out one index card (or petal or flame) for each participant, and invite participants to quietly reflect on their particular gifts as leaders. Point out that there are many different leadership skills and that no one embodies all of them. That is one of the reasons that shared leadership is so important: We each complement the gifts of the others.

Ask them to decide on the attributes of their personalities that most enable them to be good leaders and write these on the cards. Have them share their gifts and tape their cards up on the newsprint.

When the picture is complete, let everyone admire it and tell them you hope that this Coming of Age program will bring more of their leadership skills to light. Pass out Handout 24, A Youth Leader Is . . . , and remind the group that as they grow older there will be more opportunities for them to serve as leaders in the Unitarian Universalist sphere.

Sources of Conflict   10 minutes

Share with participants that leaders must deal with conflict and that being able to handle it is an important leadership skill. Invite participants to reflect on times when they have experienced conflict. Invite them to name some of the settings in which they experience conflict.

The Opinion Continuum   15 minutes

The goal of this activity is to give participants an opportunity to share their thoughts and experiences of conflict.

Introduce this activity by saying something like the following:

A conflict is a disagreement or dispute between two or more people. It's a natural part of life that many people, both adults and youth, have mixed feelings about and a range of experience with, both good and bad. I'm going to read a series of things people commonly say about conflict. After each one I read, place yourself along the continuum at the point that best expresses your feelings about that statement. You can choose to stand with "strongly agree," "strongly disagree," or anywhere in between. There are no right or wrong responses, and passing is always an option. During this exercise, there are a few things to remember: Respect the privacy of others, don't gossip about what others say and try to stay on the topic, and use "I" statements.

These are the statements to read:

- Conflicts nearly always destroy relationships.

- In every conflict, there is a winner and a loser.

- In every conflict, one person is right and one person is wrong.

- Conflict should be avoided at all costs.

- It is important to speak up for what you believe in even if others do not agree.

- It is important to speak up for what you believe in even if other people may try to harm you for doing so.

- If someone hits you, it is best to hit back.

- If you are in a conflict, it helps if you keep your feelings to yourself.

After you have read the first statement and participants have taken their places along the line, ask clusters who are standing near each other to talk together for one minute about why they are standing where they are. Then ask individual participants to share some of their reasons for choosing that point with the larger group. Make sure to solicit participation from people at different places on the continuum. If everyone in the group chooses the same position, stand on the "empty" side and articulate a viewpoint sympathetic to that position. Likewise, if only one participant is standing opposite the rest of the group, stand by that person and offer a supportive viewpoint.

Discussion   5 minutes

Use the following questions to lead discussion:

- What conclusions can you draw from this activity?

- Did anything happen that surprised you?

- Which statement did you find most challenging?

- What does Unitarian Universalism say about conflict? (Possible answers include our Principles inspire us to respect others; you can disagree and still think someone has inherent worth and dignity; acceptance of one another is not equal to agreement.)

Closing Circle   5 minutes

Use the closing ritual designed by the group.

Workshop 30
Leadership in Congregational Life

Time   75 minutes

Participant Goals

- discover some of the varied possibilities for congregational leadership

- meet leaders in the congregation

- consider invitations to adopt leadership roles now and in the future

- view congregational leadership as a fun and rewarding privilege of congregational life

Materials

- newsprint

- markers

- hints about panel members (see Preparation)

- handout describing congregational leadership roles (see Preparation)

- paper

- pens or pencils

- poster board

- tape

- name cards for panel members (see Preparation)

- a long table

- special snack, such as pizza or ice cream (remember to check registration forms to avoid allergens)

- optional: tablecloth, timer, streamers, poster saying "What's My Role?" with photographs of congregational functions, music, CD player, stage props

Preparation

- Recruit four congregational leaders for "What's My Role?" several weeks ahead of time. Aim for diversity within the panel by role, length of time with the congregation, age, gender, and other identities; if possible, include an older youth. Try to avoid congregational leaders who are so obvious that youth will guess them quickly. Many leaders play several roles within the congregation. If a youth advisor is also a greeter, recruit that person for the greeter role. Think outside the box and invite players who work behind the scenes, like the sexton; the chair of the Committee on Ministry, Denominational Affairs, or Finance Committee; or the person who manages the congregation's website. Explain how the game is played and what is required from them, including a two- to three-minute presentation on their leadership role in the congregation. Stay in touch with panel members and contact them the week before the workshop to confirm attendance and answer any questions. Ask them to arrive fifteen minutes before the scheduled time of the workshop.

- Write one-line hints about each panel member equal to the total number of "yes" answers possible in the game. Start off with hints that give away little ("member of a committee") and progress to broader hints ("works closely with the religious educator"). Witty hints are good (for example, "Always in hot water!" for kitchen committee person). You want the teams to be able to guess correctly, but not too quickly, because the hints also serve the purpose of telling them about the service this panel member provides to your congregation ("organizes the Martin Luther King Day march"). Panel members might have good suggestions for hints.

- Create a handout that describes as many congregational leadership roles as possible, including the roles your panel members play. Be broad in your definition of leadership to help youth understand that it takes many hands to keep their faith home up and running. Your congregation might already have such a document to give to new members. Ask your religious educator, church administrator, or membership chair. Add to the document, if needed.

- Decorate your room for the game show as time allows. You will need a long table with four chairs. A tablecloth will help hold the name cards and make the room more festive. Consider adding stage props, streamers, a poster that says "What's My Role?" and photographs of congregational functions.

- On the day of the workshop, show the panel where they will sit and provide another room for them to wait in until the game starts. Give members a small piece of poster board with tape on one side and ask them to print their names on the non-taped side.

Opening 5 minutes

Use the opening ritual designed by the group.

Meeting Congregational Leaders 5 minutes

Tell participants that today you will be focusing on leadership in congregational life. Ask them to name leaderships roles that exist in your congregation. Inform youth that several congregational leaders will be joining today's meeting. Brainstorm a list of questions they might ask the leaders.

Possible questions include the following:

- What do you enjoy about doing this work?

- How did you become a congregational leader?

- What other roles have you filled within the congregation?

- How has your work deepened your faith or commitment to Unitarian Universalism?

- What personal strengths come in handy in your work?

- What are some congregational leadership roles youth can fill?

- What was your involvement with congregational life when you were our age?

- In our last meeting, we talked about a couple of the challenges of leadership: finding your strengths and dealing with conflict. What other challenges have you experienced?

What's My Role?   40 minutes

Explain to participants that you are going to play a game called "What's My Role?" with a panel of four people who serve in one or more leadership positions in the congregation. Pass out the handout that describes these roles. Form teams and explain the game by saying something like the following:

- Each team can ask three "yes or no" questions. [Adjust the number of questions depending upon the size and number of teams you have guessing.]

- For every "yes" answer, I will reveal a hint to the entire group.

- At any point, a team can announce that it is ready to make a guess.

- Guesses will be written and given to the moderator.

- If the team guesses correctly, they get a point. If they guess incorrectly, they can't guess again until all questions have been asked.

- All teams must make a guess after all questions have been asked.

Ask if there are any questions about the rules, then divide participants into teams of two to four. Let each team decide how they will come up with their questions. They could let every member have one question (if needed, set the number of questions higher to allow for this possibility) or they could plan questions together. Keep track of time so that this planning step does not drag on too long. Objectively decide the order of the groups for questions. Give each team paper and pens or pencils.

Once this is all set, invite the panel into the room. Have them sit behind a table and tape their name cards on the edge of the table in front of them. Panel members should introduce themselves with their names, ages, and number of years affiliated with the congregation or years of membership.

As teams ask questions, post a hint on the wall behind the panel member for each "yes" answer. Alternate questions amongst the panel so that Person A answers one question from all teams, then Person B, then C, and so on. Embellish the game as much as you like by changing the lighting in the room or adding theme music or stage props.

After all the questioning, allow each team one last chance to guess. Then identify any panel member's role not yet guessed. Tally the points and congratulate the winning team. Thank everyone for playing and say that everyone has won a special snack. Point out that serving the congregation is a privilege, and offer the winning team the privilege of serving the group.

Questions for the Panel   15 minutes

Invite panel members to take a few minutes to describe what they do in their roles. After all panel members have spoken, ask youth if they have any questions. Use the questions from the brainstorming session and any others. If youth are hesitant, ask the panel members to look over the questions brainstormed earlier and pick one or two that they would like to answer. Thank the panel for coming.

Reflection   5 minutes

Invite participants to share anything they discovered during today's activities. Refer to the handout of leadership roles. Point out that with so many different roles, you are sure they will find a place where their interests, skills, and leadership styles intersect to create a congregational leadership role for them. Ask if anyone has already served in such a role (child care provider, religious education group assistant, chalice lighter for a service, organizer of an activity at a retreat, etc.). Let the group know of any opportunities for congregational leadership that exist now and invite them to talk to you or one of the panel members if they are interested in any of these opportunities.

Closing Circle   5 minutes

Use the closing ritual designed by the group.

Leadership Quotes

Leadership is going out ahead to show the way.
—Robert Greenleaf

We make a living from what we get: We make a life from what we give.
—Winston Churchill

You take people as far as they will go, not as far as you would like them to go.
—Jeannette Rankin

Time is neutral and does not change things. With courage and initiative, leaders change things.
—Jesse Jackson

A leader takes people where they want to go. A great leader takes people where they don't necessarily want to go but ought to be.
—Rosalynn Carter

Cautious, careful people, always casting about to preserve their reputation and social standing, never can bring about a reform. Those who are really in earnest must be willing to be anything or nothing in the world's estimation, and publicly and privately, in season and out, avow their sympathy with despised and persecuted ideas and their advocates, and bear the consequences.
—Susan B. Anthony

A leader is best when people barely know he exists. When the work is done, the people will say: We did it ourselves.
—Lao Tze

Anyone who thinks they are too small to make a difference has never been in bed with a mosquito.
—African proverb

What lies beyond us and what lies before us are tiny matters when compared to what lies within us.
—Ralph Waldo Emerson

A community is like a ship: Everyone ought to be prepared to take the helm.
—Henrik Ibsen

Leadership Role Characterizations for Actors

Informer: Define the problem and keep the group aware of the facts.

Sample lines:

What exactly is the situation?

Are these ideas realistic?

Summarizer: Clarify and summarize all the ideas that have been said. Work toward a solution. Make sure all team members know what their responsibilities are.

Sample lines:

Well, it looks like we're all in agreement. Shall we move on?

Harmonizer: Make sure the meeting builds community, not tension.

Sample lines:

How is everyone feeling right now?

Let's take a break to ease the harsh feelings.

Big Dreamer: Keep everyone's mind open to possibilities outside the norm.

Sample lines:

This makes me think of so many amazing possibilities!

Let's do something that reaches beyond the constraints of our denomination. Let's dream big!

Includer: Make sure everyone's voice is being heard.

Sample lines:

(Someone's name), we haven't heard your opinion on this yet.

That's a good idea, but remember what _____ said about _____.

Purpose Watcher: Keep the solutions in line with the purposes of the group and the Principles of the Unitarian Universalist community.

Sample lines:

Does that solution include people of backgrounds different from ours?

Does that solution show our respect for the earth?

Extended Journaling for Unit 8

Encourage participants to reflect upon the topics covered in this unit in their journals. Pose the following questions to get them started:

- Write a thank-you letter to a congregational leader who has influenced your life.

- What areas of congregational life are you interested in exploring more deeply? How will you get started?

Leadership Role Characterizations for Audience

Informer

Defines the problem and keeps the group aware of the facts.

Harmonizer

Makes sure the meeting builds community, not tension.

Includer

Makes sure everyone's voice is being heard.

Summarizer

Clarifies and summarizes all the ideas that have been said. Works toward a solution. Makes sure all team members know what their responsibilities are.

Big Dreamer

Keeps everyone's mind open to possibilities outside the norm.

Purpose Watcher

Keeps the solutions in line with the purposes of the group and the Principles of the Unitarian Universalist community.

A Youth Leader Is . . .

- someone who recognizes personal limitations and asks for help when needed.

- the "entertainer," the "informer," the "quiet commander," the person who pushes the limits, the facilitator who brings it all together.

- someone who holds the space for youth to be youth.

- someone who listens to others, not just with the ears, but more importantly, with the heart.

- someone who steps outside of his/her comfort zone to grow and evolve as a person.

- someone who can pick out the main goals and desires from another's heartfelt but disorganized ramble or rant.

- someone who can be like a booster on a rocket, helping to propel the astronauts to space but not actually going to the moon.

- someone who inspires others.

- someone who supports any youth, especially those who have dreams and ideas to share.

- someone who cares for everyone and allows no room for being judgmental.

- someone who takes the initiative to make things happen in the community.

- someone who demonstrates youth empowerment in anything from moderating the energy of a group to facilitating a business meeting.

- someone who responds well to needs of the group, whatever they are.

- someone who is responsible and reliable.

- someone who can motivate another person to create change.

- someone who shares power with adults and works with them toward a common goal.

- someone who has a combination of strength, intelligence, and passion and uses these talents to encourage other youth to voice their opinions and act on their beliefs.

- someone who doesn't tell everyone what needs to be done but allows them to come to that conclusion through their own processes.

- like any other leader, except for being a youth.

- a person people trust and respect.

- someone who knows when to step up and step down.

- willing to fill leadership roles and speak out against injustices like racism and bigotry.

- willing to make a ridiculous fool of him- or herself.

- someone who models inclusion and works actively to achieve community.

- able to see and feel beyond themselves, to be aware of how other youth are reacting, and to see how that affects the entire group dynamic.

- a vital part of the UU movement.

- a youth who leads by example, by consensus, by inspiration, and by identifying, developing, and empowering fellow youth.

—Young Religious Unitarian Universalist Leadership Development Conference Training, 2004, adapted

Closure

The young do not know enough to be prudent, and therefore they attempt the impossible —and achieve it, generation after generation.

—Pearl S. Buck

The nature of your closing celebration will be influenced by what comes before and after it, so this workshop is composed of several suggested activities. Pick the ones that hold the most meaning for your group.

If there will be no Service of Recognition, this should be your last meeting. It will be a joyful time for the entire Coming of Age community to hear credos and covenants of belief; exchange gifts, wishes, and promises for the future; and celebrate a program well done. Mentors are needed in the celebration, so make sure it is scheduled for a time when they can attend. If you can, invite families of youth in the program or, at the very least, their parents.

If there will be a worship service acknowledging the work done in the program, you might hold this workshop immediately before or after that service. It could also be held during the workshop's regular time or on a Saturday night after the rehearsal for the Service of Recognition. In that case, concentrate more on the celebratory aspects, since sharing credos and other activities will be part of the worship service.

If your program is holding a Rites of Passage retreat, some activities from this workshop could be included at that event. As written here, parents are invited to this workshop, but they probably won't be invited to a Rites of Passage retreat.

However, if you wish to include activities with parents in a retreat, you can schedule these activities before or as part of closing worship on Sunday morning, since most parents will come to the retreat Sunday morning to pick up their youth.

Workshop 31
Closing Celebration

Time   60 to 90 minutes

Participant Goals

- review their experiences in the Coming of Age program

- further solidify memories of the program

- celebrate accomplishments with the entire program community

- link the program with their future in the congregation

Materials

- small (3" x 4" or 3" x 6") brightly colored pillar candle per attendee

- matches

- two sheets of decorating beeswax per attendee, in a variety of colors

- small cutters in different shapes for the beeswax

- credos (optional)

- refreshments, plates, cups, napkins (see Preparation)

- trifold presentation board (see Preparation)

- photographs (see Preparation)

- pushpins or other attachment devices for the presentation board

- headings for presentation board (see Preparation)

- gifts for mentors (see Preparation)

- music for the party (optional)

- camera (optional)

- one sheet of plain paper per attendee (optional)

- dark-colored markers (optional)

- individual or newsprint evaluations (optional, see Preparation)

- adhesive dots in three different colors (optional)

Preparation

- At least two weeks before this workshop, ask mentors, youth, and families to contribute photographs of events that happened during the program. Post the photographs on a trifold presentation board and attach headings (for example, "Fall Retreat" or "Community Service Project"). If possible, have extra copies of the photographs for participants to take home.

- Test the markers to make sure they will not bleed through the paper and stain clothing.

- Refreshments are needed for the party. Consider asking families to provide these. Serving only finger foods eliminates the need for cutlery.

- Assemble sculptures from Workshop 20 (see page 131) or invite youth to write poems or letters as gifts for their mentors.

- Optional: If youth are receiving gifts during this workshop, make sure you collect the gifts well ahead of time.

- Optional: Create your evaluation forms. You might include boxes for youth to check if they are willing to speak at future parent-youth orientations or to write an article for the congregational newsletter. Another option is to label several sheets of newsprint on the walls with headings for the major events of the program. These sheets could include activities such as "Social Action Project," "Rites of Passage," "Worship," or "Journaling." They also could include topics like "Theology," "UU History," and "Credos." Under each topic, list activities included in the workshops conducted. For additional feedback, label one sheet "Comments."

Opening   5 minutes

Use the opening ritual designed by the group.

Celebrating Our Many Gifts   10 to 15 minutes

Invite youth to take turns sharing one thing they learned about their mentors that they had not known before. After sharing, youth should present their mentors with gifts. These could be the gifts made in Workshop 20, Connecting to the Natural World (see page 131), or poems or letters written especially for this occasion.

If youth are not being given gifts during a Service of Recognition or Rites of Passage retreat, they can receive gifts during this time. Common gifts are chalices, chalice pendants, or pins. See Services of Recognition (page 242) for other ideas.

Gifts for any other participants, such as leaders or parents, can also be given at this time.

Celebrating the Future   25 minutes

Say something like the following:

As graduates of the Coming of Age program, you represent a large piece of the future of Unitarian Universalism. Each of you brings many gifts; some may bring the gift of courage, some the gift of singing, and some the gift of their questions. We thank you for the gifts you will bring to Unitarian Universalism and for allowing us, your leaders, to share in those gifts during the program.

Display the candles and say, "These are candles of the future. Like the Coming of Age participants, they are full of the potential to shine!" Invite everyone present to decorate a candle, using the small cutters to cut out shapes from the sheets of beeswax, or rolling and pressing the beeswax into shapes that can be pressed onto the pillar candles.

If you have more time and money to spend on a longer project, provide sheets of beeswax and let participants roll the beeswax to create the entire candle. If you choose to do this, you might suggest that families and mentors work together to create one or two candles instead of providing individual candles for everyone.

Gather everyone together with their candles. Say, in your own words,

> Everyone in this room contributed to the Coming of Age program in their own way. By this, we all helped carry Unitarian Universalism forward. I'd like to share with you a reading from Albert Schweitzer: "At times, our own light goes out and is rekindled by a spark from another person. Each of us has cause to think with deep gratitude of those who have lighted the flame within us."

As you finish reading, light your candle; if there is a lit chalice in the room, light your candle from there. Turn to someone else, perhaps your co-leader, and say, "Thank you for lighting my flame." This person should light another candle, thanking that person, and so on until all candles are lit. Once all the candles are lit, ask everyone to take a moment to reflect silently upon the growth they have experienced in the past year. After several seconds, join together in saying "To the future!" and blowing out the candles.

If your congregation invites graduates to become members of the congregation and this invitation has not yet been extended, now would be a good time to do it.

Celebrating Us!   15 to 35 minutes

While those present are eating and socializing, invite them to view the photograph and memory board. If you were able to obtain extra copies of photographs, let youth know they can take home copies of photographs. Take photographs during the party, too. Music is optional.

Optional Activity

Celebrating Memories

Using masking tape, tape a sheet of plain paper to each person's back collar, including leaders and mentors. Give out markers and invite participants to write memories on one another's papers; the memories should involve something the person did during the program. Once done, everyone can take off the papers and read what people will remember about them.

Optional Activity

Evaluations

If you decided to ask for evaluations, you can provide forms to be completed during the party. If you are using newsprint evaluations, give youth five colored dots each to put on their favorite experiences. Use dots of different colors for mentors and for parents who have been heavily involved.

Closing Circle   5 minutes

Use the closing ritual designed by the group.

Extended Journaling for Unit 9

Encourage participants to reflect upon the topics covered in this unit in their journals. Pose the following questions to get them started:

- What memories of the Coming of Age program do you hope to keep?

- If you have photos, attach them to your journal.

Community Service Projects

There are several reasons why adding a community service project to your Coming of Age program is recommended. Such a project encourages youth to fulfill their responsibilities as members of a community, reinforces Unitarian Universalist values, fosters connections in the community, feeds a desire to be an agent of change, and can be fun!

Service is not a word that is always looked upon favorably in our society, yet it is crucial that young people understand the privileges and responsibilities involved in being part of a community. Whether the community is the Flower Committee, the congregation, a neighborhood, or the human race, there are certain expectations of membership. One of these is that members will support the community not just in words, but with deeds. Although no group can function well without this involvement, in many communities the majority of the work is done by a handful of members. If we wish to nurture empathetic and responsible Unitarian Universalists, we must cultivate service to our communities.

Community service projects promote an ethic of service, which upholds the UU belief in the interconnectedness of all life and emphasizes our collective responsibility to serve all of its members equally. Many activities in this handbook provide opportunities for young people to look inward; community service focuses them outward. During the project, participants will meet new people and come to understand that they belong to the same community.

These projects often focus on meeting the needs of the traditionally underserved, such as low-income families or the elderly. However, community service involves helping wherever the needs exist. Sometimes communities with a wealth of resources have difficulty meeting their needs alone. Community service should not be about helping "those poor people." It should always be performed with the recognition that we are all connected and we all need help sometimes.

The project provides a testing ground for youth to discover how their Unitarian Universalist identities and faith play out in the world. Our faith has a long tradition of coupling beliefs with action. Engaging participants in a service project lays the expectation that they will follow in that tradition. Following the community service project with a social action project could inspire youth to continue the work of making the world a better place throughout their lives.

Many youth will enjoy the project because it is a welcome change of pace from the regular meetings. It may involve physical activity and place them in an interesting and different setting; a project that involves being outside might be especially welcome. Working on the project allows youth to be together in a new way and encourages group cohesion. And youth with skills that are not evident in a workshop setting might shine at using a hammer and nails or cooking!

Setting aside time to plan and process the experience helps to specifically connect the activity to the Unitarian Universalist religious tradition and allows youth to put into words how their outlooks have been affected. In Session 2, Complete and Process the Project (see page 204), youth ask questions at three levels: "What," which asks for a description of the activity; "So what," which leads them to make meaning of the experience by asking what has changed as a result; and "Now what," which questions how the experience will affect their future actions.

For example, a youth who took part in a nursing home visit might process the experience this way: "We visited a nursing home for Christmas and had fun singing carols and eating cookies" (What). "We had decided to spend the holidays giving to others instead of just opening presents to see what others gave us. People always say it's better to give than to receive, so we put those words into action." (So what). "I don't know a lot of old people and I was a little nervous about going, but they were pretty cool. I won't be nervous next time" (Now what).

The answer to "Now what" in this example shows us that a successful community service project can help youth gain confidence in their abilities to deal with new situations, remind them to think about the less visible members of our communities, and give them confidence for taking further actions.

Planning

Community service projects in Coming of Age programs vary greatly from congregation to congregation, ranging from one-day projects to those that convene weekly and span a period of months. Serving food at homeless shelters, helping to build affordable housing, collecting newspapers for animal shelters, and conducting food drives are just a few of the projects congregations have offered. No matter what the project, thorough planning is essential and should begin as early as several months in advance, if possible.

The coordination of a successful project involves these steps:

Know your resources. Program leaders may be familiar with many service organizations in their community. Ministers, religious educators, congregational social action committees, and participating families, including youth, can all be valuable resources for identifying possible sites. Ideas can also come from the Internet and books like *When Youth Lead*, by Jill M. Schwendeman, and *The Kid's Guide to Service Projects: Over 500 Service Ideas for Young People Who Want to Make a Difference*, by Barbara A. Lewis and Pamela Espeland.

Research and clarify. Find out what types of projects youth are interested in. It can be helpful to present a variety of possibilities and let them select a project; they will be more likely to be enthusiastic about work they have chosen. If the need to plan in advance makes it impossible to solicit input from the group, perhaps the previous Coming of Age class can choose the project for the next year's group.

Clarify requirements with potential sites before confirming participation. Some organizations, including several Habitat for Humanity affiliates, require their volunteers to be at least sixteen. Others, such as food distribution warehouses, may want only volunteers who can carry at least twenty pounds on their own.

Choose projects with potential for transformation. Sites that involve personal interaction are more transformative than those where there is no opportunity to meet people. For example, an afternoon of serving food to people with HIV will make more of an impression than sorting canned goods in a warehouse. Preparing school supply packets for migrant farmworkers' children might be more comfortable than working side by side with migrant farm-worker families to build a school, but the latter project will be a richer experience because it takes youth outside their comfort zones. Similarly, baking cookies for isolated elderly people will not generate as much growth as delivering those cookies in person, along with conversation.

Build in time for group process. Schedule time before the project for framing the experience, and afterward for discussing reactions:

- Several months to a year in advance, begin contacting potential sites to learn what would be a good fit for the group in terms of age, ability, and potential for transformation. Once a few possible sites are identified, present them to the Coming of Age youth to discover which projects interest them the most.

- It is essential to receive written permission from parents for youth to participate in the community service project. It can be incorporated into the general Coming of Age permission form or obtained separately.

- Additionally, some community service sites require that participants and their parents sign a waiver of liability. If such forms are required, they will need to be obtained far enough in advance that parents have the opportunity to complete and return them.

- In making arrangements for drivers to and from the project, be sure to conform to the congregation's policy on drivers of children and youth. Ensure that every car will have at least one adult and at least one passenger with a mobile phone, if possible. Compile a list of cell phone numbers in advance, and note who is riding in the car with that cell phone number. Ideally, this list should be distributed to every adult. Provide each driver clear directions to and from the site.

During Session 1, the group will choose and plan the project and explore their expectations. In Session 2, they will process their experience. Hold the second session as soon as possible after finishing the project, either on the same day or at the next meeting. Leaders are invited to do some processing on their own before meeting with the group, using any of the activities in the session. The questions "What," "So what," and "Now what" can serve as guidelines in discussion. To be most effective, lead participants in the "What" activity first, then through one or both "So what" activities, and one or more of the "Now what" activities.

Session 1
Introduce the Project

Time 60 minutes

Participant Goals

- choose a community service project

- begin to understand what opportunities for service are available in the local community

- reflect upon how it feels to receive help

- practice group decision-making skills

- examine some of the unmet needs of the community

- bond with the group as they work toward a common goal

- develop a sense of empowerment in the face of complex and significant social problems

Materials

- list of community service project options (see Preparation)

- newsprint

- markers

- journals

- pens or pencils

- paper for drawing, crayons, markers, and colored pencils

- CD player

- CD that includes "Lean On Me," written by Bill Withers (Withers originally recorded the song in 1972, but youth might recognize a 1987 cover by Club Noveau)

Preparation

- Compile a list of project options.

- Have the music ready in the CD player.

Opening   5 minutes

Use the opening ritual designed by the group.

Guided Meditation   10 minutes

Have the song "Lean On Me" playing as participants enter. After everyone is settled, ask if anyone knows the name of the song. If not, identify it. Invite participants to take a few moments, get comfortable, close their eyes, and relax while you lead them through a short meditation. Turn the volume of the music to low. In a slow, soothing cadence, say,

> Think about a time when a group of people helped you or your family. It might have been when there was a birth or death in your family and members of the congregation or another group brought food. It might have been when a group of friends helped you move. Maybe you started a new school and your teacher and classmates helped you find your way around or figure out your new schedule. You might have started a new sport. Who helped you learn the rules and how to play the game?
>
> If you cannot think of a time when a group helped you, think of a time when one person helped you.
>
> • How did being helped make you feel?
>
> • Did you appreciate their help? Was it nice to know someone was thinking of you and your needs?
>
> • Did you feel more connected to those who helped you?
>
> • If it was with a group, did you feel good about the group because it helped you when you were in need?
>
> • Did you feel more connected to the group at the time? Recalling the memory, do you feel more connected to others in the group now?
>
> Think about capturing that experience and those feelings in either words or pictures. When you are ready, open your eyes, and use either your journal or the art supplies to capture that memory and those feelings.

Allow the rest of the time for journaling and drawing. Let participants know that in the next session they can share their memories, if they so choose. Tell them to keep the drawings and journals for the next step in this process.

Choosing a Project   15 minutes

Introduce the project by saying, "Today we are going to start our community service project. Even though this group and our congregation are communities, our project will involve service to other communities. Why do we want to encourage people to community service?"

Participants might share that our Principles and Unitarian Universalist beliefs in justice and the interconnectedness of all beings call us to community service. Other answers might include that you get to meet people you might not otherwise meet; that everybody needs help sometimes and it makes us feel good to help others; that you have a responsibility to help the communities you are part of. Affirm that these are all valid reasons. Share that as Unitarian Universalists, we believe that belonging to a community is a privilege that comes with the responsibility to help take care of the community; you cannot have the privilege without the responsibility.

Let the group know that you (or others) have researched community service projects that welcome young people and are doable within the program's time frame. As you present the options, write the name of or a phrase describing the project on newsprint, along with the community being served and how the youth are part of that community. For example, if you are presenting a project with the local animal shelter, the community is animals and we are animals, too. If it is a project at a nursing home, the immediate community is the elderly. However, these elderly live in your city, so the shared community is the city. If you are helping in a voter registration drive, the shared community is citizens.

Using consensus or voting, decide upon a project.

Planning the Project   10 minutes

Make a list of any resources needed for the project. Assign participants to bring materials or provide help in coordinating the activity. Make sure youth have the support they will need to carry out any assignments given.

Acting Out Expectations   10 minutes

Ask for volunteers to present a skit showing what they think the experience will be like. Let the actors have three minutes to plan their skit. While they are planning, play "Lean On Me" with the volume low.

Perform the skit(s). Applaud the performers. If you have time and other volunteers, perform more skits, giving actors different possible scenarios or letting them devise their own. Do not be surprised if skits become silly; participants might feel a bit of anxiety about the project, and this could surface as silliness. Between the skits, play "Lean On Me." Invite the "audience" to dance if they feel like it.

Process the skits with the following questions:

- Are there other expectations besides those presented in the skit?

- Can you describe a time when things did not happen as you expected?

- Do you think there will be things that surprise you when you are at this project?

Recognize that there are no right answers to these questions; youth's ideas will come from their own perspectives, which are likely to be different from an adult's perspective.

Logistical Questions   5 minutes

Invite and respond to questions about the work the project will involve, what items participants need to bring, etc.

Closing   5 minutes

Use the closing ritual designed by the group.

Session 2
Complete and Process the Project

Time   45 minutes

Participant Goals

- participate in an actual community service project

- reflect upon how it feels to give help

- connect to the wider community

- experience how working together as a group amplifies the community service experience

- practice being Unitarian Universalist people of faith in the community

- develop a sense of empowerment in the face of complex and significant social problems

Materials

- journals

- drawing paper

- pens or pencils

- markers, crayons, and/or pastels

- computer with Internet access (optional, see Preparation)

Preparation

- Optional: If you decide to include a guest speaker, identify someone who is familiar with policies and programs that affect the population served by the project and is comfortable engaging youth in discussion; a high-school youth who has knowledge in a relevant area can be an excellent resource. Issue the invitation a few weeks in advance. Ask the speaker to prepare a three- to five-minute presentation that reinforces the work of the project and to be prepared for questions. Stay in touch with the speaker, and confirm attendance a few days before this session.

- Optional: Prepare material on the social justice work of the Unitarian Universalist Association.

At *www.uua.org/socialjustice/index.shtml*, you will find a list of various groups, such as the Unitarian Universalist Association's Washington Office for Advocacy. Research the work of one or more of these groups. If you will not have access to a computer with Internet capability during the wrap-up, print out materials to share with youth.

Completing the Project   variable

During the project, as well as before and after, take time to connect the activity to the values and history of the Unitarian Universalist religious tradition. You might check with the minister or religous educator in advance for their suggestions.

After the project, convene the group and discuss the experience.

Opening   5 minutes

Use the opening ritual designed by the group.

"What" Activity

Picture Pairs   15 minutes

Ask participants to think of meaningful images or scenes from the project, perhaps a moment when they felt particularly helpful. Invite everyone to either journal or sketch a drawing that portrays the project experience. They should use the same medium as in the guided meditation from Session 1 (see page 202). After five minutes, ask participants to compare what they did today to their journaling or drawing from the previous session. Say something like, "Think about the feelings involved in both memories. How did your feelings while you were helping compare to your feelings while being helped?" Take a few comments before moving on to the next activity.

"So What" Activities

Choose one or more of these activities.

Learning More about the Issues   10 minutes

Introduce the speaker. Following the presentation, invite questions.

Relating It Back to the Principles   10 minutes

Lead a discussion with youth, based on these questions:

- How does your experience doing community service connect to the seven Unitarian Universalist Principles?

- Which Principles are more relevant? Which are less relevant?

- Was it a challenge to live out the Unitarian Universalist Principles during the project?

"Now What" Activities

Choose one or more of these activities.

Looking at the Future   10 minutes

Start a discussion with the following questions:

- Do you think this experience might affect how you think? If so, in what ways?

- Do you think this experience might cause you to act differently? If so, how?

What Would a UU Do?   10 minutes

Ask the group the following questions:

- What actions could a Unitarian Universalist take to address this social issue?

- What could a Unitarian Universalist congregation do to address it?

- What could groups of Unitarian Universalist congregations do together to address it?

If you have access to the Internet, show participants how to access the UUA website at *www.uua.org*. From there, click on the link "I am interested in social justice"; it will take you to a site with resources and information on the issues of current concern within the Association.

If you do not have access to the Internet, give the group the information you printed out in advance. Remind them that the Unitarian Universalist Association exists to provide resources to congregations like theirs in many areas, including social action.

Decision to Take Action   10 minutes

At this point, the group can decide whether they would like to do a social action project related to the issue(s) their community service project addressed. You or the guest speaker should be prepared with suggestions. Spend the time available working out as many details as you can. There will be time later to finish designing the social action project.

Closing   5 minutes

Use the closing ritual designed by the group.

Social Action Projects

Rather than provide direct community service, social action projects attempt to directly influence the forces and structures that oppress and cause injustice. For many congregations and their youth, this sort of social involvement is unprecedented. We are more accustomed to the activities of community service—food drives, highway cleanups, and tutoring, all designed to meet immediate needs—than we are to the activities of social justice—gathering signatures, lobbying, and making lifestyle changes, all designed to alter forces and institutions that maintain and uphold oppression and injustice.

Although social action may be new to Coming of Age participants, it is at the heart of our religious tradition and represents an exciting opportunity to join a long and proud history of Unitarians and Universalists who brought their values to life. Our Association's and congregations' work for civil marriage equality for all couples, civil rights for people of color, women's right to choose, modern slaves' right to freedom, and international peace are but a few examples of our organized social action involvement. The UUA Washington Office for Advocacy and Justice (UUAWO) employs multiple staff who work toward these ends around the clock, often providing a religious voice to counterbalance those more frequently in the public sphere.

Nonprofit organizations such as churches cannot endorse candidates, but they can take stands on social issues in keeping with their convictions. For clarification, see the UUAWO's "Advocacy Resources" at *www.uua.org/socialjustice/resources*, particularly "The Real Rules" at *www.uua.org/documents/washingtonoffice/real_rules.pdf*.

The spiral-planning process was designed by Rev. John Millspaugh to help youth think critically in creating their own social action project. (See Handout 25, Spiral Planning, page 214). It is a linear process of defined stages, in which later stages spiral back to earlier stages and mutually interact with them to give rise to the final outcome.

Session 1 presents a model you can use to help your group pick a social action project. Feel free to use all or some of the activities. Session 2 involves conducting and processing the project.

Session 1
Choose the Project

Time   90 minutes

Participant Goals

- choose a social action project
- practice the critical-thinking skills essential to social action
- practice group decision-making skills
- develop a sense of empowerment in the face of complex and significant social problems

Materials

- newsprint
- markers
- masking tape
- Leader Resource 25, Narrowing In on a Focus (page 213)

- copies of Handout 25, Spiral Planning (page 214)

- copies of Handout 26, Wisdom from UU Activists (page 215)

- copies of Handout 27, Commitment (page 216)

- five small adhesive dots per participant

- index cards

- pens or pencils

- calendar

- congregational calendar (optional)

Preparation

- The spiral-planning process is relatively rigorous. It is included because it teaches critical-thinking skills, but if you are concerned that it may be too involved for your group, decide whether to use a simplified version.

- Draw a grid on a sheet of newsprint, following the outline presented in Leader Resource 25, Narrowing In on a Focus. Leave space to list names of power brokers and their concerns.

Opening   5 minutes

Use the opening ritual designed by the group.

Generating Criteria   10 minutes

Say something along the lines of, "Today we're going to decide how we want to stand up together for social justice. We'll choose and begin to plan our social action project, using a process called spiral planning. We'll go around and around a spiral until we make it to the center, where we reach our final decision." Pass out Handout 25, Spiral Planning, and let participants look it over and comment.

Say, "The first step is "Generating Criteria," which means coming up with our ideas for what makes a good social action project. What would a good social action project be like?" Remind the group that they are brainstorming, so all responses are fine.

Note: If your group is still struggling with abstract thinking, you may want to skip this step

and leave the discussion of criteria until they are actually choosing the project, at which point you can casually bring up these considerations.

Ask for a volunteer to list responses on a piece of newsprint. Have them title the sheet "Criteria for a Social Action Project." During this and all brainstorming, encourage as wide a range of responses as possible by welcoming all contributions. Avoid the pitfall of praising some responses and questioning others. Clarifying what a speaker means is always appropriate, but using questions to advocate your own set of values (in this stage of the conversation) will only inhibit a full and honest exploration of youth's concerns and beliefs.

If youth need prompting, ask leading questions. Once the group's ideas begin to run out, you can pass out Handout 26, Wisdom from UU Activists. Invite the group to consider adding ideas from that list to their list of criteria.

The ideas from the handout are described more extensively here, to help answer clarifying questions from the group:

Value-driven. Compatible with Unitarian Universalist Principles and the religious and moral beliefs of the young people in the group. This criterion applies to the goal, the project, and the tactics.

Worthwhile. Worth the time, energy, and effort we put into it. "Worth" is not always objectively measurable. The project that stands a chance of making a positive difference proportionate to the time, energy, and other resources invested would be considered worthwhile. However, remember that projects might result in consequences that are not measurable in concrete terms. Be clear in establishing what results you hope to gain from your projects and whether these results feel worth the investment to all participants.

Manageable. Something the group can do. The project must not be too big for the group to tackle, given constraints of time, energy, and other resources.

Heartfelt. Something the group cares a lot about. Participants must not only agree about the issue at stake but also feel strongly enough about it to want to do something.

Important. Similar to "worthwhile." The possible benefits of a successful project should improve the lives of those affected by the justice issue in a significant and lasting manner.

Focused on a concrete change in human behavior. Designed to influence the significant person(s) with the power to make a difference. Social action projects are always aimed at changing specific behavior of specific people. For example, the larger goal might be "stopping pollution," but the smaller goal might be passing a piece of legislation (which requires changing a legislator's vote) or stopping ContraViva's pollution of the Bigohl River (which requires changing the behavior of a power broker at ContraViva or the behavior of a person who influences that power broker). As a general principle, if you cannot identify the person(s) your project seeks to influence your action will be directed too vaguely. At worst, it will not to be social action at all but another form of social engagement.

Likely to develop leadership skills. We want to learn and grow as a result of this project. The project should draw on the existing strengths of the group, but challenge them to enter uncomfortable territory and stretch their abilities. (Note: In adult social action, the opposite criterion is often used—actions are judged good if they are within the comfort level of the participants because that increases participation.)

Appropriate for your congregation. We do not want to impair our congregation's ability to do other important social action. Different forms of social action are appropriate for youth from different congregations. In the long term, it is more important for the congregation's social action program to maintain a credible reputation than it is to win on a particular issue. Do nothing that will impair the reputation of the congregation unless you first obtain the consent of the congregation's leaders.

Appropriate to history of the particular situation. Do not treat people as adversaries when you have not tried treating them as friends. Nonviolent social change begin with education, then progresses through various attempts at collaboration with power brokers, only resorting to more extreme tactics (such as civil disobedience) when other avenues have been exhausted. A group that jumps ahead of itself in this sequence undermines its own credibility and effectiveness.

Choosing an Issue   15 minutes

Divide the class into groups of three or four, and give each group a sheet of newsprint and a marker. Ask what the next step on the planning spiral is. The answer is "Choosing an Issue." Say something along these lines: "What I'd like you to do in your groups is discuss what issues in our community strike you as matters of social justice. Be as specific as you can, and make sure everyone has a chance to speak. After a few minutes, I'll ask you to write down the three issues your group thinks are most important. Any questions?"

If people are confused, provide examples of both large and small issues: homelessness, laws banning skateboards from certain areas, and so on.

After three or four minutes, ask each group to decide on three issues they feel are most important, write those issues down on newsprint, and hang their sheet on the wall.

Say something like, "I'm now going to give you each two stickers. I invite you to walk around the room and look at the three issues listed by each group. If you see two similar issues, let me know and we'll combine them into one. Think about which of all these issues is most important to you and which issues fit the criteria we listed. When you have seen them all, use your stickers to vote for the issue you would like our social action project to address. You can vote for two different issues or use both your stickers to vote twice for the same issue."

After this first vote, use a marker to circle the three or four issues with the highest numbers of stickers.

Say, "Okay, we have got some really good issues here! I bet all of these might work well. However, we need to choose one, so let's vote again. Take two more stickers, and this time, vote for one of the issues circled. Those are the ones that got the most votes in the first round. Whichever one gets the most votes in this second round of voting will be the one we address in our social action."

After voting, announce the winner. If there is a tie, everyone gets one more sticker to vote again between the two finalists.

Narrowing In on a Focus   10 minutes

Ask the group, "What comes next on the planning spiral?" The answer is "Narrowing In on a Focus." Say, "Now that we've chosen an issue, it's time to narrow in on a focus." Ask the following questions, and have a volunteer post the group's responses on the newsprint grid "Narrowing In on a Focus" as shown in Leader Resource 25 (page 213).

- Who has the power to influence the issue we have chosen?

Identify the person(s) with the most influence over the issue the group has chosen. These are the power brokers. Examples might include Superintendent of Schools John Smith; City Council Member Chris Brown; farmers who employ migrant laborers, including the owner of Pretty Peachtree Orchard; eighth-grade students of West Jr. High School; and so on. Be as specific as possible. You will probably be able to list only two to four power brokers for the issue you have chosen.

- Who has the power to influences the person(s) with power?

Indented beneath each power broker, list that person's major influences. These are the secondary power brokers. A superintendent of schools must be responsive to parents, school administrators, and the school board most of all; a city council member may be most responsive to the members of his/her district; and so on.

- What concerns influence these primary and secondary power brokers?

To what do the power brokers respond? List their concerns in the right column. Your list might include votes, funding streams, reputation and prestige, conscience, law, and so on.

- What do we want the power broker(s) to do?

Everything depends on the answer to this question, which the group must clearly and specifically understand for social action to succeed. What is the desired impact, and on whom? Do not move forward until the group can write down an answer this question!

Identifying Group Resources   10 minutes

Ask, "What's next on the planning spiral?" The answer is "Identifying Group Resources," including intangibles like time or talents. Ask a new volunteer to write. Ask youth to identify what resources this group could use to create a successful action. Examples include the following:

- people in the Coming of Age group

- adult sponsors and mentors associated with the group

- facilities, members, and communication channels of the congregation

- amount of time the group plans to spend on the social action

- reputation of the congregation in the community

- skill sets common to most group members: writing, walking, speaking, dramatic acting, caring, and so on

- contributions that are specific to individuals: Ming just obtained a driver's license; Tanya's father might donate supplies from his/her store; Enrique's Internet service provides free web space; Robert knows someone who works at the newspaper

Choosing a Project   20 minutes

Say something like, "Now let's take a few minutes to walk around and look at what we've done so far. We've come up with criteria, an issue, some focuses, and our group resources. Look at those and try to figure out how they fit together. What kind of project might we want to do, given what we have come up with so far?" After a few minutes, gather the group. Ask, "What can we do that will most directly influence the power brokers on this issue?" Ask for a volunteer to list ideas on newsprint.

Responses might include the following:

- Set up a group visit to a power broker's office and discuss the issue, provide informational materials, etc.

- Organize a letter-writing campaign within or beyond the congregation. (This might be done in cooperation with the Social Action Committee or one of the guest speakers from the session on community service.)

- Raise money for an organization already doing effective work in bringing about the change the group desires. The group might combine delivering the money with a scheduled tour of the organization to learn about its work.

If others have already tried reasoning with the power broker to no avail, you might consider the following:

- Make signs and invite the community to a candlelight vigil, then write and send a press release to a local news agency informing them of the event. Send a copy of the news release to the power broker as well. (For tips on getting press coverage of your event, see the "Mechanics" section of Peter Montgomery's article "Speaking to the Media as a Unitarian Universalist," available online at *www.uua.org/leaders/leaderslibrary/advocacytips*.

- Hand out flyers calling for a boycott of a store or service, and send a copy to the power broker along with a letter of explanation.

Note: Civil disobedience, physical obstructions, and other such tactics which might be dangerous or illegal are not options for a Coming of Age social action project.

After possible projects have been listed, lead the group in selecting one, using the information generated at each stage. The criteria will play a particularly critical role, but the information gathered at all stages is important. You may find that the group needs to revise the information produced at earlier stages; a particularly exciting project might make the group willing to dedicate more resources or cause them to reconsider one of the criteria.

Understanding and Dividing Components
15 minutes

Once the group agrees on a project (using a vote or consensus process), break down the project's necessary components. Accept and record volunteers who will be responsible for each component. Remind them of the standing game from Workshop 25 (see page 164), which showed that though each commitment is small, each is important, and that the group will be counting on them. Pass out index cards and ask the members to write down their responsibilities. Encourage participants to turn to their mentors for assistance in completing their parts over the coming week.

Consulting a calendar, choose a time and date for the action. You might choose to use the next Coming of Age session or do the action itself outside of the group's usual gathering time. Mark the event on your congregational calendar or submit it to the person who keeps the calendar. You may end this activity with Dorothy Day's poem "Commitment," which is provided as Handout 27 .

Note: After the session is over, send an e-mail to the mentors, informing them of the project selected and encouraging them to be in touch with their respective participants to offer help during the week.

Closing   5 minutes

Use the closing ritual designed by the group.

Session 2
Complete and Process the Project

Time   40 minutes

Participant Goals

- participate in an actual social action project

- develop some of the skills required for successful social action

211

- explore the channels for social action available in the local community

- develop a sense of empowerment in the face of complex and significant social problems

Preparation

- This session depends entirely on the successful completion of the previous session (or a modified version of it), during which participants select and plan a social action project.

- It is essential to receive written permission from parents for youth to participate in the social action project. It can be incorporated into the general Coming of Age permission form or obtained separately.

- Invite the mentors to participate in the project if they are available.

- If the project will be located at the congregation or in another building, make sure that you have made necessary room reservations and understand the resources and limits of the space.

- Write your own supply list, and account for all supplies two to three days before the event.

- In making arrangements for drivers to and from the project:

  - Be sure to conform to the congregation's policy on drivers of children and youth.

  - Ensure that every car will have at least one adult and at least one passenger with a mobile phone, if possible. Compile a list of cell phone numbers in advance, and note who is riding in the car with that cell phone number. Ideally, this list should be distributed to every adult. Provide each driver clear directions to and from the site.

- Review the information on planning in Community Service Projects (see page 201). This section also contains good ideas for pre-project and post-project activities.

Completing the Project   variable

During the project, as well as before and after, take time to connect the activity to values and history of the Unitarian Universalist religious tradition. You might check with the minister or director of religious education in advance for their suggestions. After completing the project, convene the group to discuss the project.

Opening   5 minutes

Use the opening ritual designed by the group.

Processing the Project   30 minutes

Here are several questions that might stimulate conversation:

- Did the experience unfold as you expected? If not, how was it different?

- Think back to the Snurptown activity from Workshop 25 (see page 163). What are the advantages of the actions the group took? What are the disadvantages?

- How does your experience doing social action connect to the seven Unitarian Universalist Principles?

- Was it a challenge to live out the Unitarian Universalist Principles in this project?

- Do you think this experience might change how you think or feel? If so, in what ways?

- Do you think this experience might cause you to act differently? If so, how?

- How do you think this experience might have affected others' thoughts, feelings, or actions?

Congratulate the group on their hard work and express your hope that they will continue to work to make the world a more just place. Remind them that the results of our actions are often not immediately seen, but accumulate and join others over time.

Closing   5 minutes

Close by singing a favorite UU song or by using the closing ritual designed by the group.

Narrowing In on a Focus

Power Broker #1
    Secondary Power Brokers #1
    Secondary Power Brokers #2
	concerns
	concerns
	concerns

Power Broker #2
    Secondary Power Brokers #1
    Secondary Power Brokers #2
	concerns
	concerns
	concerns

Power Broker #3
    Secondary Power Brokers #1
    Secondary Power Brokers #2
	concerns
	concerns
	concerns

Power Broker #4
    Secondary Power Brokers #1
    Secondary Power Brokers #2
	concerns
	concerns
	concerns

Spiral Planning

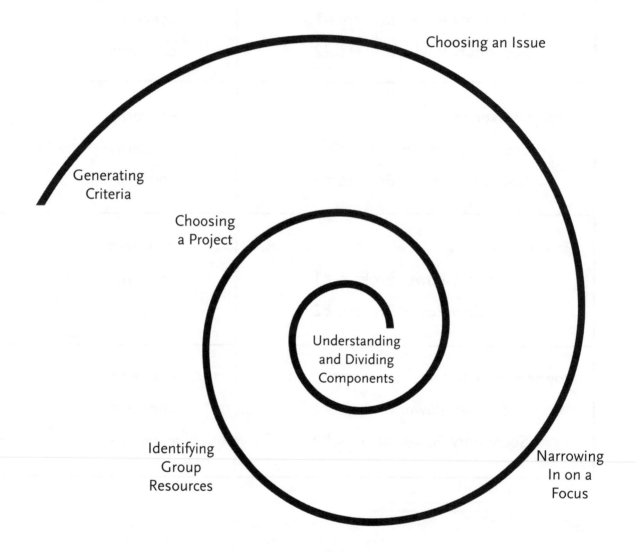

Choosing an Issue

Generating
Criteria

Choosing
a Project

Understanding
and Dividing
Components

Identifying
Group
Resources

Narrowing
In on a
Focus

Wisdom from UU Activists

Many UUs who do social action agree that a good social action project should have several of the following characteristics:

Value-driven. In keeping with UU Principles and the beliefs of the individuals in our group.

Worthwhile. Worth the time, energy, and effort we put into it.

Manageable. Something we can do so that we don't get in over our heads.

Heartfelt. Something we don't just agree on, but care a lot about.

Important. Ideally, we want to put our energy where it has the chance of making the greatest difference.

Focused on a concrete change in human behavior. Designed to influence the specific person(s) with the power to make a difference.

Likely to develop leadership skills. We want to learn and grow as a result of this project.

Appropriate for the congregation. We do not want to impair our congregation's ability to do other important social action.

Appropriate to the history of the particular situation. We do not want to treat people as adversaries when we have not tried treating them as friends.

Commitment

People say, what is the sense of our small effort.

They cannot see that we must lay one brick at a time,

take one step at a time.

A pebble cast into a pond causes ripples

that spread in all directions.

Each one of our thoughts, words, and deeds is like that.

No one has a right to sit down and feel hopeless.

There's too much work to do.

—Dorothy Day

Supplemental Activities

Many congregations have found it rewarding to ask Coming of Age participants to participate in activities outside of the regular meeting time. If your group meets during the same time as Sunday worship, you might want to consider this optional building block. Attending congregational activities gives youth an opportunity to experience a fuller spectrum of what your congregation has to offer. It provides multiple opportunities for youth and mentors to mix in a social setting that is not just one-on-one, and it expands the Coming of Age program outside the classroom and influences more variables in the lives of participants.

You may also find youth who are interested in the program, yet cannot or will not enjoy being part of regular meetings. A list like the one included here as Leader Resource 26, Sample Supplemental Activity Checklist (see page 218), can provide a way for these youth to participate. Some congregations with a small number of participants construct a program that consists mostly of youth taking part in supplemental activities and discussing their experiences with mentors or leaders. This is similar to the mentor-youth dyad model (see Leaders and Mentors, page 13).

When choosing activities to include in a checklist, decide what aspects of congregational life you want participants to experience. Balance activities to give youth a taste of the full range. For example, attending a canvass dinner gives youth an opportunity to enjoy fellowship with members of the congregation and exposes them to the financial obligations of membership. Helping in a religious education activity involving younger children gives youth a chance to provide a service to the congregation and reminds them that being part of a multigenerational community includes connecting with people younger and older.

Keep in mind your congregational culture when adding activities to your checklist. If social events will include the serving of alcohol, decide if that is an acceptable environment for youth. If there are activities where a youth presence has never existed before, be cautious of asking youth to just show up. This is not to say that you should not include these events, just that you might need to prepare all parties involved. If youth have never attended a meeting of the Board of Trustees in your congregation, be sure to talk to the board members before adding this possibility to your checklist. Consulting with all parties beforehand gives everyone a chance to extend the best hospitality possible. Youth will have a better experience, and the congregation will feel positive about its ability to welcome and include them. As a result, you may find various committees and entities within the congregation actually seeking out a greater youth presence.

Supplemental activities need not be limited to programs happening within the congregation. If youth will be working with mentors to fulfill a supplemental requirement, you might include other opportunities for the pairs to mix. Extracurricular school activities, sports, and movies are just a few activities they might share. However, keep in mind your congregational safety policy and under what circumstances, if any, youth and mentors may gather outside of the congregation.

Sample Supplemental Activity Checklist

This checklist contains activities that accompany the Coming of Age program. You should accomplish at least two activities under each of the five sections. A teacher, your mentor, or another adult (not of your family) who is present at the event must sign off on the activity. You will be awarded a point for each activity (unless otherwise noted). Those who accumulate at least fifteen points and help in fund-raising efforts are eligible to go on the Boston pilgrimage.

Learning

_____ Read and discuss Chapter 3 in *The Unitarian Universalist Pocket Guide*.

_____ Attend at least fifteen teaching Sundays in religious education.

_____ Attend all twenty-seven teaching Sundays in religious education. (5 points)

_____ Meet with your mentor at least nine times.

_____ Attend a session of an adult religious education course.

_____ Write a short report on any chapter in *The Unitarian Universalist Pocket Guide*.

Fellowship

_____ Read and discuss Chapter 2 in *The Unitarian Universalist Pocket Guide*.

_____ Invite your mentor to attend a school or extracurricular activity that you are involved in.

_____ Attend at least one all-church event.

_____ Attend a district conference or conference at The Mountain Retreat and Learning Centers. (2 points)

_____ Help set up and serve during coffee hour, a new member reception, or First Sunday lunch.

Social Action/Community Service

_____ Read and discuss Chapter 5 in *The Unitarian Universalist Pocket Guide*.

_____ Participate in the planning and execution of a Community Service Sunday.

_____ Participate in an all-church community service project, such as helping serve meals to the hungry or attending a rally, demonstration, or march for a worthy cause.

_____ Attend a Justice Committee meeting.

_____ Design and implement a service project for the Coming of Age program. (5 points)

_____ Hold a church cleanup work party.

_____ Help the office manager copy, fold, address, and mail the newsletter.

Leadership

_____ Read and discuss pages 92 to 96 in *The Unitarian Universalist Pocket Guide*.

_____ Help plan the class worship service.

_____ Help plan the Boston pilgrimage.

_____ Help during a session of religious education for younger children.

_____ Supervise a game at a congregation party for thirty minutes.

_____ Attend a meeting of the Board of Trustees or the Program Council.

_____ Examine the church bylaws and budget, and then interview the president of the

Board of Trustees (see suggested interview questions).

_____ Interview the minister, director of religious education, or music director (see suggested interview questions).

_____ Attend a meeting of another committee (Religious Education, Social Activity, Membership, etc.).

_____ Join a committee. (5 points)

Worship/Belief

_____ Read and discuss Chapter 1 in _The Unitarian Universalist Pocket Guide._

_____ Participate in a class worship service.

_____ Attend at least two worship services and make an appointment to discuss them with the minister. One of these may be an intergenerational service. (2 points)

_____ Help plan and participate in religious education chapel.

_____ Attend a choir rehearsal.

_____ Participate in a congregational worship service by telling a story, doing a reading, etc.

_____ Lead a service other than the class service. (2 points)

_____ Interview your mentor and at least one other church member about their spiritual beliefs (see suggested interview questions).

_____ Read about and discuss with your mentor (or write a short report about) the Ten Commandments, Buddha's Eightfold Path, the Sermon on the Mount, and the nine basic beliefs of Hinduism. What are their differences and similarities? Write your own rules for living. (2 points)

Suggested Interview Questions

President of the Board of Trustees

Who are the officers of the church?

How are they and the rest of the Board of Trustees chosen?

How long do they serve?

What are their duties?

To whom does the Board of Trustees answer?

What is congregational polity?

How is governance different in other churches?

Who are the church staff?

How are they hired?

What are their duties?

How were the bylaws developed?

Why are they important?

Where does the church's money come from and where does it go?

What is the best part about being president?

What is the hardest part?

Minister, Director of Religious Education, or Music Director

Why did you take on this job?

What background and training do you have?

What are your duties and responsibilities?

What are your goals for the church, both short-term and long-term?

What is the best part of your job?

What is the hardest part?

About Spiritual Beliefs

How would you describe your spiritual or religious beliefs?

What are your views on God?

What are your views on heaven and hell or any afterlife?

What are your views on how we should live our lives on earth?

What are your views on the nature of human beings?

What factors in your life have helped form your beliefs?

Do you share the same beliefs with most of your family?

Are your beliefs now the same as they were when you were fourteen?

If not, how have they changed?

How do your beliefs mesh with Unitarian Universalism?

How do they differ?

—Unitarian Universalist Church of Birmingham, Alabama

Group Trips

Several congregations have included trips as part of their Coming of Age programs for years. These trips, which can range from a few hours to a week or more, often focus on Unitarian Universalist heritage. Others may focus on social justice issues, community service, or cross-cultural exchange.

Whether your congregation already has a tradition of sending its youth to Boston during spring break or you wish to start a new tradition, this section highlights some of the benefits of group trips and provides tips for activities, sites, and planning.

Benefits

By helping answer the questions "Who am I?" and "How do I belong?" Coming of Age trips can be formative in terms of young people's identity. Youth leave their familiar environment and travel together to a new place. Along the way, they get to know each other in new ways, and their bonds grow deeper. The content of the trip helps form identity as well. If a trip is focused on Unitarian Universalist heritage, it can help young people know who they are in relation to their religious tradition. It can bring history alive for them and help them feel that they are actors in that history. With a community service or cross-cultural trip, youth are able to find new settings to live out their UU values and principles. Increasing personal experience with Unitarian Universalism within the safety of a group of peers can help make Unitarian Universalism their religion.

Where to Go and What to Do

Where you go and what you do depends largely on the aim of your program and the resources that are available to your group. If your Coming of Age program focuses strongly on Unitarian Universalist history, polity, and practices, a heritage trip might meet your group's needs. If your program emphasizes values, responsibility, and social action, then perhaps a community service or social justice–focused trip would be in order. If your program stresses identity, tolerance, and diversity, a cross-cultural trip could be a real high point of the year. There is a wide range of possibilities, but wherever you go, participants will create shared memories that will last a long time.

Heritage Trips

Many Coming of Age groups learn about Unitarian Universalist heritage with a trip to Boston and its environs. As the major locus of early American Unitarianism, a significant place in Universalist history, and the current location of the Unitarian Universalist Association's main offices, Boston offers numerous opportunities for sightseeing. The UUA's information office publishes a guide for youth groups who are coming to Boston. The guide offers advice on lodging and dining as well as historical sightseeing. Find it at *www.uua.org/documents/info/heritagetrip.pdf*. Another guide, written by religious educator Jeff Liebmann, includes more commentary on sites in the Boston area and can be found at *www.pitt.edu/~jdl1/UUcurric.htm*. Click on the "Youth Group Walking Tour of Downtown Boston" link.

For a more contemporary view of how Unitarian Universalists are effecting social change, groups can visit the Unitarian Universalist Urban Ministry (UUUM), housed at First Church. First Church is one of the oldest Unitarian church buildings in the area. UUUM was founded in 1826 to help Boston's poor and continues this mission to this day by offering after-school programs for at-risk youth, by running the Renewal House shelter for women victims of domestic violence, and by coordinating the Rice Sticks and Tea food pantry for Asian families. The UUUM is supported by nearly sixty Unitarian Universalist congregations in and around Boston. Learn more at *www.uuum.org*.

Another site to visit is the headquarters of the Unitarian Universalist Service Committee (UUSC) in Cambridge, Massachusetts. The mission of the UUSC is to "advance human rights and social justice around the world, partnering with those who confront unjust power structures, and mobilizing to challenge oppressive policies." Many UU youth have supported the committee each year through its Guest at Your Table program. Learn more at *www.uusc.org*.

Coming of Age groups may also want to visit these other sites in Massachusetts: Concord (significant to the American Revolution and Transcendentalists, and home to a historic Unitarian congregation); Hopedale (founded by Universalist Adin Ballou as a utopian community); Lexington (sites related to the American Revolution and home to two historic Unitarian congregations); Plymouth (sites related to the Mayflower and home to a historic Unitarian congregation); Provincetown (home to a historic Unitarian congregation as well as a large population of gay and lesbian people); Gloucester (home of the first Universalist church in America); Quincy (home to the historic Unitarian church of John and Abigail Adams and their son John Quincy Adams); and Salem (site of the seventeenth-century witch trials and home to historic Unitarian and Universalist churches). Winchester, New Hampshire, site of the Universalist churches' Winchester Profession of Faith, is another possibility.

Social Justice Trips

A trip to Washington D.C. could expose youth to Unitarian Universalism's role in public policy and social justice issues. The Unitarian Universalist Association's Washington Office advocates for UU values and works to enact the Statements of Conscience and Actions of Immediate Witness passed by representatives of the congregations at the UUA General Assembly each year. Washington D.C. also features a historic Unitarian church (All Souls) and a historic Universalist church (National Memorial). Its suburbs contain a number of large congregations that could potentially host a visiting group.

The Coming of Age groups at First Parish in Cambridge, Massachusetts, have embarked on some interesting trips. In 2003, youth traveled with their minister and advisors to the southern U.S. to learn more about the civil rights movement in the 1950s and 1960s and its relevance for today. They visited Atlanta, Georgia, and Montgomery, Birmingham, and Selma, Alabama, where UU clergy and laity participated in the historic 1965 march for voting rights. The group paid tribute to Unitarian Universalists Viola Liuzzo and Rev. James Reeb, who were both killed in Selma. In 2005, youth traveled to southern Florida to build housing and work side by side with migrant farmworkers and learn about their struggles.

Cross-cultural Trips

A trip that has a long-standing tradition is the "Ninth Grade Trip." Started in the mid-1960s by Denver area congregations, the trip is actually a yearlong program of personal and religious development that culminates with a ten-day journey to the Navajo and Hopi Nations in northern Arizona.

The Unitarian Universalist Partner Church Council (UUPCC) fosters and supports relationships between American congregations and congregations in other countries. If your congregation is a member of the council, research the possibility of including youth in a visit to your congregation's international partner. If your program is conducted with ninth graders or older youth, the

UUPCC Annual Youth Pilgrimage might be worth exploring. It is an opportunity for youth ages fifteen to nineteen to tour Transylvania and connect with our UU heritage and present-day congregations. If an actual visit is not a possibility, consider a virtual visit. At *www.uupcc.org/re_curricula. htm*, you can see how other congregations have developed programs that introduce children and youth to the culture of their partner church.

Community Service Trips

Trips that focus on community service can provide wonderful opportunities for youth to live Unitarian Universalist values. Community service offers youth the chance to build relationships with people they might not otherwise meet and to gain confidence in themselves as people who can make a difference. Finding a community service agency that has the resources to take on your group for a few days or even a week can be challenging, though. See Community Service Projects (page 200) for discussion of this point. The Unitarian Universalist Service Committee (*www.uusc. org*) may be able to help your group locate a suitable site.

Planning

Coming of Age trips—especially those that are a week in length or longer—most often require advance planning of six months to a year. The number of details to attend to is quite large, and coordinators may want to ask for planning assistance from others in the congregation. The tasks involved include the following:

- identifying potential sites

- confirming availability and financial feasibility of site

- investigating the congregation's insurance policy to find out if it covers out-of-state trips and rental vehicles

- researching relevant history and things to do

- communicating with any Unitarian Universalist congregation you will visit

- recruiting additional adult advisors to travel with the group

- making reservations for lodging, museums, tours, and programs (Unitarian Universalist camps and conference centers offer potential "base camps" for weeklong Coming of Age trips. See *www.cu2c2.org* to find a UU camp or conference center that might meet your needs.)

- making travel and transportation arrangements

- determining how food will be arranged for and how much it will cost

- budgeting and determining cost to participants

- fundraising (see page 224)

- having extra copies of parental permission and medical release forms ready, in case they are needed

- scheduling a parent-youth information session in advance of the trip

Understanding in advance the amount of work required to set up a trip will help your congregation decide whether to include one as part of your program.

Curricular Preparation

You may want to reserve a meeting or two before the trip for learning background information that will enhance the trip. For example, a group traveling to the South to learn about civil rights could watch some episodes of the documentary series *Eyes on the Prize* and talk with members of the congregation who are or were involved in working for civil rights. A group that will be going to Boston could study Unitarian Universalist history just before they go.

Youth Leadership and Active Participation

Opportunities for leadership can help youth gain confidence and a deeper sense of maturity. The key to successful leadership experiences is manageability; the tasks youth take on must be appropriate for their capabilities and experience. These are some good ways to involve youth in leadership during a trip:

- Assign different youth the responsibility of writing about the sites they visit each day for a collective trip journal.

- Ask various youth to be in charge of different meals, either preparing the meal or selecting a restaurant and collecting participants' orders.

- Recruit capable youth to take turns being navigators on long van rides.

- Sign youth up for different logistical roles and responsibilities. For example, one could always count luggage, another could always count youth and advisors, and another could be the lead packer for the van.

- When making decisions about sites en route, ask particular youth to facilitate the decision-making process for the group.

- Enlist youth to take lead roles in cleaning up spaces after they use them.

Structuring Learning on the Trip

Trips are often more meaningful when each day includes time for group discussion and reflection to absorb experiences. The discussion questions need not be complex; these simple questions are good ones to return to each evening:

- What did you see today?

- What did you hear?

- How did you feel?

- What meaning did you find?

- How might what you experienced today affect your actions in the future?

After days filled with work or sightseeing, youth might not have a great deal of energy for long discussions. However, they often appreciate the opportunity to mentally "unpack" and process their days.

A collective journal can also be a helpful way to structure learning. Youth can take turns writing about what they see and do throughout the trip. This facilitates reflection and can also be an aid to memory after the trip is complete.

Setting Standards for Behavior

Before leaving on your trip, you might ask the group to revisit the covenant that they established earlier in the program. Talk about whether it will hold up to the special circumstances of an extended trip; there may be a need for additions. Safety and liability issues call for clarity in what behavior is acceptable and what is not. Establishing a set of ground rules in addition to your covenant might be useful. Parents and your congregation's religious educator will want to be included in this conversation.

Fundraising

There are many ways to raise funds for a Coming of Age trip. The best place to start is to assess the resources you have in your congregation. For example, a member of your congregation who owns a candy store might be able to donate candy to your group to sell. If your congregation has a large room, you could organize a coffeehouse musical performance to benefit the group. After assessing the congregation's special resources, you can brainstorm a list of possibilities before narrowing down your choices. Approaches that other congregations have taken include the following:

- babysitting nights, when parents can drop off their little ones at the congregation to be collectively babysat by youth in the group

- pancake breakfasts before worship

- box lunches after worship

- car washes
- bake sales
- candy sales
- rock concerts/coffeehouses
- Halloween haunted houses
- recycling printer cartridges
- serve-a-thons, in which people sponsor youth for service they perform in the community or around the church
- cake auctions
- letters sent by youth to their friends and families asking for sponsorship
- direct donations solicited from members of the congregation, either through a Sunday morning collection or a direct mail appeal

Though it is hard to predict, it is helpful to estimate how much money might be raised by each of the fundraisers your group considers; you could then decide on the number of fundraisers needed and plan accordingly.

A special committee can be in charge of the various fundraisers. Parents of youth in the program might be particularly interested in serving on such a committee. The full burden of fundraising ought not be held by Coming of Age leaders alone!

Some congregations have had good success by asking participating youth to sign pledges to participate in all (or a predetermined proportion, such as four out of five) of the fundraising events. This helps youth know that the responsibility for fundraising is shared by all.

Finally, remember to get approval from your congregation's Board of Directors for any special fundraising. Many congregations' bylaws require it.

Short Trips

If an extended trip is beyond what your resources can support, consider a scaled-down version. Visiting a neighboring congregation with a unique Unitarian Universalist history can deepen youth's connection with our UU heritage. Consider joining with a neighboring congregation's Coming of Age or youth group to work on a service project. Though this type of visit might not have the same historical range as a trip to New England or provide the opportunity to interact with people from a different culture, it does enable youth to compare another congregation's culture with their own. If your congregation is located in an area that is isolated from other Unitarian Universalist congregations, a trip of this nature can help youth form new friendships and feel less alone in the wider religious community.

Another possibility is to visit local spots that have ties to local Unitarian Universalist history. A bit of research might uncover interesting connections. For example, a visit to the statehouse in Springfield, Illinois, could be coupled with a discussion on Adlai Stevenson, past governor, presidential candidate, and a Unitarian. One-day or weekend field trips can also be planned around a community service project.

Have Fun!

Trips will be most memorable for youth if they include some intentional fun. Fun need not be viewed as something separate from learning about Unitarian Universalism or living our faith—it is actually best if youth get to have fun while they do those very things! An afternoon devoted to playing games, or an evening talent show, or even a trip to a goofy museum is not time apart from the goals of Coming of Age. Bonding with other Unitarian Universalist youth is an essential component of developing UU identity. A group trip provides an excellent vehicle for doing so.

Retreats and Rites of Passage

Another building block you might wish to include in your Coming of Age program is one or more overnight or weekend retreats. During a retreat, participants have the opportunity to interact with each other in a more relaxed, leisurely manner. Activities that take longer than ninety minutes and call for a greater depth of involvement can be accommodated. The isolation from everyday interruptions enables youth to focus more intently, and the insulation of the group can tighten the bonds of community.

Preparation

Remember to estimate the costs of the retreat well in advance and decide how you will cover those costs (program fees, fund-raising, or family contribution). See Designing and Preparing for Your Program (page viii) for other tips.

Decide where you will hold your retreat. Retreats can be held at the congregational meetinghouse, but off-site locations are preferable, if possible. They make the event special and enable youth to explore a different environment, which can stimulate new perspectives on familiar material. A retreat center or campground can provide not only meeting space, but also better sleeping and dining arrangements than most congregational meetinghouses.

If you are using a retreat center, reserve space for youth, mentors, and group leaders as far in advance as possible. The retreat center ideally will have direct access to secluded outdoor areas where each youth can sit alone safely and undisturbed. Inquire whether any other groups will be using the retreat center during your scheduled visit.

Familiarize yourself with any safety guidelines of your religious education program that are specific for retreats or overnights. Your congregation might require a particular youth-to-adult ratio for retreats. Make sure far in advance that you have recruited enough adults to assist with carpooling and advising for the duration of the retreat. The Rites of Passage retreat benefits greatly from mentors' presence for its duration, and mentors can also be advisors at other retreats. It is not recommended that youth's parents be advisors at this retreat, primarily because of the social effect of some youth having their parents present while others do not.

Obtain registration forms and permission forms from parents. Provide youth and families with a list of any supplies they need to bring.

Determine which activities your group will perform on the retreat, and acquire all the necessary supplies, and food, in advance. The supply list can be long, so it is helpful for more than one person to take on this task.

When planning a retreat, it is most effective to include games, recreational activities, movies, and worship, as well as discussion-based activities. Retreats also involve several tasks for which youth can take responsibility, such as food preparation and cleanup. Make space for unstructured free time, during which youth can build friendships and make meaning of the things they have been learning.

All retreats as outlined in Leader Resource 34, Sample Program Outlines (page 252), end with worship on Sunday. Recruit youth to help plan and implement worship well ahead of time, and consider asking teams of youth and mentors to coordinate worship. Alternatively, if your retreat is being held near another Unitarian Universalist congregation, consider attending worship there. Contact the religious educator, minister, or lay leaders in advance to let them know you will be attending with youth. Youth might stay for the service or, if the congregation holds youth religious education sessions at the same time, they might prefer attending religious education.

The following example is based on a retreat from Leader Resource 34, Sample Program Outlines, and has been fleshed out into a fuller schedule.

- *Friday night:* Arrive and settle in; dinner; Peace and Put-downs; Making an Altar; games

- *Saturday morning:* Spirituality in Movement; breakfast; free time; Your God Project; Connecting to the Natural World

- *Saturday afternoon:* Lunch; The God You Don't Believe In, the God You Do; Stillness, Silence, and Meditation

- *Saturday evening:* Dinner; Starting with Us (including the movie *Mean Girls*); free time

- *Sunday morning:* Breakfast; cleanup; worship

Rites of Passage

The past twenty years have seen a growing interest among Unitarian Universalists in rituals that mark the passage into adolescence, with increasing numbers of congregations offering Coming of Age programs. The program is itself a ritual that marks this passage and, within it, there are several elements that can be ritualized: writing and sharing of credos, a group trip, and the Service of Recognition, to name a few.

Additionally, some congregations have incorporated a Rites of Passage retreat, a weekend devoted exclusively to rituals that mark the passage from childhood to youth. In the context of a Coming of Age program, the challenge is to construct rituals that focus on faith and spirituality development. After all, the program is about acknowledging and supporting youth as they enter a new phase in their lives as Unitarian Uni-

versalists, not as members of society at large.

In searching for authentic Unitarian Universalist rituals of passage, first we must ask, "What is a rite of passage?" and "What makes it meaningful?" In the classic book *The Rites of Passage*, anthropologist Arnold Van Gennep defined rites of passage as the "universal practice of ceremonializing life's major events." He identified three elements that he observed in such rituals worldwide:

Severance: a temporary separation from the context of daily life. This typically involves leaving home, family, and the congregation for the duration of the ritual.

Threshold: time spent and rituals performed in a space that is demarcated for ritual purposes, such as a specific space in the woods or a special tent.

Incorporation: a return to community and daily life, where the youth renegotiates relationships based on the internal transformation that has taken place.

Each of these elements can be part of a rite that is authentic to Unitarian Universalist religion and culture. Mythologist Joseph Campbell writes, "The function of ritual, as I understand it, is to give form to the human life, not in the way of a more surface arrangement, but in depth." Coming of Age rituals should bring depth to the lives of those who participate. They should be relevant, meaningfully marking the new identities and responsibilities of an adolescent UU.

If you choose to design a Rites of Passage retreat for your program, remember that you are marking a transition between childhood and adolescence, not adulthood. Rituals that appear to bestow adult privileges and responsibilities on thirteen-year-olds are not appropriate or true to our culture.

Borrowing Rituals from Other Cultures

As Euro-Americans have become more interested in reclaiming a coming-of-age ritual element that has been lost in their own culture, many Coming of Age programs have based rituals on those conducted by Native Americans and other indigenous peoples. These groups are often working to secure their cultural survival, and therefore the integrity of their rituals and traditions is of utmost importance to them. Because many Unitarian Universalists care about being in right relationship with indigenous peoples worldwide, and especially First Nations peoples in the Americas, it is imperative that Unitarian Universalists take seriously Native American activists' claim that cultural borrowing, no matter how well intentioned, has done harm to their cultures.

In the article "Wanting to Be Indian," Unitarian Universalist minister Myke Johnson points out that "we get used to thinking of ethics as an individual matter, where good intentions are uppermost, and right and wrong are something that each of us choose. These are important, but there is another way of thinking about ethics, which I find helpful here. That is social ethics—looking at the structures of society and their impact on people."

Some non–Native American UUs argue that they are appreciating rather than appropriating when they conduct rituals rooted in Native American traditions, such as sweat lodges, vision quests, medicine walks, and medicine wheels. Appreciation of different cultural and religious traditions is certainly a hallmark of Unitarian Universalist religious education. However, because of the structures of American society—because of the continued racism, exploitation, poverty, and cultural death that Native Americans have to fight every day—many have come to believe that it is not ethical for non–Native Americans to freely pick and choose native rituals and symbols to use in their own spiritual context. This "borrowing" functions as part of a larger cultural theft that continues the spirit of genocide and gets in the way of Native American self-determination and cultural survival.

"How," you ask, "could a group of Unitarian Universalist ninth-graders at a retreat center possibly interfere with self-determination and cultural survival?" Good question, especially because Lakota or Iroquois people might never

find out that a group of teenagers engaged in rituals based on their own. However, the second layer of appropriation is how it hurts those who borrow. Non–Native Americans have borrowed native traditions to try to fill a cultural gap of their own: the disconnection with the earth that has been wrought by modern industrialized society. This disconnection leads to the absence of meaningful, authentic rites of passage and a lack of ritual to celebrate human connection to the earth. However, our Unitarian Universalist tradition has many authentic ways of creating spiritual connection with the earth. The Transcendentalist movement of the nineteenth century taught Unitarians and Universalists that they could experience the divine by experiencing nature. The environmentalist movements of the twentieth and twenty-first centuries continually emphasize human interdependence with the earth and all of its creatures. There is no need to borrow Native American ritual in order to lead a rite of passage in a way that is respectful of and connected to the earth. Should you decide to incorporate a ritual from another culture into your Rite of Passage, proceed with respect. Leader Resource 27, Considerations for Cultural Borrowing (page 235), identifies several questions you may want to ask yourself concerning your use of the ritual.

One resource that can help you with ideas for designing rituals is *The Art of Ritual: A Guide to Creating and Performing Your Own Rituals for Growth and Change* by Renee Beck and Sydney Metrick. *Singing the Living Tradition*, *Singing the Journey*, and *Rise Up Singing* are good resources for songs, hymns, and readings. Another resource for readings is *Coming of Age*, edited by Edward Searl. Material from these resources can also be used to design an opening and/or closing worship for the weekend, and you will find a continually updated worship resource at *www.uua.org/worshipweb*. See Leader Resource 28, Readings for Rites of Passage Retreat (page 236) for other possible readings.

Activities

In designing a Rites of Passage retreat, examine the workshops in this handbook for activities you might include. A few examples are meditations from Workshop 6, Finalizing Your Credo (see page 80); Workshop 18, Stillness, Silence and Meditation (see page 126); outdoor activities from Workshop 20, Connecting to the Natural World (see page 131); and Workshop 31, Closing Celebration (see page 196).

Choosing the Masks We Wear

Time   approximately 2 hours total

This is a two-part activity. The first part involves molding the masks, and the second part, which should happen approximately twenty-four hours later, is when the masks get decorated.

Materials

- several rolls of plaster gauze, enough so that each mask can have at least three layers (available at craft and medical supply stores)

- one plastic bowl per youth-adult pair

- several pairs of scissors

- several jars of petroleum jelly (enough for participants to completely cover their faces in it)

- some tubes of a hair product called "Cholesterol," marketed for African hair

- assortment of hair ties and hair bands

- straws

- newspaper, plastic, or old tablecloths

- plastic, old shirts, or smocks

- paper towels

- variety of colorful paints (with extra red, black, white, and brown because these colors are usually popular)

- instant glue, such as Krazy Glue

- small beads, sequins, feathers, ribbon, and other decorative materials

Part 1: Mask Molding   60 to 75 minutes

Start this activity by asking the group a few questions:

- What do you think of when you hear the word *mask*?

- Do you have any masks at home?

- Do you have any stories about masks?

- What are some reasons that people wear masks?

Say in your own words,

> Sometimes we intentionally wear masks, actual masks, like the kind we are going to make. We wear them for fun, we wear them to scare, we wear them for ceremonies and rituals. When we hide our true selves, it is like we are wearing an invisible mask. Sometimes we hide because we don't feel safe to be ourselves. We may put on an invisible mask because we believe it is expected of us. For example, if someone you love is hurt and you feel sad, yet someone says you must be strong, you might put on a cheerful mask to keep your loved one's spirits up. Wearing an invisible mask is not always a bad thing. I hope, though, that you have groups of people with whom you always feel safe being unmasked. I hope our congregation, and this group in particular, can serve that function for you.
>
> We're going to pair up to mold masks. While your mask is getting made, think about the invisible masks you wear in your life and whether there are places where you can take off those masks. Tomorrow night, you'll have time to decorate your mask, and you can decide what you want it to show. Will it be the mask you wear in daily life? Will it be the "true you" that you wish the world would see?

Divide the group into pairs, either mentor-youth or youth-youth. Let the pairs decide who will first be the mask maker and who will be the model. After one mask is made, the pair will switch roles. Leaders can join in, as long as one leader is available to help the pairs with the activity. (Be aware that people will not be able to talk when there is a mask molding on their faces!)

These steps precede the molding:

- Cover the worktables with newspaper, plastic, or old tablecloths.

- Set out small bowls of water for each pair.

- Cut the plaster gauze into triangular strips: this shape is the most ideal for bending around the contours of the face. Put the strips in a pile to be used later on.

- Ask the models to cover their clothing.

- Invite models to share with their partners the type of masks they want. For example, do they want a mask with holes for the eyes? If so, how big? A hole for the mouth? If so, how big? Do they want a mask that covers their whole face or only part of it?

- Instruct models to tie or pull back their hair to keep it away from their faces.

- Have models completely cover their faces with petroleum jelly. Mask makers can help to make sure that eyebrows, eyelashes, sideburns, and other facial hair is all covered.

- It's helpful to coat the exposed roots along the hairline so hair will not get caught painfully in the plaster mask. Petroleum jelly can work for this purpose, but it is hard to wash out. The hair product "Cholesterol" is preferable.

- Cut straws in 1- to 2-inch lengths, and ask models to insert them in their nostrils. This will help them breathe easily throughout the process.

- Ask pairs to work out a method of communication by hand gestures since the model will not be able to speak while the mask is being made. What signal means yes? Which means no? Which means stop? Suggest that mask makers talk to their models throughout the molding process, checking in to make sure they are feeling okay.

Now the molding can begin. Instruct mask makers to follow these steps:

- Dip the plaster gauze strips into water, one strip at a time. After dipping each piece, hold it over the bowl and rub it with your fingers to spread the plaster mixture smoothly over the gauze.

- Place the gauze strip on the model's face, spreading it smoothly along the face's contours.

- Repeat this process, making sure that each strip overlaps.

- After the whole face is covered, create another layer. Make at least three layers for a strong mask.

- The mask will begin to "set" rather quickly. When it is firm enough to not bend when the face is moved, take it off.

- If desired, nose holes can then be filled in with more strips.

Part 2: Mask Decorating   45 to 60 minutes

Participants can decorate the masks they molded the previous night. Because glue and paint take some time to dry, it is advisable to schedule this activity for no later than the night before departure. As participants decorate their masks, remind them that their masks can reflect their inner feelings or the kind of person they want to be in the world.

Sharing Our Dreams

Time   35 minutes total

This is another two-part activity. In the evening, prepare participants for the dream discussion to be held the next morning.

Materials

- journals

- writing paper for mentors (optional)

- pens or pencils

- copies of Handout 28, Guidelines for Dream Discussion (see page 240)

Part 1: Sleeping and Dreaming   5 minutes

Let youth know that there will be time and space the next morning for journaling about their dreams and discussing them. Tell them whether they will be paired with mentors, other youth, or in small groups. Suggest that participants sleep with their journals nearby, in case they wish to jot down notes about a dream immediately upon waking. If mentors are participating, give them writing paper so they can make notes as well.

Part 2: Dream Discussion   30 minutes

As participants wake, remind them to write down any dreams they remember. Invite youth and mentors to sit together at breakfast and talk about their dreams. If mentors are not present, youth can share with another youth or in small groups. Handout 28, Guidelines for Dream Discussion, can help encourage conversation. Invite youth to consider these questions:

- Does this dream remind me of anything that is good to remember at the passage from childhood to adolescence?

- Did this dream bring up any themes worth exploring during my solo vigil today?

Both youth and mentors have the right to pass if they do not feel comfortable discussing their dreams. Sometimes it is helpful for mentors to model sharing their dreams first, then to invite youth to share. Participants who do not remember their dreams can share previous dreams that were significant to them.

Solo Vigil

Time   90 minutes to 2½ hours

The purpose of the solo vigil is for youth to experience being alone with their thoughts. It is a time for meditation, reflection, and searching inside for answers to important questions. Framing the experience is important: When mentors and leaders successfully communicate to youth that the vigil is meaningful, contemplative time, youth are more likely to have a positive and growth-filled experience. It is more than just sitting around on the ground!

Materials

- map of the area being used for vigils

- journals

- pens or pencils

- Leader Resource 29, Being Present, Being Open, Being Conscious (see page 238)

- copies of Handout 29, Questions for the Vigil (see page 241)

- rope or sticks

- whistle or bell for each youth

- rain gear, bug spray, sunscreen, jackets, pillows, as dictated by weather and the environment, for use during the vigil

Preparation

- Ask parents if their child has any medical considerations that might make a one- to two-hour vigil difficult. Plan for any youth who need special accommodations, such as insulin shots or extra food.

- Meet with camp staff to identify potential vigil sites.

Part 1: Choosing the Space   30 minutes

Inform youth that they will spend time alone in nature for this activity. Let them know that they will get more explicit instructions later, but first they will walk with their mentors to find space to hold their solo vigils. Review what to look for in a good solo vigil site:

Privacy. It is not close enough to other youth to see them, and it is far away enough from the cabins so as not to be observed.

Comfort. Is there a place on the ground, a rock, or a tree to sit? Will it be relatively comfortable for the amount of time you'll be in it? Is there shade?

Safety. Can the mentor find the site if necessary? Is it within earshot of the main gathering space so that a loud whistle or a bell could be heard in either direction? Are there hazardous spaces nearby? Is there poison ivy or poison oak? Is there somewhere to take shelter in a storm?

A gut feeling that this is the right place. It needs to feel right to the youth who will be spending time in it.

Once the space is established, mentors will help youth create borders around the space with rope or sticks. After that, youth and mentors will make a note of the space's location, return to the main meeting area, and mark the location on a map of the area or write it down so that leaders can know where all youth are holding their vigils.

After everyone has returned, review these rules for the vigil:

- You cannot take books, homework, games, or electronic devices with you.

- There will be no communication with other youth.

- You must stay at the site unless you need to speak to an adult. [Clarify the procedure if a youth needs to use the bathroom.]

- Should you need adult assistance for any reason, use the whistle/bell.

- You may take rain gear, bug spray, something to sit on, a jacket, sunscreen, a pen, your journal, and the handout provided.

- Questions are provided on the handout to help you with reflection. Feel free to use them or not. If you use them, it's up to you whether to write down answers or not. You can write answers in your journal or directly on the handout.

Pass out copies of Handout 29, Questions for the Vigil, for contemplative questions that can bring structure and meaning to youth's time on their own.

If the group is not already in a circle, invite them to sit or stand in a circle. In this circle, comment on the significance of the solo time that they are about to experience by saying something like the following:

As an infant and toddler, you needed to be watched during all your waking hours. As a small child, you learned to spend some short periods by yourself, and as an older child, you learned to spend longer periods by yourself—but always sheltered. Today, you will mark your entry into adolescence by spending time in solitude.

You will be by yourself, but not alone. Sometimes it is in solitude that we can best know what friends, family, and community mean to us.

The solo vigil time is a time to stand on the cusp between childhood and adolescence and to ask: Who am I at this time? Who do I want to be? How do I want to be? What are my core values? Who is my core community? What are my roots, and what are my wings?

Offer the guided meditation in Leader Resource 29, Meditation: Being Present, Being Open, Being Conscious, in preparation for the solo vigil.

Part 2: Solo Vigil   1 to 2 hours

Excuse youth to walk in silence to their solo vigil site. During the vigils, have adults take turns listening for emergency whistles. Such whistles are rarely blown, but if they are, adults need to respond fast. Mentors and leaders may also wish to check on youth's safety by silently observing them from a distance every fifteen minutes.

Wisdom Circle

Time 25 minutes

Materials

- talking stick or other object to be passed among speakers (optional)

Preparation

- Mention to mentors that they will be sharing personal stories in this circle along with the youth. Encourage them to share in ways that feel comfortable, and emphasize that appropriate sharing in this context keeps youth's needs front and center. All sharing by adults should be in the service of helping youth learn and grow.

Invite everyone to sit in a circle.

Give the following instructions in your own words:

We adults know that as you leave childhood behind and enter a new time of life, you have many questions, perhaps some that we can help you answer. We also know that people never outgrow questions: Perhaps there are some questions that you can help the adults answer. In the time and space that follows, we will hold each other in honesty and with respect. We will regard one another as full, complex, growing human beings. In this spirit, we ask that all stories shared in this group remain anonymous outside this group. We want you to discuss the things you learn from this circle with others; yet because some of the stories are sensitive, we ask that you not connect any person's name—or identifying characteristics—with the stories you hear. This is to be done out of respect for each other and love for this group. We also ask that everyone take turns speaking, and that on any given question, no one speak twice until everyone who wants to has spoken once. After each question appears to have been answered, we will sit in silence for a moment to cre-

ate space for voices that might otherwise be lost.

If taking turns or keeping open space for the quieter members of the group to speak into will be a challenge, consider using a talking stick or another object that is passed around, giving the holder permission to speak.

Questions can be solicited from youth and adults, or you can use the following questions:

- When times get tough for you, what keeps you going?

- Who is your community? Who is your family?

- Who are your role models for being adult?

- What role has your faith played in becoming the person you are today?

- To adults: What do you know now that you wish you had known when you were the age of these youth?

- To youth: What do you know now that you want to remember as you become an adult?

- To youth: What do you fear losing as you grow older? What do you look forward to gaining?

- To adults: Looking back, what have you lost and gained in becoming adults?

- What do you hope to gain by being part of a UU community? What do you hope to contribute?

Close the conversation with this final question to the adults: What are your wishes and blessings for this group of youth as they grow in their UU faith?

Sample Outline for a Rites of Passage Retreat

- *Friday night:* Arrive and settle in; dinner; a community-building game; Choosing the Masks We Wear, Part 1: Mask Molding; Sharing Our Dreams, Part 1: Sleeping and Dreaming

- *Saturday morning:* Breakfast; Sharing Our Dreams, Part 2: Dream Discussion; Workshop 20, Connecting to the Natural World

- *Saturday afternoon:* Lunch; Solo Vigil; unstructured free time and/or a movie that deals with spiritual issues

- *Saturday evening:* Dinner; Wisdom Circle; Choosing the Masks We Wear, Part 2: Mask Decorating; Workshop 6, Finalizing Your Credo

- *Sunday morning:* Breakfast; cleanup; closing worship

Considerations for Cultural Borrowing

Motivation

Why am I doing this? What is my motivation?

Goal

What is the goal?
Why do we want multiculturalism?

Context

What is the context in which I will use the cultural material?
What is the cultural context from which it is taken?
What are the controversies and sensitivities surrounding this material?
What are the power relationships in this context? The privileges? The history?

Preparation

What am I willing to do to prepare for this experience?
Have I done my homework on this material?
What sources and resources have I used?
Have I asked people from the culture for feedback on my plans?
Have I asked people from the culture to create or co-create the material?
Did I invite people from the culture to participate? To speak for themselves in this plan?

Relationship

Am I in relationship with people from this culture?
Am I willing to be part of that community's struggle?
What is my relationship with the source?
What can I give in return? What do I offer?
With whom do I ally myself with this usage?
Am I working alone?

Identity

How does this work nurture self-identity and group identity?
How does this strengthen UU identity?
How does it help UUs be religious?
What does this say about UU faith?
How does it relate to UU spirituality or spiritual practice?
What can UUs learn from other traditions?

Adaptation

With printed material, who holds the copyright?
Have I received permission to use the material?
Who has the right to adapt? Why?
Who might be insulted or offended by this adaptation?
With whom do I ally myself with this adaptation?
What is the difference between symbolic and real ritual, and how am I using this ritual?
If I am using a translation is it accurate, authentic, and current?

Language

Am I using current, authentic language?

—Lifespan Faith Development working group, Unitarian Universalist Association of Congregations

Readings for Rites of Passage Retreat

The Unitarian Universalist Association hymnbook, Singing the Living Tradition, *has many readings that can be used at a retreat. The readings that follow are intended to supplement the hymnbook. You may also access a continually updated worship resource at www.uua.org/worshipweb.*

We light this chalice
To symbolize our unity and diversity.
Just as the flame in this chalice has patterns and
　differences,
So do we have patterns and differences with each
　other.
Just as the base of this chalice forms a solid foun-
　dation for the flame to grow on,
So do we form solid foundations for others to
　grow on.
And just as the fire in this chalice creates light
　and warmth for all around it,
So do we create light and warmth through love
　and friendship for all around us.

　—Natty Smith

In the name of all that is good and holy, with the
　Spirit of Life and Love
which dwells within and among and beyond us,
We bless you.
May your journey know joy and contentment and
　satisfaction.
May it also know pain and disappointment in
　just enough measure to grow within you good
　character and compassion.
May both character and compassion guide your
　lives.
May you never feel alone.
May you always feel love around you from family
　and friends and from that
　　great holy source beyond us all.
May you always offer your love to the world.

May you walk your path, through the light and the
　darkness, with hope and faith and grace.
We bless you.
Amen.

　—Dana E. Worsnop

Deep down you know the truth. You must cross the border. You must take the step. You must inherit your life. You must grow, because growth is required in order for you to survive. . . . You are no longer innocent about what life is about. The grim truth is that you must find a way to survive in it.

　—Steven Foster and Meredith Little

This is the true joy in life: The being used for a purpose recognized by yourself as a mighty one. The being a force of nature instead of a feverish, selfish little clod of ailments and grievances complaining that the world will not devote itself to making you happy.

I am of the opinion that my life belongs to the whole community, and as long as I live it is my privilege to do for it whatever I can.

I want to be thoroughly used up when I die, for the harder I work the more I live. I rejoice in life for its own sake. Life is no "brief candle" for me. It is a sort of splendid torch which I have got hold of for the moment, and I want to make it burn as brightly as possible before handing it on to future generations.

　—George Bernard Shaw

To live content with small means; to seek elegance rather than luxury, and refinement rather than fashion; to be worthy, not respectable, and wealthy, not rich; to listen to stars and birds, babes and sages, with open heart; to study hard; to think quietly, act frankly, talk gently, await occasions, hurry never; in a word, to let the spiritual, unbidden and unconscious, grow up through the common—this is my symphony.
—William Henry Channing

Being Present, Being Open, Being Conscious

Relax and be quiet within. Close your eyes.

Be aware of your body: its posture; the points of contact it makes with your clothing; the floor; the air moving around you.

Take a long, slow breath in. Exhale silently, slowly.

Feel your whole body. Where there is stiffness, loosen.

Where there is pain, feel the pain and let go of it.

Where you feel tension, release it.

Where there is fatigue, acknowledge it and move through it.

Feel each breath: inhale slowly and silently.

Exhale slowly and silently.

Acknowledge your feelings.

Name those you are experiencing, now, to yourself.

One by one, as you exhale, release these emotions from you.

Affirm your intellect. You are the product of your lifelong striving to learn, grow, reason, and make sense.

As you exhale, move away from this intellect.

Follow the circuit of your breath.

Listen:

This morning, you were invited to find a place for your solo vigil.

This is a place where you will soon be for an extended time.

How will that place engage you? What will you see there? What will you smell? What will you hear? Use each of your senses to discover this place.

Listen:

You have traveled a long time and a great distance to find this place. You have met and named allies and recognized their gifts to you—the ones you found in our congregation and the ones we find each day. You have, throughout your time in Coming of Age, explored yourself and your relationship with Unitarian Universalism, with the earth, and with all beings. You have explored your gifts of life and spirit. All you have discovered, all you have gained insight into, is yours. You have realized your strengths: values that guide and support; courage; loyalty; responsibility balancing freedom; self-discipline; mindfulness; respect; compassion. Be aware of them. Understand them. Practice them.

Listen:

You will be at this place for an extended time. You will explore and examine, drawing from your power and wisdom to meet the challenges ahead.

Be aware: This is new and unfamiliar. You may be uncomfortable. You may need to deal with distractions: external interruptions; physical discomfort; social unease; emotional needfulness; mental scatter. You may feel bored, abandoned, unstimulated, adrift, dumb. Your mind and body and emotions may send you messages that you cannot do this.

If this happens, do this: Sit comfortably. Breathe from the diaphragm. Begin counting: "1" on the in-breath; "1" on the out-breath. Continue up to "10" and "10." Then begin again. Breathe very calmly. Breathe to your own rhythm. Concentrate on the breath coming in and going out of your body. This breath connects your mind and body.

If you start to think, "This is really boring," it's a signal of resistance, and you know it's time to start counting. When you begin to feel physically uncomfortable, start to count. When you wish you were with a friend, start to count. When you want to be entertained, start to count. Address the distraction. Confront the tension. And start to count. Acknowledge your mind chatter and get rid of it. Don't believe it. Don't waste your time on it.

By acknowledging these blocks and working through them, you will be open to receive. You will be open to discover:

Who am I?

What do I need?

What are my strengths and gifts?

How can I serve?

Draw from your strengths; they are there. Use your wisdom; it's yours. Refocus if you need to; you know how to.

And now, gently draw your attention back to the circle and open your eyes.

—Prairie Star District Coming of Age program, early 1990s, adapted

Guidelines for Dream Discussion

One

All dreams speak a universal language and come in the service of health and wholeness. There is no such thing as a "bad dream"—only dreams that sometimes take a dramatically negative form in order to grab our attention.

Two

Only the dreamer can say with any certainty what meanings his/her dream may have. This certainty usually comes in the form of a wordless "Aha!" of recognition. This "aha" is a function of memory, and is the only reliable touchstone of dream work.

Three

There is no such thing as a dream with only one meaning. All dreams and dream images are "overdetermined," and have multiple meanings and layers of significance.

Four

No dreams come just to tell you what you already know. All dreams break new ground and invite you to new understandings and insights.

Five

When talking to others about their dreams, it is both wise and polite to preface your remarks with words to the effect of "if it were my dream . . ." and to keep this commentary in the first person as much as possible. This means that even relatively challenging comments can be made in such a way that the dreamer may actually be able to hear and internalize them. It also can become a profound psychospiritual discipline: "walking a mile in your neighbor's moccasins."

Six

All dream group participants should agree at the outset to maintain anonymity in all discussions of dream work. In the absence of any specific request for confidentiality, group members should be free to discuss their experiences openly outside the group, provided no other dreamer is identifiable in their stories. However, whenever any group member requests confidentiality, all members should agree to be bound automatically by such a request.

—Jeremy Taylor, *The Dreamwork Tool Kit: Six Basic Hints for Dream Work*

Questions for the Vigil

Reflections upon your surroundings:

You are out in nature, alone. How does it feel?

What do you see?

If you look really closely, what more do you see?

Look, smell, hear, touch, interpret, imagine, create, affirm, feel, plan, ask questions, wonder, experiment, be aware of the natural world. Pretend you are an ant or small insect, and take a microhike in the grass or soil. Become something in nature in your imagination: a tree, animal, rock, etc. What does this thing represent or symbolize to you? What is it trying to tell you? What is its perspective of the world?

Reflections upon you:

What are your birthrights? (A birthright is something that you are born into, like an ethnic tradition, a religion, or a way of being.) What do they mean to you? How will you use them?

What from your childhood do you want to outgrow, and what from your childhood do you want to keep always?

How do you choose to define yourself?

Reflections upon your connections:

South African archbishop Desmond Tutu writes about *Ubuntu*, the essence of being human: "We say a person is a person through other persons. We don't come fully formed into the world. We learn how to think, how to walk, how to speak, how to behave—indeed how to be human—from other human beings. We need other human beings in order to be human. We are made for togetherness, we are made for family, for fellowship, to exist in a tender network of interdependence."

Who is in this tender network of interdependence for you?

Who is your community?

What is your spirituality—your way of connecting to the miracle of life?

Services of Recognition

Coming of Age programs often culminate in a congregational worship service of recognition. Some congregations ask youth in the program to design a Sunday morning service in its entirety; others' services are planned by the congregation's professional staff or a worship committee. Many include the reading of credos; most also include some form of ritual to acknowledge the youth, mentors, and parents who have been involved in the program. Some congregations, particularly larger ones, choose to have an evening event (rather than a Sunday morning worship) to honor youth and hear their credos. This chapter provides resources that your congregation can use to plan a worshipful service of recognition that suits its needs.

Making the Service Worshipful

If you choose a Sunday morning worship service, take special care to create a service that is not only meaningful to youth and their parents but also worshipful for everyone in the gathered community. Like a high school graduation ceremony, this service will create many pairs of moist eyes in its audience. The key difference between a good high school graduation and a good Coming of Age service is that the latter involves worship as well as recognition of one of life's transitions.

Worship in a Unitarian Universalist setting connects the gathered community to that which is sacred within them, among them, and beyond them. Those who gather for worship on a Sunday morning include people from infancy to old age, lifelong Unitarian Universalists as well as people who are visiting for the first time. Among them are happy people, but there are also people grieving a loss, people caring for sick parents, and those who are lonely and depressed. While coming of age is most often a happy transition, it can be valuable to ask, "What elements of our Coming of Age worship service can speak to those who come with sadness in their hearts?" A worshipful service is able to speak to all who have gathered, by lifting up both the universals and the particulars of the human experience. Such a service invokes reverence for life, celebrates the bonds of community, and upholds the congregation as home for people in all life stages—from birth to death. A worshipful service touches the congregation's longings for human connection, meaning, and purpose through its use of ritual, readings, reflections, music, and aesthetics. It also involves authentic personal sharing, which can be both worshipful and transformative.

A Coming of Age service is well suited to authentic personal sharing. The more a youth's credo is able to speak to the honest depths of the youth's experience and understandings, the more authentic it is and the more likely to touch similar depths in listeners. Parents (or a representative of the group of parents) can be asked to speak authentically about what it means spiritually to accompany their child on the transition from childhood to adolescence. Mentors, too, can have a role in speaking about how the experience of mentoring has been meaningful in their own spiritual development.

See Handout 11, Typical Elements of a Traditional Worship Service (page 137), to help structure your recognition service.

Planning

Early in the church year, your program's planning team will need to decide whether to have a Coming of Age recognition service. The congregation's staff and worship committee can then plan the annual worship calendar accordingly. At this time, you can also begin the conversation about who will be involved in the service and what roles they will play. If the minister and religious educator will participate that Sunday, they should know far in advance.

As the date of the service nears, you will want to choose someone—a program leader, a mentor, or the congregation's religious educator—to be the point person. This person can also work with various groups to answer questions like these: Will youth deliver credos? Will there be a ceremony of recognition, and if so, who will be involved and how long will it take? Will the minister deliver a sermon or homily? Will parents be involved? What will the mentors' role be? If credos are to be a main feature of the service, how much time will be allotted for them? And how much time per youth does this allow? Further, if there are to be gifts given to youth during the service, they should be ordered well in advance. Chalices, books, necklaces, or T-shirts are common gifts for a congregation to offer in a Coming of Age service.

The point person can work with the program leaders, the religious educator, the minister, the worship committee, and the youth to make decisions about the remaining elements of the service, including the choice of readings and hymns. An Order of Service can then be drafted.

A Coming of Age service typically needs two full rehearsals: one a few days before and one the day of the service. Scheduling the rehearsals well in advance will give participants enough time to make accommodations in their schedules. Practice makes the whole service run much more smoothly and lets youth gain comfort and skill in speaking from the pulpit. If you can find someone with public speaking and/or pulpit experience to coach youth, the service will be better for it. The worship committee is a good place to find such a volunteer or a referral.

Order of Service

Because Coming of Age services often include elements, such as rituals, special readings, or credos, that are unusual in a Sunday service, it is likely that your congregation's traditional Order of Service will have to be adapted. The degree of adaptation is subject to conversation with your congregation's professional leadership and worship committee. It is generally advisable to include several elements that are typically part of a Sunday Order of Service, such as opening words, chalice lighting, offertory, etc. The worship service will then feel familiar to the gathered congregation even as you introduce new elements specific to the occasion.

At *www.uua.org/worshipweb*, you can find several chalice lightings, opening words, prayers/meditations, and closing words that can be used effectively in a Coming of Age service. Leader Resource 30, Sample Orders of Service (page 245) includes additional ideas.

Rituals of Recognition

Create a ritual in your congregation that suits the spirit and traditions of your community. The following samples have been used by some congregations:

Bridging from childhood to adolescence. At the beginning of the ritual, youth stand on the left side of the stage with their parents to signify childhood. One by one, youth hug their parents, then walk to the center of the stage with their mentors, and receive a chalice necklace from their minister and religious educator. Youth then proceed to the right side of the stage, to be welcomed by current members of the youth group. The Coming of Age youth then meet their parents again at center stage, recognizing and affirming the new relationship between parent and adolescent child. Short statements read by a parent, a mentor, a youth group member, and a member of the congregation's staff, on behalf of all the others in these groups, can be particularly poignant.

The symbols of childhood and adolescence. Youth each bring two objects: one that symbolizes the childhood they are leaving behind, and one that symbolizes the future they want to claim. The objects are placed on two altars on either side of the stage. Youth stand at the childhood altar before they are recognized (and/or before they give their credos) and move to the future altar afterward.

Credos

Some congregations invite youth to deliver their credos during a Sunday morning Coming of Age service. Other congregations find it more meaningful to focus the worship service on recognition and ritual rather than credos. Some print the credos in the Order of Service instead of asking youth to read them aloud.

In deciding what role credos will play in your service, consider these factors:

Size. How large is your congregation? In larger congregations, it is likely that there would not be enough time for all youth to read their credos. Larger congregations also tend to have multiple staff members who collaborate to design highly structured worship services, and a credo-oriented service might not fit with their usual worship style.

Number of services. If a congregation has more than one Sunday worship service, will youth deliver their credos at one? Both? Neither?

History. Is there a history of presenting credos in past Coming of Age recognition services? History, of course, does not dictate how it should be done in the future, but it does shape expectations and should be taken into account.

Interest. Are all interested parties—youths, parents, leaders, and the congregation's staff—all supportive of credos' inclusion in the worship service? Or are they more supportive of credos being shared at a smaller evening service?

Length of service. Is your typical worship service one hour in length? One hour and a half? How much time can be allotted to credos, and is that

enough time per person for youth to share what they have written?

There is no one right decision about whether to include credos in a Sunday morning worship service. Each congregation must come to its own decision on the matter.

Homilies and Reflections

Whether credos are included in a worship service or not, consider including a homily (a short sermon of five to ten minutes) or one or more reflections (one- to three-minute first-person narratives). In selecting speakers, you can choose from ministers, religious educators, parents, mentors, and youth. Leader Resource 31, Living by Choice (page 247), is a copy of a homily delivered by Rev. Galen Guengerich at All Souls Unitarian Church in New York City. His words demonstrate that a homily can frame credos and Coming of Age in a meaningful way.

Responsive Readings

Often Coming of Age services include an opportunity for the wider congregational community to acknowledge this important transition. Responsive readings with parts for parents or the entire congregation can fulfill this need. Leader Resources 32 and 33 (pages 250 and 251) are two examples of responsive readings tailored specially for a Coming of Age Service of Recognition.

Resources

In addition to the leader resources that follow, you can also look to Unitarian Universalist congregations in your area for ideas. Whatever route you decide to take with your service of recognition—youth-designed, adult-designed, credo-inclusive, ritual-focused—collaboration and careful planning will help your service be deeply meaningful for all involved.

Sample Orders of Service

Buxmont Unitarian Universalist Fellowship, Warrington, Pennsylvania

This midsize congregation has joined with another nearby congregation to offer a Coming of Age program. Youth in the program had a role in planning this service and conducting its various parts.

Prelude (an original song performed by a COA youth)

Greeting (by the minister)

Welcome/Chalice Lighting (by COA youth)

Opening Hymn (Hymn 348, "Guide My Feet")

Story for All Ages

"Blues Now In Peace" (a variation on "Go Now in Peace," played by a COA youth)

Announcements and Greeting of Visitors (by a COA youth)

Sharing of Joys and Sorrows (by a COA youth)

Offertory ("Money" by Pink Floyd)

Introduction to Coming of Age Program (by the minister)

Introduction of Youth and Credos

Song (led by a COA youth)

Introduction of Teachers and Mentors (by the religious educator)

On Being a Mentor (by a mentor)

Anthem (sung by the choir)

Giving of Gifts (by the religious educator)

Antiphonal Reading

Invitation to Reception (by a COA youth)

Closing Hymn (Hymn 162, "Gonna Lay Down My Sword and Shield")

Closing Words (by the minister)

Postlude (a song performed by a COA youth)

First Unitarian Church of Dallas, Texas

This large congregation has several youth enrolled in its Coming of Age program each year. In 2005 there were more than twenty. Because of the size, there is not enough time in the service for youth to all read their credos. Instead, the congregation prints and includes each youth's credo it in a program that all worshippers receive. Coming of Age participants and their parents are recognized in the service. The Order of Service and the music are planned by the congregation's professional staff.

Announcements (by an adult layperson)

Lighting the Chalice (by an adult layperson)

Prelude (classical music)

Opening Words (by the youth director)

Hymn

Affirmation (the congregation's weekly unison reading)

Doxology (the congregation's weekly unison song)

Welcome (by the minister)

Offertory (classical music)

Responsive Reading (Reading 649, "From Generation to Generation," led by the religious educator)

Prayer (by the minister)

Interlude (classical music)

Homily (a short sermon by the minister on the theme of credo)

Hymn

Coming of Age Ceremony

Reflections from Advisors

Invitation for COA Class and Families to Come Forward (by youth director)

Presentation of COA Class Members by Their Families

Blessings (by minister and religious educator)

Welcome: Young Religious Unitarian Universalists (by three members of the youth group)

Hymn

Closing Words (read by religious educator)

Postlude (classical music)

Extinguishing the Chalice (by one of the COA advisors)

Living by Choice

In 1945, the celebrated novelist and essayist E. B. White wrote a curious essay—it's only three pages long—titled "About Myself." It begins like this:

> I am a man of medium height. I keep my records in a Weiss Folder Reorder number 8003. The unpaid balance of my estimated tax for the year 1945 is item 3 less the sum of items 4 and 5. My eyes are gray . . . My social security number is 067-01-9841. I am married to U.S. Woman Number 067-01-9807. Her eyes are gray. This is not a joint declaration, nor is it made by an agent; therefore it need be signed only by me—and, as I said, I am a man of medium height . . .
>
> I hold Individual Certificate Number 4320-209 with the Equitable Life Assurance Society, in which a corporation hereinafter called the employer has contracted to insure my life for the sum of two thousand dollars. My left front tire is Number 48KE8846, my right front tire is Number 63T6895 . . . I brush my hair with Whiting-Adams Brush Number 010 . . . My shaving brush is sterilized.

And so on for three pages. The title of the essay, as I mentioned at the outset, is "About Myself." One wonders why. It seems an odd title for an essay that provides precious little insight into the self the world came to know as E. B. White—the person who wrote books like *Charlotte's Web*, *Stuart Little*, and *The Trumpet of the Swan*. If I had a black dog with cheeks of tan, as White tells us he did, could I write like him? Or maybe if I sprayed my nose with De Vilbiss Atomizer Number 14, or sometimes stopped the pain with Squibb Pill Number 3K49979, also known as aspirin. In other words, if the circumstances of my life were more or less the same as E. B. White's, would I be the kind of person he was and be able to write like he did?

Not likely. Circumstances tell us something about a person, but often not a lot. Being of medium height will not make you a novelist, nor will having a black dog with cheeks of tan. Almost none of the people who were born in New York City in 1979 can sing like Norah Jones. Wearing cufflinks will not enable you to play piano like Yefim Bronfman, nor will taking a ginseng supplement make you into a CNN news personality. These incidental qualities do not make us who we are.

What does, then? If I say that I am going to tell you about myself, what you expect to hear is something significant and substantive. You don't want to know what I had for breakfast or the number on my left rear tire or even if I have a left rear tire. You want to know what I hold in my heart—what moves me from within and compels me to act, what frightens me and keeps me awake at night, what aspirations I nurture and what longings I hold close. You want to know about my self.

That's where the idea of a credo first came from, though it's not what it means today. In Latin, the word *credo* is the first person singular form of the verb meaning "to believe." Literally translated, credo means "I believe." The most common contemporary usage of this phrase appears in the Apostles' Creed, widely used among Western Christians in their worship services. It is repeated regularly by Christians to remind them of the essential doctrines that define their faith. The Apostles' Creed goes like this:

> I believe in God, the Father almighty,
> creator of heaven and earth.
> I believe in Jesus Christ, God's only Son, our Lord,
> who was conceived by the Holy Spirit,
> born of the Virgin Mary,
> suffered under Pontius Pilate,
> was crucified, died, and was buried;

he descended to the dead.
On the third day he rose again;
he ascended into heaven,
he is seated at the right hand of the Father,
and he will come again to judge the living
　　and the dead.
I believe in the Holy Spirit,
the holy catholic church,
the communion of saints,
the forgiveness of sins,
the resurrection of the body,
and the life everlasting. Amen.

It should now be crystal clear why we as Unitarian Universalists do not have a creed. Even if you and I were inclined to place our faith in a set of beliefs concerning things like the resurrection of the body or which hand of the Father Jesus is seated at, if indeed he is seated and if in fact there is a Father, it's hard to imagine even two or three of us agreeing on which facts are the essential ones. Besides, creeds like this one relate mostly to other worlds and other dimensions of experience. What concerns you and me in our worship is this world and our everyday experiences—our fears and dreams, our aspirations and longings.

In other words, what we gather here to ponder is not a creed in the modern sense, but a credo in its ancient form. The Latin word *credo* was derived from two other Latin words, *cor*, meaning "heart," and *do*, from the verb meaning "to give." In its original meaning, *cor-do* meant "I give my heart." To believe in something is to give your heart to it.

In my view, a credo statement is not primarily about whether you believe the Bible is true or God is spirit or the earth is round. It's about what you aspire to give your heart to. A credo is an ideal we set for ourselves, a goal by which we measure our conduct and our accomplishments. Because it emerges from the depths of our hearts, it defines who we are—not by describing our circumstances or specifying our beliefs, but by revealing the choices we have made about how we intend to live.

To say that you believe in your family means that you intend to give yourself to the cause of seeking their good. To say that you believe in love means that you intend to act in ways that enhance the well-being of others. To say that you believe in peace means that you intend to extend the domain of compassion in human relations. These choices define who we are. They set us on a course in life and give us markers to evaluate whether we have made anything of ourselves.

John Fowles, one of the leading novelists of the latter part of the twentieth century, wrote many books, including *Daniel Martin*, *The Magus*, and most famously, *The French Lieutenant's Woman*. His first novel, *The Collector*, was published in 1962. Shortly thereafter, Fowles wrote a short essay titled "I Write Therefore I Am." In it, Fowles describes how he had chosen to be a writer ten years before—chosen in the existential sense of having deliberately made the choice. He says, "I constantly had to renew the choice and to live in anguish because I have so often doubted whether it was the right one. So I have turned down better jobs; I have staked everything on this one choice . . . I think, now, that even if the book had not been accepted, even if I had never had any book accepted, I was right to live by such a choice." He concludes, "I am surrounded by people who have not chosen themselves, but who have let themselves be chosen—by money, status symbols, by jobs—and I don't know which is sadder, those who know this or those who don't."

A decade later, Fowles wrote a short novel titled *The Ebony Tower*, about David Williams, a young art critic who visits an old painter named Henry Breasley in his rural French retreat. The two are a study in contrasts: One is young, the other old; one is a passive observer of life, the other is an active creator of it; one has mostly let others direct his life for him, the other has relentlessly made his own choices and followed his own imagination. As Fowles tells the story, the young critic's time in France is his chance to choose a different course, to claim his life for himself.

He ultimately fails the test, and he knows it. When he returns home, Williams realizes that "[the time away] had been a mirror, and the existence he was returning to sat mercilessly reflected in its surface . . . How shabby [his life] now looked, how insipid and anodyne, how safe. Riskless, that was the essence of it. . . . [His time in France] had remorselessly demonstrated what he was born, still was, and always would be: a decent man and eternal also-ran." Fowles concludes with young Williams looking among the rooftops outside his hotel window, where in the angles of the roof lines he sees "the collapsed parallel of what he was beside the soaring line of all that he might have been."

What I believe is that a credo is about setting our sights along the soaring line of all that we might become and giving our hearts to following that course. It's about making choices and committing ourselves to following through. As John Fowles reminds us, it's also about taking risks and having doubts. In this community of faith, we talk with each other about what we aspire to give our hearts to. In so doing, we set ideals for ourselves and set standards by which we measure our conduct and our accomplishments. These choices about how we intend to live define, at least in part, who we are as people of faith.

What we are here to celebrate today is that Henry, David, Tara, and Raymond have made a laudable start along the soaring line of all that they might become. Henry has wisely reminded us that a fulfilling life consists of an ample measure of productive work, along with an equally ample measure of relaxation and enjoyment. David has reminded us of how important perseverance, patience, and love are to our well-being, as well as how much we need the support that comes from our family and friends. Tara has wisely reminded us that much of what makes life meaningful comes to us through our imaginations, which make us each unique and give us each our own dignity and worth. Raymond has reminded us of the importance of stories in our human quest for meaning—both stories that are factual and stories that are true, as well as stories that are both factual and true.

Henry, David, Tara, Raymond: I am proud of the courage you have shown and the choices you have made. My challenge to you this morning is to continue to set your sights along the line of all that you can become. Take risks in life. Set high standards for yourself and those around you. Continue to challenge us and make us proud. When you struggle or have doubts, share those too. We'll do the same. This is how we will make the journey through life: we make it together. This I believe; to this I give my heart.

Recognition

Henry, David, Tara, Raymond: You have each presented us today with a thoughtful statement of your convictions concerning a certain aspect of the life of faith. In so doing, you have demonstrated your commitment to the aspirations that we share as a congregation—to live with open minds and open hearts, to act justly, love mercy, and walk humbly. In recognition of your presence among us and your contribution to our worship this morning, I hereby recognize your coming of age as people of faith. Congratulations from all of us, and welcome.

—Galen Guengerich, All Souls Unitarian Church, New York City, 2003

Sample Reading for a Recognition Service

As infants, named as unique beings, we are welcome in this community

AND WE ARE EMBRACED BY OUR CHURCH

As children, putting down roots and trying our wings, we are welcome in this community

AND WE ARE EMBRACED BY OUR CHURCH

As youth, wrestling with questions of who we are and want to be, we are welcome in this community

AND WE ARE EMBRACED BY OUR CHURCH

As adults, seeking nurture and focus amidst the fragmenting demands of the week, we are welcome in this community

AND WE ARE EMBRACED BY OUR CHURCH

As imperfect beings, making mistakes and disappointing ourselves, yet also rising to unexpected heights, we are welcome in this community

AND WE ARE EMBRACED BY OUR CHURCH

As individuals seeking companionship amidst the triumphs and tragedies of day-to-day living, we are welcome in this community

AND WE ARE EMBRACED BY OUR CHURCH

Through all ages and stages, all the ups and downs of a lifetime, we are welcome in this community

AND WE ARE EMBRACED BY OUR CHURCH

—Colleen McDonald

Coming of Age Ceremony

Parents and Youth:

Until now:

Parents:

Our job with you has been to fix the unfixable, to guide, to mold, to expose you to beauty and to the wonder of the world.

Youth:

Our job with you has been to bring you broken bones, tears from laughter, half-dead flowers, silent fears, amazing stories, both true and fiction.

Parents:

Our job with you has been to give you unconditional love, time to reflect, places to remember, shelter and safety.

Youth:

Our job with you has been to stretch your patience, your boundaries, and your willingness to accept our inevitable growth into now.

Parents and Youth:

It's been an incredible journey—our jobs are changing; we will acknowledge this and accept that:

Parents:

Our role with you will become more passive but no less loving.

Youth:

Our role with you will be to live out what you have sown, growing into new beings through our own experiences.

Parents and Youth to the Congregation:

We ask your help in realizing our recommitment to each other and to you.

Congregation:

We, the members of the _____, welcome your presence among us. For your fresh vision and inspiring energy, we welcome you. For your questions and your challenges, we welcome you. May you continue to grow—may we all continue to grow—in mind and body and spirit, our hearts always open to one another. We give you our blessing.

—David Maywhoor, First Unitarian Universalist Church of Columbus, Ohio

Sample Program Outlines

The following schedules are built of workshops and other building blocks in this handbook and cover several possible scenarios. You can use them, adapt them, or create your own that are compatible with your congregation's religious education calendar and its goals for Coming of Age.

On a few occasions, these samples mention mentors' involvement. However, mentor presence is not limited to only these sessions. As you plan the calendar, it is helpful to consider when and how to integrate mentors throughout. Other building blocks, such as journaling and worship, can also be easily added in greater numbers to these schedules.

Remember to adjust for holidays, multigenerational worship services, regional events, length of program meetings, leaders' scheduling conflicts, and anything else that will affect your calendar.

September-to-May Program

This program includes two retreats, one overnight, one community service project, one social action project, and a trip. Sunday meetings are held from 10:30 to 12:00 and run concurrently with 10:30 worship.

Previous spring

Leaders and mentors recruited

August/September

Parent-Youth Orientation held before the Opening Overnight

Mentor Orientation held before the Opening Overnight

September

Opening Overnight: Covenant and Community Building; Unitarian Universalist Values; The Community Building Continues!

3rd Sunday: Your Autobiography; journaling

4th Sunday: Introduce the Community Service Project; meet mentors and review Supplemental Activities Checklist

October

1st Sunday: Unity and Diversity; *UU Pocket Guide* discussion on "Sharing Our Faith"

2nd Sunday: The Web of Interdependence; Complete and Process the Community Service Project

3rd Sunday: Learning to Lead Worship; journaling

4th Sunday: Attending Worship

Parents' Small Group Ministry sessions start this month

November

Fall Retreat (with mentors): (Friday night) Peace and Put-downs; Making an Altar; (Saturday morning) Spirituality in Movement; Your God Project; Connecting to the Natural World; (Saturday afternoon) The God You Don't Believe In, the God You Do; Stillness, Silence and Meditation; (Saturday evening) Starting with Us; (Sunday morning) worship

2nd Sunday: Introduction to Spiritual Practice; journaling

3rd Sunday: Rituals of Our Faith; *UU Pocket Guide* discussion on "Our Ministry"

Holiday weekend

December

1st Sunday: Prayer; worship

2nd Sunday: Good and Evil; *UU Pocket Guide* discussion on "Our Worship"

January

2nd Sunday: Writing Your Credo; check-in

3rd Sunday: Understanding Social Action; *UU Pocket Guide* discussion on "Our Faith"

4th Sunday: How UUs Make a Difference; journaling

February

1st Sunday: Choose the Social Action Project

2nd Sunday: The Meaning and Practice of Leadership; UU Pocket Guide discussion on "Our Work for Social Justice and Diversity"

3rd Sunday: Complete and Process the Social Action Project

4th Sunday: Leadership in Congregational Life; check-in

March

1st Sunday: Life, Death, and the Afterlife

2nd Sunday: Our Unitarian Universalist Story; *UU Pocket Guide* discussion on "Important Dates in Unitarian Universalist History"

3rd Sunday: Weeklong COA trip during spring break

April

1st Sunday: The Local Story; worship

2nd Sunday: Talking about Unitarian Universalism; journaling

3rd Weekend: Rites of Passage Retreat

4th Sunday: Finalizing Your Credo; invite mentors; review Supplemental Activities Checklist

May

1st Sunday: Closing Celebration; check-in

2nd Sunday: Coming of Age Service of Recognition

January-to-May Program

This program includes one retreat, two overnights, and one social action project. Sunday meetings are held from 10:30 to 12:00 and run concurrently with 10:30 worship.

Previous spring

Leaders recruited, mentor recruiting begins

Previous fall

Leaders and mentors recruited

January

Parent-Youth Orientation held before the Opening Overnight

Potential Mentor Orientation held before the Opening Overnight

3rd Weekend Opening Overnight: Covenant and Community Building; Unitarian Universalist Values; The Community Building Continues!

3rd Sunday: Your Autobiography

4th Sunday: Unity and Diversity; journaling

February

1st Sunday: The Web of Interdependence; check-in

2nd Sunday: Attending Worship

3rd Sunday: Learning to Lead Worship; journaling

4th Sunday: Introduction to Spiritual Practice; worship

March

Retreat Weekend: (Friday night) Peace and Putdowns; Making an Altar; (Saturday morning) Spirituality in Movement; Rituals of Our Faith; Your God Project; (Saturday afternoon) Connecting to the Natural World; The God You Don't Believe In, the God You Do; (Saturday evening) Starting with Us; Good and Evil; (Sunday morning) cleanup; worship (invite mentors)

2nd Sunday: Writing Your Credo; journaling

3rd Sunday: Our Unitarian Universalist Story; check-in

April

1st Sunday: Life, Death, and the Afterlife

2nd Sunday: Leadership in Congregational Life; worship

Spring Overnight: Understanding Social Action; Deciding on a Social Action Project; Talking about Unitarian Universalism; Finalizing Your Credo

4th Sunday: Complete and Process the Social Action Project

May

1st Sunday: Closing Celebration; check-in

2nd Sunday: Coming of Age Service of Recognition

Retreat-based Program

This program includes an average of ten hours of programming per weekend. This model could also be adjusted for a day-camp program, with five days at eight hours of programming a day. It includes time for a Rites of Passage ceremony.

1st Weekend: (Friday night) Covenant and Community Building; Unitarian Universalist Values; Learning to Lead Worship; (Saturday morning) The Community Building Continues!; Unity and Diversity; (Saturday afternoon) Good and Evil; Rituals of Our Faith; Your Autobiography; (Saturday night) Our Unitarian Universalist Story; The Local Story; (Sunday morning) worship

2nd Weekend: (Friday night) Peace and Put-downs; The Web of Interdependence; (Saturday morning) Introduction to Spiritual Practice; Spirituality in Movement; Connecting to the Natural World; (Saturday afternoon) Your God Project; The God You Don't Believe In, the God You Do; Life, Death, and the Afterlife; (Saturday night) Starting with Us; (Sunday morning) worship

3rd Weekend: (Friday night) Understanding Social Action; Prayer; (Saturday morning) Stillness, Silence, and Meditation; Writing Your Credo; (Saturday afternoon) How UUs Make a Difference; The Meaning and Practice of Leadership; (Saturday night) Talking about Unitarian Universalism; Making an Altar; (Sunday morning) worship

4th Weekend: (invite congregational leaders to join you for dinner on Friday): (Friday night) Leadership in Congregational Life; Rites of Passage; (Saturday) Rites of Passage; free time; Finalizing Your Credo; (Sunday morning) Service of Recognition; Closing Celebration

Resources

Books

Many of the books listed below are available in the Unitarian Universalist Association Bookstore. To order, call 1-800-215-9076 or visit the website at *www.uua.org/bookstore*.

Armstrong, Thomas. *The Myth of the A.D.D. Child: 50 Ways to Improve Your Child's Behavior and Attention Span Without Drugs, Labels, or Coercion.* New York: Dutton, 1995.

_____. *Multiple Intelligences in the Classroom.* Alexandria, VA: Association for Supervision and Curriculum Development, 1994.

Arnason, Wayne, and Rebecca Scott. *We Would Be One: A History of Unitarian Universalist Youth Movements.* Boston: Skinner House Books, 2005.

Beck, Renee, and Sydney Merrick. *The Art of Ritual: Creating and Performing Ceremonies for Growth and Change.* Berkley, CA: Celestial Press, 2003.

Blood, Peter, and Annie Patterson, eds. *Rise Up Singing: The Group Singing Songbook.* Bethlehem, PA: Sing Out Publications, 2004.

Bumbaugh, David E. *Unitarian Universalism: A Narrative History.* Chicago: Meadville Lombard Press, 2000.

Erslev, Kate Tweedie. *Full Circle: Fifteen Ways to Grow Lifelong UUs.* Boston: Unitarian Universalist Association, 2004.

Fowler, James W. *Stages of Faith: The Psychology of Human Development and the Quest for Meaning.* San Francisco: Harper and Row, 1981.

Gardner, Howard. *Intelligence Reframed: Multiple Intelligences for the 21st Century.* New York: Basic Books, 1999.

Gilbert, Richard S. *The Prophetic Imperative: Social Gospel in Theory and Practice.* Boston: Skinner House Books, 2000.

Hoertdoerfer, Patricia, and Fredric Muir, eds. *The Safe Congregation Handbook: Nurturing Healthy Boundaries in Our Faith Communities.* Boston: Unitarian Universalist Association, 2005.

Hurd, Tracey L. *Nurturing Children and Youth: A Developmental Guidebook.* Boston: Unitarian Universalist Association, 2005.

Lewis, Barbara A., and Pamela Espeland. *The Kids' Guide to Service Projects: Over 500 Services Ideas for Young People Who Want to Make a Difference.* Friday Harbor, WA: Turtleback Books, 1995.

Patton, Sally. *Welcoming Children with Special Needs: A Guidebook for Faith Communities.* Boston: Unitarian Universalist Association, 2004.

Pipher, Mary. *Reviving Ophelia: Saving the Selves of Adolescent Girls.* New York: Penguin Publishing Group, 1994.

Pollack, William. *Real Boys: Rescuing Our Sons from the Myths of Boyhood.* New York: Random House, 1998.

Rydberg, Denny. *Building Community in Youth Groups.* Loveland, CO: Group Publishing, 1985.

Schwendeman, Jill M. *When Youth Lead: A Guide to Intergenerational Social Justice Ministry, Plus 101 Youth Projects.* Boston: Unitarian Universalist Association, 2007.

Searl, Edward, ed. *Coming of Age: A Treasury of Poems, Quotations and Readings on Growing Up.* Boston: Skinner House Books, 2007.

Singing the Journey: A Supplement to Singing the Living Tradition. Boston: Unitarian Universalist Association, 2005.

Singing the Living Tradition. Boston: Unitarian Universalist Association, 1993.

Tatum, Beverly Daniel. *"Why Are All the Black Kids Sitting Together in the Cafeteria?" and Other Conversations About Race*. New York: Basic Books, 1997.

Wiseman, Rosalind. *Queen Bees and Wannabees: Helping Your Daughter Survive Cliques, Gossip, Boyfriends, and Other Realities of Adolescence*. New York: Three Rivers Press, 2002.

Websites

KidSource Online, *www.kidsource.com*

National Center for Learning Disabilities, *www.ld.org*

National Study of Youth and Religion, *www.youthandreligion.org*

Search Institute, *www.search-institute.org*

Worship Web, Unitarian Universalist Association, *www.uua.org/worshipweb*

Acknowledgments

The author wishes to thank the following for their contributions to this handbook:

Rev. John Gibb Millspaugh for writing Unit Six and Chapter Five on social justice; Anne Principe for activities in the spirituality unit; Shawn Newton for his contribution to the Unitarian Universalist history unit; Kevin Durkin for his meditations; Rev. Dan Harper for information about the mentor's role from his mentor manual for First Parish in Lexington, Massachusetts; Susan O'Connor for material from the "Roots and Wings" Coming of Age program for First Parish Universalist Church in Stoughton, Massachusetts; Rev. Jory Agate, minister of religious education at First Parish in Cambridge, Massachusetts, for the mentor training session outline; Samaya Oakley and Lynn Sanbourin of North Shore Unitarian Church in West Vancouver, British Columbia, for the sample mentor information sheet and the sample mentor recruitment letter; Jan Taddeo and River Road Unitarian Church of Bethesda, Maryland, for the sample code of ethics; Beth Brownfield et. al. for information on mentoring from the Prairie Star District Coming of Age Program; Rev. Geoff Rimositis, minister of religious education at First Unitarian Church of San Jose, California, and Amanda Ayling, youth program coordinator at University Unitarian Church in Seattle, Washington, for providing copies of their mentor materials; Rev. John Buehrens for some of the journaling/credo questions; and all the Unitarian Universalist congregations and individuals who sent ideas and activities from their Coming of Age program materials to us for review.

Much thanks also to Judith Frediani, Adrianne Ross, and Rachael Brown for all the hours of work contributed to this project.